THE SPY NET

THE SPY NET

THE GREATEST INTELLIGENCE OPERATIONS OF THE FIRST WORLD WAR

HENRY LANDAU

Biteback Publishing

First published in Great Britain in 1938 by Jarrolds Ltd.
This edition published in Great Britain in 2015 by
Biteback Publishing Ltd
Westminster Tower
3 Albert Embankment
London SE1 7SP
Copyright © Henry Landau 1938, 2015

ISBN 978-1-84954-906-6

10 9 8 7 6 5 4 3 2 1

A CIP catalogue record for this book is available from the British Library.

CONTENTS

INTRODUCTION

HENRY LANDAU WAS serving with the British Army in 1916 when he was recruited into the British secret service, the organisation we now know as MI6, in order to reorganise the British networks in Belgium that were watching the German troop trains travelling to and from the Western Front. These train-watching networks allowed the British to work out the locations and numbers of German regiments.

Landau, who was born in South Africa, was talent spotted when he dated one of the secretaries to Mansfield Cumming, the first head of MI6 (then known as MI1c) and the original 'C'. On finding out that Landau spoke French, Dutch and German, she told him he was 'just the man my chief is looking for'. He was summoned to see Cumming's deputy, Colonel Freddie Browning, at the secret service headquarters in Whitehall Court.

He informed me that I had been transferred to the intelligence corps, and that, as I had been attached for special duty to the secret service, he would take me up to the chief immediately. Up several flights of stairs I went, until I reached the very top of the building. Here, in a room that resembled the stateroom of a ship, I was confronted with a kindly man who immediately put me at ease. It was the chief, Captain C. He swung round in a swivel chair to look at me – a grey-haired man of about sixty, in naval uniform, short in stature, with a certain stiffness of movement, which I later discovered to be due to an artificial leg. After a few preliminary remarks, he suddenly came to the point: 'You are just the man we want. Our train-watching service has broken down completely in Belgium and north-eastern France – we are getting absolutely nothing through. It is up to you to reorganise the service. I can't tell you how it is to be done – that is your job.'

Landau went on to run *La Dame Blanche*, a group of more than 1,000 Belgian and French agents who monitored the movement of German troop trains to and from the Western Front. Named after a mythical White Lady, whose appearance was supposed to presage the downfall of the Hohenzollerns, it was arguably the most effective intelligence operation of the First World War and, according to Cumming, produced 70 per cent of Allied intelligence on the German forces.

At the end of the war, Landau was rewarded for his work with *La Dame Blanche* by being offered one of the plum jobs in the post-war intelligence service. 'I was informed by the chief that, in recognition of my services, he had awarded me the best of his appointments abroad in the post-war re-arrangement of the secret service. I was to open an office in Berlin.'

With Bolsheviks causing mayhem and threatening a German revolution to match that in Russia, Berlin was expected to be the service's most important overseas station. But Landau not only struggled to come to terms with the work, he also found himself in severe financial difficulties. He left the secret service and went to America, where he became a US citizen and published a book on his wartime intelligence experiences called *All's Fair: The Story of the Secret Service Behind the German Lines*.

The book was a bestseller in America, but was not published in the UK for fear of legal action by the authorities. Appearing only a year after Hitler had come to power, its revelations about those who had worked for the British during the First World War and had remained in Germany – in a number of cases, still working for the British – put them at risk. Landau also named his successor as MI1c's head of station in Berlin, Frank Foley, who would subsequently become better known for his work helping Jews escape from Nazi Germany. Shortly after the publication of *All's Fair*, the German authorities warned the population to be on the lookout for foreign spies. 'A large number of spies are busy in Germany collecting all particulars, especially with regard to the possibilities of economic mobilisations,' they announced. 'Spies must be energetically brought to book. Great reserve must be shown towards all foreigners encountered in public houses, railway compartments etc.'

A second book was also published in the US to avoid legal action, but this book, originally called *Spreading the Spy Net*, was the most comprehensive, published in both the US and the UK in 1938. Although Landau had let much that it contained out of the bag in his previous two books, it was still surprising that British secret service chiefs decided against taking any action.

Quite why is not clear, but it might well have something to do with the man Landau describes as 'the Dane', in what is a deliberately disguised account of the work of the best MI1c agent inside First World War Germany. Karl Krüger was not, in fact, a Dane. He was a German naval engineer. Codenamed variously TR16, H16 or, as here, R16, he had been recruited by Landau's wartime boss, the head of MI1c's Rotterdam bureau, Richard Tinsley. Krüger had extensive access to the German North Sea and Baltic ports and provided the British with often extraordinary and highly accurate detail, both of damage caused to the German Navy by its British counterpart and of the capabilities and vulnerabilities of the new ships and submarines the Germans were building.

Krüger had continued to work for the British after the First World War and, by the time *Spreading the Spy Net* was published, was providing detailed information on the build-up of German forces under the Nazis. But he was already under suspicion, and taking action against Landau's book would only have alerted the Germans to the British concerns for his safety.

It is unclear whether the Germans ever discovered the full extent of Krüger's work for British intelligence, but, shortly after the start of the Second World War, they announced that he had been beheaded by axe (although there is some evidence that he frustrated his would-be executioners by committing suicide). It was initially assumed within MI6 that Landau's account of Krüger's work was responsible for his death – and when the Americans entered the war in December 1941, there was even an attempt to have Landau arrested – but, in fact, when Krüger came under suspicion, the British had put one of their best Dutch agents on his tail to make sure he wasn't being followed. The Dutchman assigned to cover Krüger's back was also working for the Germans, and it was he who informed them that Krüger was a British spy, thereby sealing his fate.

Michael Smith
Editor of the Dialogue Espionage Classics Series
May 2015

CHAPTER 1

FROM BOER TO BRITON

I WAS BORN TO be what by chance I became; no child could have been ushered into the world under better conditions or in a more fertile environment for the dangerous and varied service into which I was thrown at the time of the Great War. By blood, by breeding and education, by the very country and atmosphere into which I was born, and the circumstances through which I grew to manhood, I was a composite of many inheritances and many backgrounds.

I was born of a Dutch mother and an English father, in Boer South Africa. My earliest memories centre about the arduous, almost medieval life of the veldt, and my first vivid impressions were those of war. Hazily I can remember the long trek in ox wagons from the Orange Free State to our farm in the Transvaal, when I was between four and five years of age; the long spans of red Afrikander oxen, the kaffirs with their long ox whips, the campfires, the hunters returning with their day's bag of springbok and koorhaan remain in my mind pictures at once remote and vivid.

I have visions, too, of my mother superintending the making of household essentials, which the Boer women of those days had to attend to – remedies for simple illness, soap, candles, and dried beef or *biltong*. She was an excellent horsewoman and a fine shot, and, in addition to her many household duties, it came naturally to her to handle the kaffirs and the stock in my father's absence. I can see her, at the approach of one of those South African thunderstorms which always seemed to come suddenly from nowhere, calling to the kaffirs to bring in the calves and other small stock, and herself scurrying off to direct them. Married at sixteen, she probably knew more about farming and stock-raising than my father, for she came of a long line of French Huguenots and Dutch, who had lived on the land in South Africa for close on 200 years, ever trekking northward to escape British rule, and in search of freedom. There was something elemental in her make-up, a ruggedness of character which breathed of the veldt itself. Her main qualities were dependability and resourcefulness; she was the master of every situation which arose, largely because of her own experiences and a fund of general knowledge carefully handed down by her pioneer mother.

From seven to ten, I lived in the midst of the fighting of the Boer War, and though I had relatives fighting on both sides, my boyish sympathies were all with the Boers. The coming and going of small groups of horsemen, with their tales of heroic encounters with the British, their ambushes and skirmishes, their marvellous skill with the rifle, their hairbreadth escapes, their hiding places, their foraging for food, all filled me with the glamour of war, which later on as a young man, on the British declaration of war, sent me trudging to Whitehall in a frenzied endeavour to get into the great adventure before it was too late.

My English father, a burgher on account of his long residence in Boer territory, was forced to join the Boer forces, and was placed by General Joubert at the head of the Commissariat in the Standerton District; but during the latter part of the Boer War, guerrilla warfare removed all need of a fixed commissariat, and so my father's application for leave of absence was readily granted. Through the back door of Portuguese east Africa and Delagoa Bay he was able to get to Europe to attend to the disposal of a large consignment of wool, which he had shipped at the outbreak of war, and which was being held up in Portugal. Finding himself unmolested on a visit to England, he was bold enough to try to return to the Transvaal via the British base at the Cape. All went well until, on the second day after his arrival in Cape Town, he ran into a group of Boer prisoners from his home district, who were being marched under guard through the street. Their yells of greeting led to his prompt arrest and internment.

My mother and the children were now stranded in the Transvaal, and, as our studies had been sadly disrupted during the war, my father decided to send us all to Europe to complete our education. Passes were eventually obtained permitting us to leave the country. My father was also liberated, as the war was now in its last stages. Mafeking and Ladysmith had been relieved; Lord

Roberts had occupied Pretoria; most of the Boer leaders had surrendered; it was merely a question of rounding up De Wet and the few followers that still remained with him.

I was destined by this removal to lose my home for good; it is true I was to travel with my mother for some time, but I never knew a real home again. The chief impressions it had made upon me, however, strongly survived, because of the dominating character of my father, who had so largely filled my early horizons. A born raconteur, he had filled my boyhood fancies with pioneer tales of the past. In 1874, after a six months' voyage out from London in a sailing ship, he had landed at the Cape to find that his elder brother, whom he was to join, had returned to England. Thrown entirely on his own, he had lived in succession the life of a transport driver, farmer, trader, and merchant. He had trekked with the Boers from the Cape, to take up new lands in the Transvaal and Orange Free State; he had participated in Kaffir wars; he had been connected with the diamond mines in Kimberley; he had ridden over the Witwatersrand and the site of the city of Johannesburg before the discovery of gold, and when there was hardly a farm-house in sight. He had wonderful tales of the illicit diamond buyers, cattle thieves, and the thousands of wildebeest, springbok, blesbok, and other game, which warmed the veldt in those days. No wonder I grew up into restless manhood, ever ready to follow every impulse and opportunity which led to adventure and travel.

My first sight of the sea and the three weeks' voyage from Durban to Southampton was a thrill. When I arrived I found the grey treeless veldt, the kopjes, and the wide expanses of the Transvaal exchanged for the green fields, hedges, and lawns of England.

Gone were the ox wagon and the unclad kaffir. I was deposited in London, to experience at the impressionable age of nine the delirium of a nation at the signing of peace, the Coronation of Edward VII with all its pageantry, and the metamorphosis of my own self from Afrikander to European, by means of school days and vacations on the Continent.

My recollection of my first school – Dulwich College – is vague. Memory brings to the surface odd events and impressions of no importance now, but which were probably of great interest to me then: my first Eton suit and bowler hat; P. G. Wodehouse, a prefect at Treddie's house; the Bedford and Haileybury football matches; Dr Gilkes, the head master, stern and forbidding; and the Latin school song, which impressed me greatly.

Christmas found me in Dresden with my mother and sisters, and later on I was placed in a German school instead of returning to England. Dutch, which, of course, I spoke as fluently as English, helped me with German, and within six months I was speaking the language like a native. I have pleasant memories of Dresden, young as I was; I liked the Saxon people. The parents of my school companions were immensely interested in this boy from South Africa. I am afraid, urged on by repeated questioning, I sometimes gave them exaggerated descriptions of life on the veldt. Rucksack on back, I spent week-ends and vacations with my German companions and some of their parents on short walking tours in Saxon Switzerland. I recall the glorious scenery of the Basteibrücke, Schandau, Pillnitz, and other resorts, and the delightful wayside inns where we slept at night. With the inquisitive eyes of youth, I was absorbing all I saw of German life and customs; partly from my affection for the country, and partly from the fresh vividness of my boyish impressions, I was effortlessly creating a foundation of assured familiarity with Germany which proved of value later on.

I had now reached an important turning point in my life; the rest of my boyhood and young manhood was to be spent in boarding school and universities. My parents I saw less and less often, for my mother, on her return from Europe, was to obtain a divorce from my father. True to her Boer traditions, she returned to the land to conduct her own stock farm, while my father threw himself with enthusiasm into the multiple developments which were now taking place in South Africa under British rule. At the end of the year in Europe, it was decided that I should return to South Africa, where my father placed me immediately in the Durban High School. I remained there until my sixteenth year.

It was a splendid school, fulfilling the best traditions of the finest of the English public schools, and its faculty was composed of Oxford and Cambridge men. Here I was changed into an Englishman; I was taught to play the game; I excelled in athletics, and I was turned out a scholar. At prize-giving, I was patted on the back by Sir Matthew Nathan, the governor of Natal, in whose brother's rooms at the Albany in London later on, I was often to sit answering rapid-fire questions on the political situation in Belgium and Germany.

Natal, with Durban, its chief port and city, was at this time a British crown colony, almost more English than England herself. It prided itself in being free of Boer settlers, and it was not until some years later, when it was forced into the Union of South Africa, that Dutch was taught in its schools. French was the modern language used instead, and here, in the Durban

High School, over a period of five years, I gained that thorough knowledge of syntax and grammar, which later, aided by long stays in France and Belgium, and by close contact with their people, made me master of the French language.

Most of my vacations were spent on some farm or other, where my chief occupation was riding and shooting. What other country can boast of three kinds of partridges, quail, bustard, spur-wing goose, pau, muscovy duck (as big as turkeys – they had to be shot with a rifle), snipe, and three or four different species of smaller antelope, all within easy reach of an ordinary farm? It was enough to keep any healthy boy in the saddle from morning to night; I virtually lived on horseback.

At sixteen, I was ready for entrance to a university, but my father judged me too young to proceed overseas. Accordingly, I was entered as a student in the government Agricultural College, at Potchefstroom, in the Transvaal. Here I was in my element. I loved farming; it was in my blood. No course could have been more interesting to anyone who had been raised on the land. For an institution of its kind, we probably had the finest equipment and the most valuable stock in the world, for it was to serve not only as an agricultural college, but as a farm from which thoroughbred cattle, horses, pigs, sheep, poultry, and seeds were to be supplied to the whole of South Africa. I liked everything about the college, and even though I was in competition with boys and men much older than myself, many of them university graduates, my enthusiasm and application enabled me to pass out top of the whole college at the end of the first year.

At this juncture, the South African government decided to award about a dozen scholarships of £400 a year, for four years, to students for the purpose of study in American and English agricultural colleges. In the light of my success at Potchefstroom, one of these scholarships was mine for the asking, but my father, feeling that he could afford to pay the cost, decided to send me to Cambridge University at his own expense. It was a decision which changed my whole career. Wrongly or rightly, I believed these twelve government students would be given preference over me on their return to South Africa, and so, upon proceeding to Cambridge, I abandoned agriculture for a mining career.

Why I changed from agriculture to mining, instead of to some other profession, I do not know. I was probably influenced by my father's elder brother, who had made and lost several fortunes in mining: he was one of the first to develop the mines on the Rand, and at one time had owned Auckland Park, the finest residential section of Johannesburg. Later the Witbank Collieries were named after him; he eventually died in Spain developing a cinnabar mine. Or, perhaps, it was that other mining uncle of mine who was on a continual treasure hunt, searching for a fabulous sum in gold bars, which the Boers had instructed him and four other men to bury, one night, on the eve of the British entry into Johannesburg. When they were able to reach the spot in safety, two years later, they were unable to locate the exact site; if he is alive, he is probably still digging. No doubt, it was the love of adventure which played the leading part in my decision.

My three years in Cambridge were the happiest days of my life. The friends I formed there are the only ones I have kept close to my heart. Some were killed in the war; some at odd intervals I still hear from. The will to succeed was driving me on, and scholastically I was a brilliant success: at the end of my first year at

Caius College I was elected an exhibitioner; in my final examinations, in 1913, taking four sciences instead of the usual three, I passed the Natural Sciences Tripos with first-class honours. I mention this point, not in a spirit of braggadocio, but because my precocity played an important part later on in my wartime advancement at a very early age to a position of great importance.

To Cambridge I owe a debt which I shall never be able to repay. Its traditions, its customs, its old colleges with their priceless architecture, their quadrangles, libraries, lawns, and 'backs', and, above all, the companionship and the association with the products of England's finest public schools, all left their imprint on me; they contributed to the moulding of my character, and inspired in me a love of learning and an appreciation of the finer arts. It is the genius of the English schools that they turn out persons who are above all equable and affable, but controlled, reserved, and self-contained – the type that can get along with anyone anywhere without losing its own dignity and self-sufficiency. If I lack anything of these attributes the fault is mine; I was certainly shown the way.

At Cambridge, almost half the year is taken up with vacations, and all of them I spent travelling on the Continent. My bicycle accompanied me always through Germany, Holland, Belgium, and France, and as I spoke the three languages of these four countries fluently, I was continually on the move. I covered hundreds of miles. I rode the *pavé* from Brussels to Ghent; I climbed the hills in the Ardennes. Walking tours carried me through the Black Forest and the Hartz; I explored the Rhineland from Heidelberg to Düsseldorf, sometimes pedalling my wheel, sometimes gliding lazily on river steamers. It was the people that interested me above all: their customs, their way of living, their philosophy of life. I was Bohemian in my tastes: sometimes I frequented the homes, cafes, and places of entertainment in the poorer sections; but other times, in the great cities, such as Berlin, I afforded myself the luxury of the big international hotels, the 'Adlon' and the 'Bristol', and restaurants such as those of Hiller, Borchart, and Horcher.

To see a country, to study its language and the ways of its people, to look under the façade which is dressed up for the tourist, and finally to learn its topography, there is no better way than a walking or bicycle tour. The energy expended is well repaid in rich dividends of experience and information gained. If I never visit Holland again, I shall ever remember that the road from Rotterdam to Amsterdam, via The Hague and Haarlem, is as flat as a pancake, and that, on the contrary, there are appreciable hills around Arnhem. Even if memory failed, the muscles of the legs would jog it.

Here, then, for almost four years, six months in the year, I was learning the 'feel' of Europe – absorbing a knowledge of the actual land and furthering a familiarity with its intimate life. It was a continuation of the days at Dresden, but with the field vastly greater, and the enjoyment enhanced by mature observation and judgement. All unwittingly, I was preparing myself for the role which I was to play during the war.

CHAPTER 2

GETTING TO THE
FIRING LINE

I N JUNE 1913, having graduated, I left Cambridge with
still two years to be spent at a mining school, if I wanted
to qualify myself thoroughly as a mining engineer. To this
end, three mining schools presented themselves: the one in London, Freiburg in Germany, and the Colorado School of Mines.

Ever ready for an excuse to travel, I decided on a personal
tour of inspection, beginning with the college most remote. In
July I sailed for Quebec as a steerage passenger in the company
of two other Cambridge men. After a day's experience, two of us
decided to transfer to regular accommodation, however expensive it might prove. We were willing to suffer hardships, but we

were afraid of disease: cleanliness was not an inherent characteristic of the steerage passengers from Galicia and southern
Russia. Our chief occupation during the rest of the voyage was
sneaking food out of the first-class saloon to pass on to our companion left in the steerage.

I was duly impressed by the usual round of sights offered to
the tourist in the United States, but my one urge was to get out
west. In Denver, I ran short of money. I was thoroughly unprepared for the difference in the cost of living in Europe and the
United States, and I dared not apply to my father, who had not
been consulted about my American trip. On impulse, I decided
to work out the six weeks on a cattle ranch, and managed to be
hired by the Carey Brothers, whose place is one of the biggest in
the United States. I spent a happy six weeks oblivious of mining
and studies, earning $2 a day, plus the best of food and lodging.
The work, pitching hay, or tramping it down on the top of a hay-
stack, was hard, but I was young and healthy, and the work did
me a world of good. I thoroughly enjoyed the company of the
cowboys, listening to their tales of early times in the West, and
putting up with the many tricks they played on me; they broke
me into the intricacies of the western saddle, and on privileged
occasions I was allowed to ride the ranges.

Toward the end of September, I went to Golden, ready to
give the Colorado School of Mines a trial. The London School
of Mines opened on 15 October, so I knew I could still reach
London in time for the opening if I wished. To a graduate accustomed to Cambridge with its serene reserve, its lecture and
tutorial system, its traditions, its culture, its beautiful old colleges with their lawns and walks, the Colorado School of Mines

was a direct contrast. Set among mines, where students could get practical experience, it was then, and probably is today, the finest mining school in the world; but my sole memory of it is the general instruction of the classroom system, which was too much for me, and the ragging of the freshmen, which as a post-graduate I was permitted to escape, but which, as a privileged spectator, I was allowed to witness. I wonder if the freshmen are still forced to roll eggs with their tongues across the stage of the local movie theatre, or whether enduring raw egg shampoos, and coats of green paint are still the order of the day?

If I had stayed in Colorado, the following years might have been very different for me; but on an impulse, which was per-haps homesickness and perhaps fate, I returned to England, and entered the London School of Mines as a post-graduate.

During this year, I worked incessantly, and the records of the School of Mines will show that I repeated my Cambridge suc-cesses by heading the lists in most of my classes. But though work was my chief interest and almost my whole occupation, the most memorable event of the time was my first innocent debut in diplomacy – the diplomacy of romance. Once again, it was chance that played the leading role.

One evening, dropping into the Empire in Leicester Square, I saw a young and beautiful girl among the demi-mondaines of the theatre's then notorious promenade. She was so obviously out of place that my curiosity was piqued and I spoke to her. She told me her sad little tale: a stepfather in Lincolnshire, family trouble, the leaving of home to find work in London, no success, hunger, a chance acquaintance who had showed her the easy way, and had loaned her a dress. This was her second week as a daughter of joy. Had I been older, I would have treated her story with a shrug, but I was young and romantic, and I believed her. I found that her flat was being paid for by an Australian, a young Cambridge student to whom she introduced me. By agreeing to put up £10 a month for six months, I got him to agree to do likewise to enable her to go straight.

With an appropriate story about her being one of his relatives, he introduced her to a charming London family. Only an irresponsible youth could have done such a thing, but it all ended very happily: cultured and coming from a respectable family, she was able to pass it off with success. In later years, I often met Elsie; she married a colonel in the British Army and was for a time divinely happy. He was killed in the war, leaving her quite well off. I often saw her riding and her happy smile amply repaid me for anything I had done. There were only two of us who knew her secret, and she knew we would keep it well.

I met the sister of my young Australian friend, who was stopping with her mother in London. Time with her passed by as a delightful dream; she brought a tenderness into my life which I had never experienced before. I had known very few girls, and this was my first love. In March 1914 she and her mother sailed for Melbourne. They were to return in six months for our marriage.

The summer of 1914 I spent surveying in a lead mine in Flintshire, where I heard the first news of the British declaration of war. War was furthest from my mind at the time; I was happily in love, and filled with ambition. I had my life mapped out: one year more at the School of Mines to qualify as a mining engineer; then the mines on the Rand and in Rhodesia for experience; and after that London as a consulting engineer. But this was not for me.

Restlessness seized me, and in short order my mind was made up. It was a surprised mine manager who saw me dash into my lodgings one morning to pack my bag in time for the London train leaving within the hour. But I scarcely made a coherent explanation to him. Here was the great adventure.

My first thought in the morning was to join the Honourable Artillery Company, a volunteer corps, but at their headquarters I was informed that for the time being they had no vacancies. I secured a personal letter of introduction to Lord Denbigh, the commanding officer, and was on my way back to HAC headquarters for a second attempt, when chance took me into the Royal Colonial Institute, of which I was a fellow. Here I ran into Mousely, a New Zealander, an old Cambridge man, who was on his way to Australia House to join the Australian Volunteer Hospital, which was then in the process of formation.

People were saying the war would be over in a few weeks, and in view of my rebuff that morning, and of my never having had any military training, I jumped at Mousely's suggestion that I should accompany him for an interview. The Hospital was due to leave, he said, in a few days. Here, at least, was a sure way of getting out to France. By nightfall, we were members of the Australian Volunteer Hospital, under orders to leave for France as soon as the unit had been completed. Quarters for the time being were the Ranelagh Club, where the polo field proved a splendid training ground for us, and the club rooms excellent quarters for our officers; we slept in the horse boxes, and were glad of them at the end of a day's drilling.

The next morning, regular army uniforms were handed out to about eighty of us, who comprised the rank and file, and we found ourselves in the presence of our officers: Colonel Eames, the commanding officer, and a group of Australian doctors who had been recruited from the London hospitals. I still remember with respect the regular army sergeant major, who knocked us into soldiers in those few days. We broke his heart at times, but we were willing. Infantry drill and stretcher drill was the order of day from reveille to dusk. At the end of about ten days, we were ready to join the Expeditionary Force. We were inspected by a RAMC colonel from the War Office, and orders were given to entrain. All was excitement. We had been trained as a field unit, and we had visions of ourselves dashing under shell and rifle fire to the rescue of the wounded. We thought we should be at the Front within forty-eight hours.

We embarked at Southampton in a troop ship, and found ourselves in the midst of other units, mostly infantry battalions which had been rushed home from Gibraltar and Malta. When we reached Havre, the retreat from Mons was rapidly proceeding. For a week we never moved from the wharf. Wrapped in our blankets, we slept on the hard cobblestones and the filth of the dock; we missed the horse boxes of Ranelagh. Rumours were rife: Uhlans had been seen on the outskirts of Havre; spies had been caught at the headquarters of the Allied forces. Confusion was all we knew to be a fact. Troops, including the French Marine Corps, kept arriving and departing.

Suddenly, at a moment's notice, we were piled into a transport, packed to capacity with units from a dozen regiments, and we were off into the unknown destination. We slept on the deck where we stood. There were rumours of Bordeaux, but eventually we heard that our destination was St Nazaire.

There, some public building probably a school, housed our unit. We had expected to see service as stretcher bearers; instead we found ourselves as orderlies carrying coverings, bandages, trays, bedpans, attending to the pitiful unceasing demands of an overcrowded hospital. The wounded kept coming in until some had even to be left on their stretchers.

I cannot describe the horror of the next few weeks. Nothing I subsequently saw in the trenches equalled it. Most of the wounded had lain for days in cattle-trucks, with only a rough field dressing for the most desperate cases. Practically every case meant amputation; here was horror worse than any battlefield. I subsequently saw men shot down next to me with limbs torn off by shells; but here I saw them slowly die in agony; I heard their cries for water and their groans. There was no supply of anti-tetanus serum on hand, and of the many who developed the dread disease all succumbed. With rubber gloves on, to protect ourselves, we stood helpless and watched them slowly die. I can still see the convulsive twitching of their haggard faces, the contorted look of horror of locked muscles, the frenzied, lost despair in their eyes.

The doctors and nurses did more than gallant service; they worked night and day. Many of the wounded were saved; but if so many died, it was certainly not the fault of the hospital or its staff; gangrene had set in and the tetanus germ was there long before these men, desperately wounded, ever reached St Nazaire.

I think it was in November that we eventually left St Nazaire. Entrained in cattle-trucks, we had great hopes that at last we were going to the Front, for we still had all our field hospital equipment with us. But our hopes were again dashed; after several days of shunting and slow progress, we detrained at Wimereux, and realised that a base hospital was to be our lot.

The war had already resolved itself into trench warfare, and Lord Kitchener was appealing for volunteers on the basis of a three years' war. To serve in a base hospital was not what I had joined up for; at all costs, I wanted to get to the Front. I am afraid Mousely and I had made nuisances of ourselves; we had repeated interviews with Colonel Eames, the commanding officer, and with Lady Dudley, the wife of a former governor of Australia, who was intimately connected with the hospital, until finally, probably in order to get rid of us, our applications for a commission were recommended. In December 1914, I was gazetted a second lieutenant in the Royal Field Artillery, and was appointed to the brigade of a division, then in the process of formation at Ewshot.

I thoroughly enjoyed the four months of training we went through. Most of the subalterns were overseas Englishmen, who had hurried home at the outbreak of the war. There were men from India, China, South America, and other parts of the globe – an interesting group who were excellent company. The remaining officers were mostly 'dug-outs' – retired officers whom the exigencies of war had once more called to active service – and, as the training proceeded, we received a few 'regulars', chiefly recovered wounded, and a few 'rankers'. The traditions of the regiment and of the officers' mess were kept up; we all tried very hard to do the correct thing, and I am sure even the 'dug-outs', who were very critical, agreed we did very well, though I did once, flustered by having a general seated on my right, start the port in circulation in the wrong direction.

Most of the officers were good horsemen, but few of the drivers could ride; they were chiefly from the East End of London, chosen because of their small stature. Horses they managed with difficulty, but the South American mules, of which we had many, played havoc with them until they learned to keep out of reach of vicious heels. However, perseverance, practice, and willingness of spirit, carried the day; eventually they were turned out a credit to their instructors, upsetting the theory that horsemanship must be learned from youth up. Gradually as the few months went by, we acquired discipline, training, and, above all, equipment. Old French guns, even wooden guns, were all we had, until about a month before leaving for France. The officers went off to Lark Hill for a course in gunnery; brigades and their batteries went through target practice on Salisbury Plain; we were reviewed by the King and by Princess Mary. We were ready for the Front.

Life had been very pleasant for four months, at the government's expense. We had had everything a healthy man desires: good, clean exercise, good sport, fine companions, the best of food and accommodation, the joy and responsibility of authority, hard work, and London, with its amusements, within easy reach on week-ends. This was all to change now; we had to get down to the grimness, the hardship, and, above all, what was the most terrible, the monotony of war.

In April 1915 I found myself once again on a transport ship under sealed orders for a port which turned out to be Boulogne. We entrained for the St Omer area, where we remained in rest billets for a few days. Then we slowly moved into the line in the Armentières sector, probably the quietest at that time on the Western Front. Everything was prepared for us: gun pits, telephone lines, observation posts, and billets; it was simply a question of relieving and taking over from the outgoing division. Simple as it was, I probably experienced the greatest thrill I ever got in the firing line: it was my first contact with the enemy, my first entry into a zone where I imagined death was constantly lurking in the form of a bullet or a shell. Later, I was to laugh at those first fears, for, in reality, it was the calmest of nights.

Relieving was done at night. It was an eerie feeling, approaching the front line for the first time: it was a pitch dark night, and the dazzling white Very lights, shot out rocketwise at regular intervals, clearly marked the position of the firing line. Bursts of machine-gunfire, interspersed with an occasional rifle shot and the howl of a shell, drowned at odd intervals the muffled sound of our gun wheels, horses' hoofs, and the champing of bits. Once the gun pits were reached, the relief was quickly carried out, and we were soon wrapped in our blankets, trying to sleep. At first everything was new. Every operation, every scene was avidly taken in. It was great sport firing at objectives behind the enemy's trenches, and a stinging thrill to watch a direct hit through field-glasses, after regulating by telephone the fire of a battery 3,000 yards away from the observation post. The routine of a week at the battery, a week as forward observing officer in the trenches, and a week at the wagon lines some 8 or 10 miles behind the Front, was eagerly gone through at first, but as the months dragged on it became terribly monotonous.

In 1915 we were suffering from shell shortage. Our ammunition was cut down each week, until eventually we were not allowed to fire more than six rounds a day, except in emergencies.

The winter came on, and with it the rain, snow, and mud. The trenches became a quagmire. We were up to our thighs in water each day; and at night, we slept in dug-outs on wire bunks, sometimes only a few inches above the water. Add rats and fleas to make the picture complete. Rheumatism and trench foot were causing more casualties than the enemy's fire.

I had my share of land mines, Big Berthas, Whizz Bangs, and Minnies, and saw men killed and wounded. I had an observation post razed to the ground while I sat in its sand-bag cellar for a couple of hours, wondering whether it would hold out against the 'crumps' that were being poured on it. In the front line, I spent a sleepless seventy-two hours as FOO cutting wire and directing an artillery barrage during a diversion we tried to create at the time of the Loos attack. But all this was tame to what the division had to go through on the Somme, and in many a subsequent battle later on, after I had left it. Actually, I saw more of death in the three weeks in the hospital at St Nazaire than I saw here during our whole nine months' stay in the sector. Armentières remained to the end of the war the de luxe sector of the Western Front, a convenient terrain in which to give the new Kitchener divisions their first baptism of fire. If we could have relaxed, it would not have been so bad, but we were continually keyed up expecting something to happen which never did.

Our only relief from this dull routine was our three days' leave in England every three months. We also had good food: the army rations were excellent, and this was supplemented by hampers which we were permitted to order from Harrod's. For water, we used Perrier, as the ordinary supply was bad, and the local beer was even worse. How the peasants of north-eastern

France could drink it, I never could fathom. I could get a little consolation out of letters. Most of my relatives were disappointed that I had abandoned a promising career for the service; they were too far away to realise that the best of England's youth had joined up. My fiancée, cut off from me in Australia, wrote less and less, until finally we ceased to correspond. The end of the war seemed indefinitely postponed, and communication, because of censors and delays, became almost impossible. I seemed effectively cut off from the world.

Just when we began to think that we never would be transferred, we got orders to move. All immediately was excitement and bustle. The usual rumours flew around as to our destination. We were even going to the Dardanelles, and then it was to Mespot. Imagine our dismay when we found ourselves relieving the Guards at Laventie, a sector at that time almost as quiet as the one at Armentières. But we were really on the move: we only stayed there for a couple of weeks. At the commencement of March 1916 we started south again: the concentration for the Somme offensive had begun.

For the rest of my short stay on the Western Front, I was never again to complain of monotony. Events moved quickly. Before leaving Ewshot, I had been promoted to the rank of first lieutenant; I was now a captain. My battery commander had been placed on the sick list and was subsequently retired on account of advanced age; Captain Wells, who had succeeded him, had been wounded at Laventie; I now found myself in command of the battery.

We covered miles in intermittent snow over muddy roads. The displacement of guns, ammunition wagons, horses, and men over such a distance was an undertaking. We spent hours in the saddle each day, our hands and feet numb with the cold. It was ceaseless work, which called for endurance. At dusk, billets had to be found, and, when all the men and horses had been looked after, maps and orders had to be studied for the next day's march. I enjoyed it; it was the only part of the war which recalled to me my boyhood memories and conception of war. We still had the mud, but I was in command of a fine group of men; I felt a good horse under me; we were on the move; we were going somewhere.

At Souchez, we moved into the line again, taking over gun positions vacated by the French. Here I was immediately faced with an ordeal: the French battery had already left, and I was faced with no indication as to the position of our front line trenches or that of the enemy. There were no telephone lines, nor any information as regards observation posts; the only thing for me to do was to reconnoitre for myself over ground which had been taken and retaken a dozen times, where not an inch was left unpitted by shell craters. I crawled through rotted fragments of French and German dead whose clothes had long since crumbled away, so that the only distinguishing marks were the long top boots of the Germans and the shorter ones of the French. Covered with mud, raked by machine-gun and shell fire, I reached our front line trenches, where I quickly established contact with battalion headquarters. Telephone lines were laid. As soon as I could get back to the battery we got the range, and were ready for all eventualities.

On the third day after taking up this position, my leave fell due. The enemy were to have one more crack at me, however, before I entrained. At railhead, sparks from the locomotive betrayed us to a raiding German plane. In the darkness of the night, we heard the drone of its motor, the whistle of the bomb, then crash! We scattered as fast as our legs could carry us while three more bombs fell in quick succession. We had visions of an enforced return to the trenches; but, to our relief, the train was untouched, and other damage we did not care about. Within the hour, we were on our way to Boulogne and 'Blighty'. I was not to see the Front again.

CHAPTER 3

I ENTER THE BRITISH
SECRET SERVICE

L EAVE FOR MOST of us colonials and overseas men, with no family or relatives in England, had resolved itself into a mad three days without sleep, doing a round of night clubs and shows, with companions of the opposite sex, not always well chosen. I had been no better or worse than the others. For all we knew, we might never return on another leave.

To me all this had brought a reaction of strong distaste, and on this particular leave I was grateful and happy to have a letter of introduction from a brother officer to his sister. She was a charming, highly intelligent girl, with a job at the War Office. We saw a great deal of each other, dining together, and seeing some of the better plays; starved for companionship, I told her a great deal about myself, especially about my travels. She listened with her eyes shining, but I was not allowed for a moment to fancy that she was a modern Desdemona – her excitement was all for the service.

'What a pity you cannot get into intelligence!' she cried. 'You are just the man they are looking for. They have the greatest difficulty in finding an officer with military experience who speaks French, German, and Dutch, and who is thoroughly acquainted with the countries. The difficulty, of course, is Dutch,' she added. 'It is remarkable how few Englishmen speak it. It is typical of us as a race – we always expect the foreigner to speak our own language.' I laughed at her remark. Wasn't I returning to France that evening?

On arrival at Folkestone, ready to embark for Boulogne, we wretches leaving 'Blighty' were told that since a German submarine had been sighted outside, we could return to London, and report back the next evening. I woke next morning at the Waldorf Hotel with a fever and a body rash. Frantically I dashed to the nearest military hospital. My case was diagnosed as German measles, and to bed I was ordered. Entrance into a hospital in England automatically transferred one from the Overseas Command to that of the War Office. I realised that this meant I was now free to apply for the post my enthusiastic friend had mentioned. As I convalesced, I turned the matter over in my mind, and over the phone, I discussed it with her. She promised to talk to her chief about it.

A week later, I received orders to report immediately at the War Office. I hurried there, hoping to find out at once what my new duties would be. Instead, I was confronted by three examiners in succession; I was in for a language test. The examination, both oral and written, presented no difficulties. I had, in fact, the advantage of the Dutch examiner: I was speaking my native language, the first language I had learned as a child.

Next day a telephone call at the 'Waldorf' instructed me to report to Colonel B. at Whitehall court. He informed me that I had been transferred to the intelligence corps, and that as I had been attached for special duty to the secret service, he would take me to the chief immediately. Up several flights of stairs I went, until I reached the very top of the building. Here, in a room which resembled the state-room of a ship, I was confronted with a kindly man who immediately put me at my ease. It was the chief, C, a captain in the navy. He swung around in a swivel chair to look at me – a grey-haired man of about sixty, in naval uniform, and short in stature.

After a few preliminary remarks, he suddenly came to the point:

I know all about your past history. You are just the man we want to join T in Rotterdam, leaving tonight via Harwich and the Hook. Our train-watching service has broken down completely in Belgium and in north-eastern France – we are getting absolutely nothing through. It is up to you to reorganise the service. I can't tell you how it is to be done – that is your job. You have carte blanche.

Use T as 'cover'; communicate with me through him. Within reasonable limits, he will supply you with all the money you need for the organisation. You will find others in T's office in charge of other branches of the secret service; co-operate with them.

You are in complete charge of the military section; responsibility for its success or failure is on your shoulders. consult with Colonel Oppenheim, our military attaché at The Hague, as to the kind of information we require. A handbook and other information about the German army will be given you by Colonel Oppenheim. We will also send you questionnaires from time to time through T.

Urgent military information you obtain about the Germans will be telegraphed in code by Colonel Oppenheim direct to GHQ. Hand T all written reports concerning less important information; he will send it to us through the diplomatic bag. Anything else you want to know, ask T. Here is his address. Commander S. in the next room, will furnish you with your ticket and expenses, and will tell you when your train leaves Victoria.

He offered me his hand, wishing me good luck.

It was in somewhat of a daze that I found myself out in the street – events had moved so rapidly. I had envisaged a job in some government office in London, probably connected with the censorship; a commission in Holland, practically as a freelance, had been furthest from my mind. I had only the afternoon in which to get together some civilian clothes, and in a scramble like that of a nightmare, where everything happens at once and nothing seems accomplished, I bought underclothing, hats, and shoes, and routed out suits and coats long-forgotten in storage in Harrods. The pleasant friend to whom I owed my new career dined with me at 'The Piccadilly' to celebrate our common delight and excitement at my new enterprise. At eight-thirty that evening I was on my way to Harwich.

Again, chance had changed my whole career; as a matter of

fact, it had saved my life. Had I developed the measles six days earlier or later, I should have been in France with my battery. A few weeks later, as I subsequently learned, it was wiped out completely on the Somme; every officer in it was killed.

Normally I should have got to the Hook in the morning, but with a group of several ships convoyed by destroyers, the speed of the convoy is that of the slowest ship. A fog further delayed our arrival until the evening. A short journey by rail brought me to Rotterdam too late, as I thought, to get in touch with T. After a good night's rest at the Maas Hotel, where I had stayed in pre-wartimes, I called on T in his office, which occupied the whole of the first floor of a large building on the Boompjes. A man on guard at the entrance took my name, and after few minutes' delay I was ushered in to T.

I found myself facing a short, though broad-shouldered man, ruddy of complexion, with small piercing eyes, who looked like the combination of sea captain and prizefighter. I spent the whole morning listening to his summing up of the situation. He was dreadfully worried. The whole of his organisation covering Belgium and north-eastern France, comprising over forty train-watching posts, had broken down, and nearly all the agents had been arrested. Frankignoul, his agent in Maastricht, had been striving to establish a new organisation, but so far had been unsuccessful, and absolutely no information was coming through. T seemed somewhat dubious as to whether I would be able to do anything, but he told me that he would give me every assistance, as he had been instructed that I was to be at the head of the military section in Holland. He placed a room at my disposal and introduced me to the men with whom I was to be associated: Power, the head of the naval section; de Mestre, the head of the counter-espionage; de Peterson, the son of the Russian consul-general at The Hague, and, as far as I could gather, general factotum at the office; and, finally, Meulkens, the cashier and book-keeper. T further informed me that he had been ordered to supply me with such sums of money as I required, but that I would have to justify the expenditure to him, and added that it was simply a question of results; there would always be ample funds available for the right kind of information.

From T's remarks, and from those of C, the chief in England, I knew my stay in Holland was entirely dependent on my own activities. I had obvious qualifications in the way of my knowledge of languages, especially Dutch and Flemish, my intimate acquaintance with the topography and people of Germany, and the occupied territories, and my military experience at the Front; but, although there were generals in the British Army at the end of the war no older than I was, my age was a handicap. I realised that if I were unsuccessful, I would be recalled after a few months; and as far as the expenditure of money was concerned, C would pay only for dependable and effective reports. If, subsequently, I was never refused any sum I asked for, it was only because of the vital information which was secured by the organisations which I built up. Youth carried with it an enthusiasm and an adaptability, which today, as an older man, I marvel at. Pitkin may be right about life beginning at forty, but in the field activities of war youth has the advantage.

During my stay in Holland, right up to the end of the war, T lived up to his promise. I think he was always loyal to me. The 'cover' he provided was sufficient to protect me from the Dutch authorities; I never had the least trouble from them, although they obviously knew what I was doing. He certainly had great influence with them. The head of the River Police, and other police authorities, were always ready to rush to his office at a moment's call. They accorded him every privilege he demanded. He had lived in Holland a great number of years, the owner of a successful shipping business, and had a great number of powerful friends; but above all, he had the prestige of the British government behind him. It was also the policy of the Dutch government to be friendly to both the Allied and the German secret services; they realised that they could not prevent their country from being overrun with secret service agents, and so wisely chose to keep in close touch with the respective chiefs, who could thus be held responsible for the behaviour of their agents.

T's outstanding quality was that he was a fighter; he was ever ready to fight with the Belgian authorities when we complained of interference with our agents, and even with the British War Office at times. Since he was living as a civilian in a neutral country, with ample private means, the chief in England always had to handle him carefully.

T spoke little Dutch, and knew no French or German. He had known nothing about Frankignoul's train-watching organisation. Frankignoul had held all the threads in his own hands, and when they broke, T was naturally unable to do anything on his own.

He was, however, a shrewd executive, and helped to keep the various branches of the service under him in close co-operation. His chief function, the handling of the Dutch authorities, he carried out admirably. He undoubtedly rendered splendid service, and fully merited the CBE (Commander of the British Empire), with which he was decorated at the end of the war.

My first care on leaving T was to find a comfortable apartment, and with the help of de Peterson I soon found one on the Heemraad Singel. De Mestre, the head of counter-espionage, with a twinkle in his eye, informed me that the Maas Hotel, where I was staying, was overrun with German agents.

It took me two or three weeks to orientate myself, and in this I was helped considerably by a young Englishman who had spent several years in Brussels before the war, and who had been in Holland since the outbreak of hostilities. I was fortunate enough to get him transferred to me from the CE department, and to the end of my stay in Holland, he remained my faithful assistant and companion.

Those who were living in Belgium and in Holland at the time will realise the difficulties we had to contend with. The Germans had created excellent barriers against the passage of information; along the Belgian–Dutch frontier there stretched deadly high-voltage electric wire, with an unbroken cordon of sentinels at small intervals within sight of each other, and a swarm of German Secret Police patrolling the frontier on both sides. But the German devices and men were a definite, concentrated force, much simpler really to combat than the vague but potent pest of Dutch and Belgian freelance agents with which Holland was swarming. Hundreds of Belgian refugees had settled there, and before the Germans had established their effective barriers, many of them had found it easy to get information out of Belgium, and had made a lucrative living by peddling it to the British, Belgian, and French secret services, sometimes selling the same information to all three. Conditions had now changed; they were producing no further information, but they were all rushing around interfering with every attempt we were making to establish communications with the interior of Belgium.

The first essential was to obtain trustworthy Belgians in Holland whom we could rely on to keep their mouths shut, who would submit to discipline, and who would be governed by patriotism and not by money, providing their living expenses were paid. I was delighted to come in contact with Moreau, a former high official of the Belgian Railways, who, after learning our problem in a long talk with me, offered to get his son to enlist the aid of picked Belgian railwaymen – there were a large number of them in Holland at the time who still looked upon him as their chief. The son presented himself in due course, and as he impressed me favourably, I outlined my plan to him. Accordingly, at odd intervals he brought me, one by one, some fifty or more men who could be distributed at strategic points on Dutch soil from Maastricht to the coast in Zeeland, in a manner so reasonable as to avoid suspicion.

Each of the Moreau agents was made responsible for a definite strip of the Dutch frontier, with instructions to find some means of regular communication across the frontier with the occupied territory. We explained that there were three possible channels to be used: '*Pasteurs*' who could go back and forth across the electric wire on dark nights by means of india-rubber gloves and socks; boatmen, who though under strict surveillance of the Germans, were allowed to ply their barges all the way from Rotterdam to Antwerp; and farm labourers who had fields under cultivation bordering the frontier, and who could toss messages across the wire when the sentry was not looking.

To each agent a number was given, and the son assumed the name of 'Oram'. It was agreed that Oram was to be their immediate chief, that they were to obey him implicitly, that once located, they were not to move from their prescribed areas, and that Oram would arrange couriers to pick up the reports. Each one was sworn to secrecy not to divulge whom he was working for, nor to try to discover the identity of any of Oram's other agents.

Thus was started an organisation in Holland which gradually increased in efficiency until eventually, during the last two years of the war, we had open continuously at least six '*tuyaux*', or means of communication, with the interior of Belgium. When one broke down we had the other five in reserve, and others were continually being established.

The next problem was to post agents throughout the interior of Belgium in such a manner that, as a group, they would cover the whole of the occupied territory; to instruct them as to the information required; to establish contact men in the interior with whom reports could be deposited; and finally to find trustworthy couriers who should collect the reports and relay them for passage at the frontier.

There were three ways of establishing agents in the occupied territories. One was to send Belgians or Frenchmen back into Belgium or France by passing them through the electric wire on a dark night. Another was to use a courier in the interior to carry a letter from one of our agents in Holland to friends in Belgium, soliciting their help. Here again Moreau furnished us with the names of many railwaymen in Belgium who were glad to work for their old chief; they turned out to be some of our best agents. And finally we were often able to establish contacts with old organisations which had functioned in 1915, and which had lost contact with the exterior when the frontier became practically sealed in 1916. Each agent in the interior could also be relied upon generally to recruit two or three others.

The establishment of couriers in the occupied territories presented a special difficulty. Owing to the identity card system, which was rigidly enforced, no one could travel more than 30 miles from the address written on his card without facing arrest. The German Secret Police, circulating in Belgium, paid special attention to people on the road, or in any means of conveyance. They realised as well as we did that no information was of any value until it had crossed the frontier.

The system of communication from the spy in the occupied territories to me in Rotterdam can be summed up briefly as follows:

The chief of each spy group in the interior concentrated the reports sent in by his agents, and then deposited them at Antwerp, Liège, or Brussels at an address ('letter box') furnished by us. A courier carried these reports from the letter box to the tuyau, or passage at the frontier, where they passed into Holland. Here they were collected by Oram's frontier men and relayed to me through Oram. The frontier passages, the letter boxes, and the couriers between the letter boxes and the frontier passages were mounted from Holland under the direction of Oram and myself only. Each spy chief, whose agents were collecting information in the interior, had his own independent letter box, frontier courier, and passage at the frontier, the whole

*personnel of which, with the exception of the letter box, was unknown
to him; the letter box in his turn did not know the identity of the
couriers who deposited and picked up the reports. Once the reports
containing the information were deposited at the letter box, it was
my responsibility to get them to Holland for transmission to GHQ.*

Duplication and secrecy based on ignorance of the general system was necessary; it was the solid basis of our policy. Our main care was to build up a number of small groups, each isolated from the other, so that if one worker was caught, he could only involve at the most four or five others. Even the bravest patriots could not be relied upon to keep silent in the face of the German third degree methods; and the prisoners were often cruelly beaten until they confessed. Drugs were sometimes administered to break the resistance of the sternest will.

We had learned our lesson from the Frankignoul disaster, for I found, after investigating his organisation, that he had tied 200 agents in the interior to one solitary channel of communication with the outside: the tram which ran daily across the Belgian frontier to Maastricht. In this tram the reports had been hidden each day in Belgium, to be taken out by Frankignoul's agents on their arrival in Holland. His method of communication was ideal because it was so direct and simple as to forestall detection for a considerable time; but it had worked so smoothly for months that he had lulled himself into the belief that it would go on working forever. He had made the additional error of allowing the identity of all his agents in Belgium to be known to each other. Hence when the link of communication fell into the hands of the Germans, they had time to seize all the reports and trace down all the agents, since Frankignoul had no means to warn his men of this danger.

In the course of my activities I was continually in communication with Colonel Oppenheim at The Hague. He was the exact opposite of T: fairly tall, and somewhat frail, scholarly in appearance, highly strung, and retiring in disposition. One of his functions was to analyse information and telegraph reports, and having nothing to do with the procuring of information or with secret service organisation, I sometimes thought he did not quite realise the difficulties with which we had to contend. He was, however, a brilliant staff officer, as I found out afterwards from his masterly analyses of the reports I sent him. He got every scrap of information there was to glean from them, and in the examination of train-watching reports, he was an expert in gauging the exact volume of each troop movement.

From Colonel Oppenheim I learned exactly what information was required. It will probably astonish the layman to know that this was chiefly data on the movements of trains! I myself in other times would never have pictured secret service as an organisation devoted to, or even interested in, noting the arrivals and departures of railway units; yet this became a ruling interest of all our lives. The use of the trains by the Germans meant the movement of German troops, and the movement of troops often presaged a mass attack. On our information often depended the Allies' hope of preparing to defend a position, or to surprise an attacking force. The Germans never did have enough troops to initiate an offensive on both fronts at the same time, and so each offensive was always preceded by a large transfer of troops from one front to the other. Hence Colonel Oppenheim's emphasis on the importance of getting all possible information about every troop movement, and the identity of the units involved. To assist identification of the different German regiments and units, he furnished me with handbooks of the German Army, which made me thoroughly conversant with its organisation and the various uniforms and distinguishing marks. All of this it was necessary to know in order to follow the movements of German troops with definiteness and assurance.

Urged on by him, we gradually built up a train-watching system which covered every strategic line in Belgium and north-eastern France. The time and composition of each troop train was noted; at each junction we followed the movement, and so were able to trace each division from its point of entrainment to its place of detrainment. Troops coming from the Russian Front on their way to the Western Front were reported as they passed Herbesthal; from our Liège posts we knew whether the fifty-two trains which composed the division had branched off to Namur or to Brussels; at Namur or Brussels we caught them again and followed them through the various junctions until they detrained. By a system of duplicate train-watching posts we were able to check any errors, and special agents definitely settled in the detraining centres and rest areas identified the troops as they arrived. Divisions coming from a distance invariably went into a rest area before being put into the front line; or, in the case of an offensive involving several divisions, they were first concentrated in the back areas. Movements in the front line could be checked by taking prisoners, or by seizing letters and documents, but back of the Front it was chiefly on careful watchers that the High Command depended for its information.

It will be shown later how our train-watching posts caught all the east to west, and west to east movements. Even though there was often a delay of three to four days before we got the reports, this was of no importance, as it took weeks for the Germans to concentrate for an offensive. The transfer of a division through a given junction required at least two days, and as a rule four or five days, since, in addition to the fifty-two troop trains comprising the division, there were the trains carrying food and war material which had to be run through as well. Many divisions were required for an offensive; so it can readily be seen that we could get our reports out in ample time for GHQ to be warned about the various movements.

As I shall indicate later, we also obtained a variety of other information, such as enemy plans for the launching of offensives, the formation of new divisions and regiments, change in equipment, new inventions and new types of guns, new methods of attack, the arrival of drafts to replace losses, and targets for aerial bombardment; but by far our most important achievement was the continual check on the movements of the enemy, and the identification of the units involved. The interest and excitement of this service developed into a terrific tension toward the end of the war, for it became common knowledge that the German Command was working toward a climactic movement, the big offensive, designed to bring the war to a crashing and decisive end. It was a matter of chief importance to detect any traces of plans or first movements toward the big offensive, and we were on the alert constantly to note any massing of troops which might indicate the location chosen for it and the types of service troops destined to serve in it.

This, then, is a résumé of our objective, the difficulties we had to contend with, and a few of the technical details which I have had to explain in order to enable a better understanding of the tales of secret service which I am able to narrate. In order to avoid repetition, I intend mentioning only a few typical organisations. During the last two years of the war we had over 2,000 agents in our employ at different times; it would be impossible for me to relate the individual exploits of each one of them, or even to tell about all the organisations which we mounted.

CHAPTER 4

VAN BERGEN STARTS MY
FIRST ORGANISATION

O N MY ARRIVAL in Holland in May 1916, in view of the total lack of information coming through from occupied territories, I decided to begin by interrogating all refugees crossing the frontier. There were a few of them braving the electric wire from time to time on dark nights under the guidance of *passeurs,* who, knowing the frontier well, and having a supply of rubber gloves, got from 500 to 1000 francs from each refugee they conducted.

My object was not only to get military information, however meagre it might be, but also to enrol agents for service in the occupied territory, or to get addresses of people in the interior who might be willing to work for us, if we could establish connection with them.

It took a very courageous and patriotic man to return to Belgium or France after having successfully braved the dangers of the electric wire. Hundreds of photographs which I have seen, and which the Germans purposely circulated, bore eloquent proof of the high mortality among those refugees who ventured to cross alone; corpses burned and scarred by the high voltage were exposed, horrible and terrifying to look at. Besides for those who were caught returning there was the great danger of arrest, which meant certain death by a firing-squad; even for those who were seized in the act of merely escaping into Holland, a long term of imprisonment or dispatch to a civilian concentration camp in Germany was meted out. Added to this was the risk of gossip: once a man had fled to Holland, his neighbours knew it; if he returned, they were quick at surmising that he had come back as a spy, and even though sympathetic, their talk could undo him. Among the civil population, there were also a number of traitors in the pay of the Germans, who spied on their neighbours, and who were sharp to catch any secret service activities on the part of returned citizens.

Henri van Bergen was our first recruit, a native of Louvain; he had crossed the frontier north of Antwerp by means of a *passeur*. Within twenty-four hours, I was interrogating him in our office on the Boompjes. The first thing that struck me about him was his bowler hat and his clothes, which he had donned on the previous day, before setting out on his hazardous trip. Immaculately dressed, he looked as if he had just stepped off the boat or train, instead of having come through the electric wire. I found myself talking to a man of about forty-five, with dark piercing eyes, a lawyer by profession, keen and alert, who made an excellent impression. Having met with refusals to serve from several other refugees, I was surprised at the ready consent which he gave as soon as I had convinced him that he could render better services to the Allies by returning to Belgium than by proceeding to France to enlist as a soldier.

Oram was immediately ordered to arrange for a passage at the frontier, while I quickly instructed van Bergen as to the information we required, laying special stress on the mounting of train-watching posts. I explained fully to him the working of the posts and the details of information required – such as the composition of each troop train, the time of its passing. Nothing had to be repeated; his brief sharp nod, his concentrated gaze, showed me that his disciplined brain was already working with me. To avoid incriminating notes, he committed to memory the name and address of a cafe owner in Antwerp to whom he was to hand or send his reports; he himself was to be simply M. 60, a number which was at the same time identification and password. He understood at once the necessity of concealing his actual identity from the Antwerp letter box man. It was with a feeling of satisfaction that I dismissed so intelligent an agent, and yet I felt strangely sad as I said goodbye to him. As a soldier I had seen death in many forms, but in the guise of a civilian in Holland, the sanctity of human life was much more apparent to me. Right to the end, I could never shake off the terrible responsibility I felt in sending these men back into the occupied territory, many of whom I knew were going to their death.

The moon being favourable, within three days he was on

his way to the frontier near Eindhoven, in the hands of Charles Willekens, who was to prove himself one of our best *passeurs*. Crawling on their stomachs to the electric wire, in the blackness of night, Willekens took his man through successfully, thanks to the rubber gloves and socks. We afterwards learned, on his return, that he had conducted van Bergen to a small village called Moll, and then had sent him on his way alone.

Anxiously we waited for news. Each week contact was established with the cafe owner or 'letter box' in Antwerp, which was connected to our *tuyau* at the frontier by means of a courier. At the end of the third week, Oram brought us the first news, in the form of a train-watching report from a post at Ilerent, just outside Louvain, on the Louvain–Brussels line. It was written in indian ink on the typical service *papier pelure,* fine tissue paper, so that the courier could hide the report in his hat band, lining of his clothes, shoes, or elsewhere, in case he was stopped and searched on his way from the letter box to the frontier. In addition to this report there was word from van Bergen that he was trying to mount other posts, but that it was difficult, as he had not only to find the right men, but also persons who had houses overlooking the railway line. Shortly afterwards, he established another train-watching post at Louvain on the Liège line. We were now getting all the traffic passing through Louvain, since by subtraction we could get the traffic along the relatively unimportant Louvain–Malines line.

The reports came through regularly for four months. Van Bergen wrote hopefully of friends at Ghent, who had promised to mount posts there. I was much pleased, for some of our other organisations had just started sending out their first reports, and gradually the network was spreading. Suddenly we heard that our courier from Antwerp to the frontier had been arrested. Later, from another Antwerp agent, whom we had asked to investigate the affair, we found that the owner of the cafe who had acted as letter box or contact man, had also been caught. We never heard from van Bergen again. After the Armistice, on my arrival in Brussels, I discovered that he had been shot, together with our two Antwerp men and the men who had been working for him in Louvain.

What led to his arrest, I was never able to find out for certain. It was obvious, however, that since neither van Bergen's nor the Antwerp frontier courier's identity was known to the letter box, nor that of the courier to van Bergen, the German Secret Police must have delayed making an arrest until they had followed all the active threads of the organisation. I am of the opinion that van Bergen himself was probably the first one to be caught. Well dressed, and with the obvious appearance of a gentleman, his association with the railwaymen whom he employed as train-watchers, and with the Antwerp cafe owner, who catered chiefly for boatmen in the poorer quarters of the city, may have attracted attention. We had advised him to secure an intermediary to reach these men, and to content himself with directing and keeping in the background, but he had probably not heeded our warning. A German agent may have followed him or his courier to the letter box, and there seen him handing over the reports. The Germans had probably proceeded, according to their usual method, to seize anyone making any contact whatever with an agent whom they had under suspicion. Our problem was that of the kidnapper trying to collect money from the relatives of his victim, with the police looking on. We were never able to solve this problem completely. All that we could do to avert the Frankignoul catastrophe and the complete stoppage of information coming out of Belgium was to follow our cumbersome plan of having a dozen organisations functioning at the same time, each group being entirely independent of the other in every detail, from the train-watching post right into Holland.

After the war, in Brussels, I met a priest from Ghent, belonging to the order of the Petits Frères, who told me that he was the man from Ghent about whom van Bergen had written. He had already established two train-watching posts which were just ready to function when contact with Louvain was severed. He had arranged with van Bergen to enlist other members of his Order in different parts of Belgium, but with the arrest of the letter box he had no means of communication, and so was forced to abandon his plans. Many priests were employed in the different organisations which we mounted later. They were excellent agents, as they were often able to bridge over the gap which existed between the Belgian business and professional men and the ordinary workmen; they could frequent both classes without arousing suspicion. We needed men with brains, and yet we could not dispense with the railwayman, the smuggler, the small cafe owner, the boatman, and the peasant working on the frontier. It was often hard to make connections between them.

During his visit to me after the Armistice, the priest and I visited the grave of van Bergen, and as we stood beside it with bared heads, we mourned the death of a brave man. The keen-faced, quiet lawyer had rendered very great service, for his Louvain post controlled the Liège–Brussels line, one of the most important railway lines through Belgium. For a considerable time, until we succeeded in mounting a duplicate post, it supplied the only information which the Allies were getting at that time concerning troop movements along this important artery.

CHAPTER 5

THE WHITE LADY OF THE HOHENZOLLERNS

VAN BERGEN AND his organisation had been arrested by the Germans, and although Morreau's train-watching posts at Brussels, Namur and Liège were then still functioning, together with some other independent posts of ours, we had to replace our losses and also increase the number of our posts, as we knew that the span of life of each of our organisations was strictly limited. The Germans kept making arrests and each agent was in continual danger of the firing-squad.

When, therefore, directed by one of our frontier agents, I received the visit of an emissary from Belgium under the assumed name of St Lambert, who said that he represented a large group of patriots in the interior desirous of organising an espionage service in the occupied territory, my enthusiasm knew no bounds. Here was half the work done; I only had to supply the *tuyaux*, or passages at the frontier, furnish the money, and send the necessary instructions in as to the kind of information required.

The more we talked, the more enthusiastic I became. It was explained to me that the group in the interior was made up of intellectuals: college professors, professional men, bankers, and a sprinkling of the Belgian nobility. Already in my imagination I could see this super-service working. I was getting ready to dismiss St Lambert with instructions to meet me again in the afternoon, when suddenly he shot at me, 'There is one condition however; they insist on being enrolled as soldiers before they commence work.'

I looked at him in blank amazement, even though I could understand the desire. Every agent in the interior was serving his country, incurring even greater risks than the soldiers in the front line; they were facing danger alone, without the beat of drums, without any means of self-defence, without uniforms, without even the pageantry and excitement of war. But, for the moment, the demand seemed quite impossible. How could the War Office make British soldiers out of Belgian subjects? How, even, could the Belgian authorities do it, when it would be far too dangerous to send the names out across the frontier? Above all, how could either of them make women soldiers? – for there were several women in the group.

I was on the point of voicing my sentiments openly, when I noticed the look of expectation and determination on St

Lambert's face. I parried by asking him how he thought it could be done, and how he thought the oath of allegiance could be administered?

'I don't know,' he replied. 'The War Office will have to find the formula. My instructions are to take the matter up with the Belgian authorities in Havre, if I cannot get satisfaction from you.' I knew that even if the Belgian military command were to accede to their request, the Belgian secret service could not supply them with a safe means of communication at the frontier. I doubted whether the Belgian service was getting any information at all out of Belgium at that time.

Never in my life have I been afraid to make a rapid decision. I have ever been a gambler, ready to take a risk if there is something big to gain by it. I knew that here was the chance of building up the organisation I had dreamed of, but that I would have to make a promise which, perhaps, I couldn't keep, or which, perhaps, would get me into trouble. I told St Lambert that I would communicate with the chief in England, and that within a day or two, I would give him a reply.

It was useless for me to refer the matter to higher authorities; I knew that even if the War Office was willing to grant their request, it would be necessary to get the consent of the Belgian government, and that many useful months would be lost. The next day, at peace with my conscience, I told St Lambert that their request had been granted, and that he could write a letter to this effect, which I would cause to be delivered to any address he indicated in Brussels or Liège.

After the Armistice, it took a great fight to make good my promise. Later on, it will be told how this was achieved. Their eventual militarisation was a just reward for the splendid services they rendered.

St Lambert, an engineer and executive in one of Belgium's biggest engineering works, was an intelligent man. There were many questions he could have asked me; he could have embarrassed me by demanding guarantees or an official letter from the War Office. He was a practical man, however, whereas he had told me that the leaders of the group in Belgium were idealists. I think he realised the audacity of their demands, and having obtained a favourable reply from me, he was glad to let the matter drop. He wrote the letter I requested, gave me two contact addresses, and left for Havre to place his services at the disposal of the Belgian government. He kept the promises I exacted from him; he never mentioned the matter to a soul until after the war.

Our first message contained St Lambert's letter, instructions as to the sort of information required, suggestions as regards organisation, and the sum of £500 for preliminary expenses. We instructed our courier to make his own arrangements with the letter box, or contact man, in regard to the days and the time he should pick up the reports.

We received a prompt reply, containing some military information and a promise of train-watching posts at Liège, Namur, and Brussels. We were also informed that the organisation would be called *La Dame Blanche*, after the legendary White Lady whose appearance would herald the downfall of the Hohenzollerns. The name was appropriate, for they certainly did their share in contributing to the defeat of the German Army, and ultimately to the abdication of the Kaiser.

The organisation developed rapidly. In a brief time, there

were close upon 200 agents enrolled in this organisation. At its head were two leaders: one Walthère Dewé a brilliant engineer, formerly in the employ of the Belgian government, and the other Herman Chauvin a college professor. There was no need to tell these men how to organise. They had lived in contact with the Germans for nearly three years, and knew the danger they were running. They realised the importance of organising their service on our basis of independent and isolated nests. They studied the methods and movements of the German Secret Police, and were able to outwit them at every turn.

With Belgium covered so efficiently by *La Dame Blanche* and our other organisations, it was not long before we were established in the occupied territory in France. For two years, none of the Allied services had received any reports from this area so close behind the Front. *La Dame Blanche* did their work well, and soon the first reports on the important Hirson–Mézières artery commenced to come in. Colonel Oppenheim was elated; it thrilled me, too, to read the copy of his telegram to GHQ reporting the first troop movements through Hirson. Once again, we got a telegram of congratulations from GHQ, which we transmitted in code to the interior.

We now had three independent passages at the frontier connected with *La Dame Blanche*, and these we safeguarded night and day. The electric wire, the German sentries, and the German Secret Police – these were the enemies we were ever watching, watching so that we could slip the reports through right under their noses. We were handicapped by the fact that at the frontier of Belgium, we were forced to use Belgian peasants of a mental capacity far inferior to our agents in the interior; the Germans would have been suspicious of any other type, and besides, the peasants in tilling their soil, had an excuse to approach the wire. But the difficulties we faced made the game more exciting; it was a case of the fox and the hounds.

La Dame Blanche organisation was ever growing in size; like a great octopus, it was spreading its tentacles over the whole of the occupied territory, including both Belgium and France. Its need of money kept growing. The train-watchers and other agents had to be on duty night and day, and most of them had families to support. We were now sending in to *La Dame Blanche* about £10,000 each month, not counting the *tuyaux*, or men at the frontier, whom we paid separately. This money was sent in chiefly in the form of 1000-mark bills, but even in this large denomination, it meant passing 200 bills each month; this meant bulk, and bulk meant danger, when one ran the risk of being searched at any moment. There was a danger, too, of tempting the peasants at the frontiers. We were entirely in their hands: if they chose to steal the money, we had no means of redress; they could even plead innocence, blaming one of the many others through whose hands it had to pass. But the loss of the money was the least annoyance; we were afraid that because of theft the *tuyaux* men might cease working. We were very fortunate, however; we knew most of the money got through, for *La Dame Blanche* acknowledged receipt of each sum.

Our three *tuyaux* functioned smoothly for almost a year; then, suddenly, the men at one of them were arrested. They had probably aroused suspicion by approaching the wire too often. We were able, however, to warn *La Dame Blanche* in time, so that their courier could be kept from making contact with the *tuyau*, and as his identity was not known to the frontier men, no further arrests were made. The Germans captured the last batch of reports, which were at the frontier ready to be passed. This meant no direct danger to *La Dame Blanche*, as everything compromising was in code, but by the bulk of the reports, it warned the Germans that there was a huge organisation functioning in the interior, and this meant increased surveillance.

By far the biggest annoyance to us was the fact that most of the money had been sent in through this particular *tuyau*. *La Dame Blanche* immediately proposed to us that for the time being, they should borrow money in the interior from a banker who was one of their members. Once again, I took prompt action; without referring the matter to London, and thereby avoiding a waste of valuable time, I told them to go ahead. £30,000 was borrowed in this way before we could send money in regularly again. As with the militarisation, the chief in London, once again, helped me to fulfil my promises after the Armistice. He transferred the money to me in Brussels, in 1919, and I was able to write a cheque out to them for the sum, repaying in full the amount borrowed.

A few months before the big German offensive in 1918, *La Dame Blanche* added one more extension to their organisation – the development of a group of agents in the Valenciennes section of occupied France. Here an old Allied service had functioned in the earlier stages of the war, in 1915, but had lost contact with Holland. It was now resuscitated, and was able to send us train-watching and *promeneur* reports of the greatest value during the last stages of the war.

The final development in the *Dame Blanche* service was an attempt at establishing telephone connection with us in Holland.

But for the Armistice, this would have been achieved; it would have been a crowning triumph added to the already brilliant successes of this magnificent organisation. One of the chiefs, a professor of physics at one of the Belgian universities, knew, from his familiarity with electricity, that if the earth is used as a return circuit in a field telephone installation, messages could be intercepted by another similar installation, with its connecting wire running parallel to that of the first. He had also discovered that in the Maastricht sector of the Belgian–Dutch border there was a spot on the river separating the two countries where, because of the water, there was very little surveillance; 100 yards of wire could have been run underground between two cottages on the Belgian side; and on the Dutch side opposite there was a big estate owned by a man who was very pro-Belgian, and who was willing to allow the second line and set of apparatus to be installed there, with prying eyes kept away from it.

I knew the installation would work, for we had intercepted German messages in this way at the Front, when the distance between our trenches and those of the Germans was much greater than the distance between the proposed two wires. Furthermore, our lines would be parallel, an ideal arrangement for interception. No time was lost in developing this scheme, and telephone apparatus had already been dispatched to us from London, when the Armistice brought an end to hostilities.

No account I can give can render adequate justice to the splendid achievements of *La Dame Blanche*. They were *undoubtedly* the finest espionage organisation created in the occupied territory. The information they sent us was of priceless value to the Allies; again and again telegrams of congratulation from GHQ bore this out. Prior to the big German offensive, which broke in March 1918, their train-watching posts, over fifty in number, gave all the troop movements through all the junctions in Belgium, and through many in occupied France. Their *promeneurs*, especially those of Fabry in the Avesnes area, signalled the massing of troops in their neighbourhood – proof positive, to my mind at least, as I identified division after division, detraining there, and marching there from other sectors, that it was from this sector that the big German offensive was to be launched.

La Dame Blanche owed its success, first of all, to the genius of its two leaders, a professor and an engineer; secondly, to the discipline which it was able to secure through its militarisation; and finally to the splendid calibre and intelligence of its agents drawn from the Belgian intelligentsia. After the Armistice, the two chiefs, Dewé and Chauvin, were decorated with the CBE (Commander of the Order of the British Empire), military division, and the remaining 1,000-odd agents received lesser awards from the British government.

I cannot close this chapter without some reference to Dieudonne Lambrecht, hero and martyr, whose organisation in the early months of the war was the nucleus around which grew *La Dame Blanche*, or the 'White Lady'.

On a hill-side which dominates the city of Liège, lies the suburb of Thier-à-Liège. Here in one of those small brick houses with low, violet-tinted, slate roof, and diminutive garden, so typical of the area, Dieudonne Lambrecht was born on 4 May 1882 and grew to manhood.

For a few years he worked in one of the Belgian administrations, but his ardent nature revolted against the narrow, hide-bound, official routine of a government office. With his brother-in-law, he established an engineering workshop, which soon grew into a small factory, producing high grade precision machinery. Happily married, blessed with a small baby girl of four months, a permanent income assured, a keen participator in all church activities, Lambrecht's life was fixed. The vista of a peaceful existence stretched before him.

All this was suddenly changed by the war. Into the turmoil of that conflict went all that he had built up.

He resolved to consecrate his intelligence, his fortune, his influence, his life itself if necessary, to the task of freeing his country's soil from the German invader. Naturally, his first thought was to join the Belgian Army.

But, as happened to so many Belgian refugees, as soon as they reached Dutch soil, he was approached by one of the Allied secret service agents who swarmed in Holland at that time. It was into the hands of Afchain, a Belgian in the employ of B, chief of an intelligence service connected with British GHQ, that Lambrecht fell.

Now a man of thirty-two, his sensitive mind keenly alert, Lambrecht listened attentively to Afchain, weighing how best he could serve his country. It needed little persuasion to get him to return to Belgium for the purpose of organising an espionage service.

In the Catholic circles of Liège, Lambrecht found support. Two Jesuit priests, Father Dupont, and Father Des Onays, and his brother-in-law, Oscar Donnay, helped him recruit a number of former railway employees. With this band of faithful followers, train-watching posts were soon established at Liège, Namur, and Jemelle, from which all troop movements by rail through these important centres could be observed.

The most dangerous work Lambrecht reserved for himself. In spite of rigid surveillance by the Secret Police, he travelled around the country enrolling new agents and identifying German divisions in the various rest areas. As far afield as Belgian Flanders he went spying and recruiting; he even penetrated into the Grand Duchy of Luxembourg. On one occasion, at Jemelle, a heavy westward movement of German troops was in progress for several days from the Eastern Front. Realising that concentration for an offensive was probably under way, Lambrecht, without hesitation, jumped on the buffer of a passing troop train, and accompanied it through the night, until he had definitely established its destination. The very boldness of his act outwitted the German Secret Police – a troop train was the last place to look for a spy, as Lambrecht cleverly realised.

In addition to this hazardous work, he often acted as his own courier, the most dangerous role in wartime spying. Slipping past the frontier guards at night, and avoiding the revealing rays of the searchlights, he carried the precious reports, written with a mapping pen on fine tissue paper, and sewed into the interior of the cloth buttons on his clothes, through to Holland. A friend manufactured these buttons in Liège, and it was an easy task to substitute the filling. Good as the concealment was, however, it only protected him in case of a casual search in Belgium itself. Caught at the frontier, his fate would have been sealed – the knives of the German Secret Police would soon have laid bare the compromising contents of those ingenious buttons.

For eighteen months Lambrecht and his faithful assistants kept watch. Night and day, every train passing through the railway centres of Liège, Namur, and Jemelle, every troop movement through Belgium between the Eastern and Western Fronts, was reported to British GHQ. These reports definitely announced coming offensives, and were far more valuable than any information obtained from stolen or captured documents. The documents might be false, or the Germans might have changed their plans after the dispatches or orders had been written, but the troop movements were established facts which could not be altered.

To Lambrecht also belongs the credit that he helped to devise these means of controlling troop movements. Train-watching posts had never been used in any previous war, and it was the initial reports of such pioneers as Lambrecht which enabled intelligence officers at British GHQ to work out from the number of constituted units passing by a given train-watching post, their accurate system of gauging the exact volume of a troop movement.

The mass of information transmitted by Lambrecht to British GHQ is astonishing.

In May 1915, for example, his train-watching posts at Jemelle and Namur rapidly and accurately reported the transfer of several German divisions from the Serbian Front to Flanders. This was of vast importance because it was an indication that all the German divisions on the Serbian Front were being transferred to France. In August 1915, his posts noted a heavy movement of troops from the Eastern Front to Champagne. This concentration of troops was intended to parry the offensive which the Germans knew the French were preparing in this sector. As a result of this information, the French advanced the date of their offensive several days.

Lambrecht also accurately reported the German preparations for their attack on Verdun. Much of the information he obtained through the indiscretions of a German major, billeted in his sister's home. But not satisfied with this, he sent agents into occupied France to determine the destination of the troops which were pouring past his train-watching posts in a westerly direction.

The following letter from Afchain, dated 26 January 1916, speaks eloquently for the valuable services rendered by Lambrecht and of the high hopes entertained of him:

> *I have just received a telegram of congratulations from our chief at British GHQ. The 26th Division, which you reported passing through Jemelle, on 15 December, coming from the Eastern Front, has been contacted in the front line.*
>
> *Do your best to establish train-watching posts in the Grand Duchy of Luxembourg, and in occupied France. I know how difficult this will be; but the merit will be all the greater, if you are successful. Knowing your great tenacity, I am sure if anyone can succeed, you will.*

Events now began to move quickly.

Eighteen months of experience had taught the German counter-espionage service all the tricks used by refugees, and by the Allied secret services, and efficient means had been devised to seal the Belgian–Dutch frontier. In the interior, every Belgian, man and woman, was forced to carry an identity card, with photograph, name, and address attached; and special permission had to be obtained to travel from one town to another. At the frontier, a high-voltage electric wire, a cordon of sentries every

100 yards, mounted patrols, police dogs, and, finally, an army of plain-clothes Secret Police, guarded its entire length.

The Belgian refugees in Holland who had dabbled in secret service could well shut up shop. And it was a good riddance – they had exploited the patriotism of their countrymen in the interior, and they had sold their information to the highest bidder among the Allied secret services, sometimes to several of them at the same time. The results cost the life of many a brave man or woman in the occupied territories.

But the secret service game had become a problem even to the official services. After months of fruitless effort many of their representatives were recalled from Holland, to leave the field clear for the few who still seemed to have the chance of success. There was a period in 1916 when no information of any kind was coming out of the occupied territory. The Allied secret services had lost their initiative. New methods had to be devised to penetrate the formidable barrier which the Germans had built up at the Belgian–Dutch border.

It was not surprising, then, that Lambrecht found himself suddenly cut off from all communication with Holland. His precious information piled up only to become valueless as the days dragged by. Frantically, he waited for a courier from Holland to pick up his reports at the letter box, which he had established in Liège.

In Holland, Afchain was working feverishly to find some means of reaching Liège. He could no longer pick a trusted courier from a dozen volunteers. He would be fortunate if he could find anyone at all to undertake the dangerous mission.

His chief at British GHQ wired him impatiently. He took

a risk. Whether he handed a letter for Lambrecht to an intermediary, who was duped, or whether he himself was tricked, is not known exactly. The letter, however, fell into the hands of Keurvers, a Dutchman in the employ of the German counter-espionage service.

Lambrecht's 'letter box' in Liège was a small cigar store owned by one of his relatives, a man called Leclercq. While Leclercq was out Keurvers called at the store and introduced himself to Madame Leclercq as a Dutchman who had just arrived from Holland with an urgent letter for her husband. Madame Leclercq, fully aware of her husband's dangerous activities, was suspicious. This man with his red, bloated face, and small vicious eyes, repulsed her; besides, his accent seemed more German than Dutch. She refused to accept the letter. But Keurvers, not to be put off, countered with the password: 'The seven boxes of tricolour cigars have arrived safely.' Madame Leclercq was nonplussed: she recognised the words, but still she could not bring herself to trust the man. After some hesitation she replied that her husband had told her nothing about the cigars, and that they were not expecting any letters from Holland.

As soon as Keurvers was out of sight, she hastened to Lambrecht with the news. To her surprise, instead of praising her discretion, he scolded her for being overcautious. 'He gave the right password, didn't he? What more did you want?' Thoroughly dismayed, she hurried back to the store, where she found Keurvers had returned in her absence and left the letter with her servant together with a message that he would be back the next morning at ten o'clock. The message and the letter were quickly conveyed to Lambrecht.

Lambrecht eagerly opened the small roll containing the letter, and found that it was in Afchain's familiar handwriting. It was dated 24 February 1916, and contained the following message:

> *I confirm the long list of merchandise orders delivered to you, 28 January, care of our friend Dupont (Leclercq's service name), but regret having received no reply.*
>
> *Our delivery man, who brought you the above orders, being unable to continue with his duties, I am using the present carrier, who will contact you once a week. I believe he is the only one who can do this at the present moment. I hope you will be able to pull us out of our present critical situation by giving him a report, as complete as possible, of all the merchandise in your store. It is absolutely necessary to make use of the present opportunity, as none of our competitors are in a position to deliver.*

If Madame Leclercq had sowed any doubts in his mind, they were quickly dispelled by Afchain's letter, which was undoubtedly genuine. Lambrecht was ready to welcome Keurvers with open arms, so relieved was he that regular communications with Holland had once more been established. His thoughts immediately turned to the accumulation of six weeks' reports which he had in his possession. He knew they would be too bulky as they were, and so the night was spent making a résumé of all but the most recent ones.

At ten o'clock next morning, Lambrecht was at the Leclercq cigar store, in the rue de Campine. As he entered, he saw a man in conversation with Leclercq. It was Keurvers. Leclercq immediately called Lambrecht aside into the small parlour at the back of the store. He, too, shared his wife's suspicions of this man. But Lambrecht could not be persuaded: there was Afchain's letter, and the man had given the right password. So Keurvers was called into the back room, and the reports were handed over to him.

On his way home Lambrecht noticed that he was being followed. Such was his trust in Keurvers and his solicitude for his men that his immediate thoughts were not for his own safety, but for that of the courier, and the precious reports in his possession. By jumping on to a passing tram, he managed to get rid of the man who had been following him.

Lambrecht knew that he had a chance of finding Keurvers in one of the cafes on the Grand Place, for most visitors in the city gravitated to this centre. As he looked through the large windows of the Café du Marronnier, he saw Keurvers sitting with Landwerlen and Douhard, two of the German Secret Police, whom Lambrecht knew only too well by sight; they had figured in nearly every spy arrest in the city.

Instantly Lambrecht knew he was trapped, that the Secret Police were following him to discover his associates. He had a chance to get away. He had shaken off the man who had been on his trail. He had a number of friends who would gladly have hidden him until an opportunity presented itself to get across the frontier. But Lambrecht decided to return home to advise his wife, and to get her to warn Leclercq. He thought he could get there before the police.

It was a fatal step. As Lambrecht walked in at the front door, the Secret Police were waiting for him on the inside – his wife had been arrested shortly after he had left for his rendezvous with Keurvers. It was known afterwards that the Secret Police had been watching the Leclercq cigar store for several days before Keurvers presented himself there, that they had photographed Afchain's note, and, of course, had understood its meaning. As usual, their object had been to track down associates, and above all to secure the reports – the evidence to convict.

Lambrecht knew he could not save himself. He could, however, save the thirty-odd agents who had been working for him. (The Leclercqs did not know their names.) His one care now was not to betray them. Every third degree method familiar to the Germans was employed to break down his resistance, but Lambrecht allowed no name to escape him. He even succeeded in proving to the Secret Police that his wife had no idea he was engaged in espionage activities, and that the Leclercqs did not know the purport of his correspondence with Holland.

His friends did everything within their power to save him. Brand Whitlock, the Marquis de Villalobar, and van Vollenhoven, the various neutral ministers to Belgium, were all persuaded to intercede with von Bissing, the German governor-general of Belgium. Even the German chaplain of the prison was so moved by the heroic attitude of Lambrecht that he wrote to the German Cardinal von Hartmann, at Cologne, asking him to intervene.

All these efforts were in vain. Lambrecht was condemned to death.

Lambrecht faced his death with sublime resignation. The following letter, written to his wife on the eve of his execution, reveals his nobility:

17 April 1916,
The citadel of the Chartreuse.

MY WELL-BELOVED JEANNE:

I have just been transferred here from the prison of St Leonard. As I suspected, it was to inform me that the sentence of death, which was passed on the 12th, has been confirmed, and that the various petitions for mercy have been refused.

God calls me to Him – let His will be done. We can only but incline ourselves before His supreme wisdom.

Oh! My well beloved, what a terrible blow to you, who had such high hopes! Poor wife! Poor parents! My soul is filled with intense sadness thinking of you all.

He who dies is quickly rid of his pain. But for you others, how much suffering! Let my resignation be a comfort to you. May God give you the courage, which He has never ceased to grant me, so that your suffering may be less.

In heaven, I will watch over you, and will pray to God to reserve for you those happy days which I myself had hoped to provide you. God has not permitted me to do this – let us incline ourselves before His wishes. If He causes us to suffer now, it is but to reward us better later on, when we are near Him.

Think of my life as having been given up for my country – it will make my death seem less painful to you. After my faith, my country is what I hold most dear; in sacrificing my life for it, I am only doing what so many have done before me, and will do again.

Life passes so quickly here below – it lasts but a moment. We will meet in a better world. It is in moments such as these, through which

I have just passed, that one appreciates the inestimable good that parents do their children in giving them a Christian education, and faith in God.

Console my poor parents for whom the blow is going to be terrible. Draw from your love for me, the necessary force to show them an example of courage.

Take refuge in prayer, my beloved. I will leave you, as a last souvenir of me, the cross you sent me, and I will place on it kisses for you, Riette, and my parents. I will join to it my wedding ring.

Jeanne, in heaven we will meet again. For our darling little daughter, for my parents, and for you, receive on this letter, the last affectionate kisses of he who was.

Your Donné

Lambrecht was shot 18 April 1916.

After the Armistice, Lambrecht was posthumously decorated with the OBE by the British, and was mentioned in dispatches by Field Marshal Sir Douglas Haig. King Albert bestowed on him the Chevalier of the Order of Leopold, with *lisérés d'or*; he was also mentioned in the order of the day of the nation, and was accorded the Civic Cross, first class.

Valuable as his work had been during the eighteen months he had faithfully served the Allies, it was in death that he exerted his greatest force. His example was an inspiration to others to carry on his work; his friends swore to avenge him, and out of the scattered remnants of his espionage service emerged the 'White Lady', the greatest spy organisation of the war.

CHAPTER 6

MILITARISATION OF THE 'WHITE LADY'

T HE 'WHITE LADY' now entered upon a new phase of its activity. Permission to militarise the service gave fresh life to Dewé and Chauvin, the chief organisers; abandoned projects were resuscitated, and the militarisation was immediately put into effect. When the service was first founded, they had tried to organise the different sections, or sectors, as separate and independent nests, with centres at Liège, Brussels, Namur, and Charleroi; they had even intended to create individual 'letter boxes' for each section, to enable their reports to be picked up by independent couriers from Holland, and passed through four distinct passages at the frontier. They soon realised, however, that a single frontier passage was all Liévin could manage; in addition, lack of experience kept the heads of sections continually in consultation with headquarters in Liège. The result was that though certain individual agents, more exposed than others, were isolated, yet as a whole the service had remained closely knitted together. The militarisation and increased experience gained by the heads of sections during the past year, at last gave Dewé and Chauvin an opportunity to attain, in a slightly modified form, what they had been striving for from the beginning.

Three battalions were created with centres at Liège, Namur, and Charleroi. Each battalion was divided into companies, each company into platoons. Thus the Namur sector became Battalion II, with companies at Marche, Namur, and Chimay; and the Marche company had its platoons at Marche, Arlon, and Luxembourg; the Namur and Chimay companies were similarly divided up into platoons. Each unit covered the area designated by its name.

Each fourth platoon in a company occupied itself exclusively with collecting the reports from the three other platoons, and depositing them at a 'letter box' allocated to the company. Each battalion also had a special unit, some of whose members collected the reports at the company 'letter boxes' and deposited them at the battalion 'letter box', while a special member carried the reports from this 'letter box' to the headquarters' 'letter box' in Liège. In Liège there were three 'letter boxes', one for each battalion. These 'letter boxes', and the couriers serving them, were kept as completely isolated as possible. They knew nothing about the service except their own particular duties; it was forbidden them to try and discover the identity of any member of the service.

Each battalion had a secretariat where the reports picked up at the battalion 'letter box' were typed out, after they had been scrutinised by the battalion commander. At Liège, the reports from the three battalions were examined and criticised by Dewé and Chauvin, and were then passed on to the headquarters' secretariat, where they were prepared for transmission to Holland.

A special courier carried the reports from the headquarters' secretariat to the frontier 'letter box'. Here the duties of the War Office service commenced. It was up to it to pick up the reports at this 'letter box' and convey them across the frontier into Holland. The role of frontier 'letter box' was the most dangerous in the organisation, and so not only the agent occupying it, but everyone coming into contact with him, was especially isolated. The typing of the reports served a twofold purpose: it diminished the bulk, and it removed the evidence which handwriting would have supplied, if the reports were seized.

GHQ consisted of the two chiefs, a supreme council of eight members, a chaplain, a counter-espionage section, a section to deal with finances, a courier section, the secretariat already mentioned, a section to attend to the hiding of compromised agents, and to make arrangements for their escape across the frontier into Holland, and, finally, a section to study all new extensions, and, if approved by the supreme council, to carry them into effect.

All members were required to take one of the following oaths of allegiance:

> (i) I declare that I have engaged myself as a soldier in the military observation corps of the Allies until the end of the war.
>
> I swear before God to respect this engagement; to accomplish

*conscientiously the duties which are entrusted to me; to obey my
superior officers; not to reveal to anyone whomsoever, without formal
permission, anything concerning the service, not even if this should
entail for me or mine the penalty of death; not to join any other espionage service, nor to undertake any work extraneous to the service,
which might either cause an inquiry or my arrest by the Germans.*

*(ii) The same oath of allegiance as above, but instead of the phrase
'to accomplish conscientiously the duties which are entrusted to me',
it was allowed to substitute the following: 'to accomplish conscientiously the duties which I have undertaken, or shall undertake in
the future'.*

To each was given a lead identity disc, with his name, date, and place of birth, and matriculation number engraved on it. This disc was to be buried immediately, and was not to be disinterred until after the war.

In addition to the reorganisation already mentioned, the militarisation and the oath of allegiance had other far-reaching effects. Hitherto, being civilians, Dewé and Chauvin had been forced to discuss all projects with agents before they would carry them out. This not only involved loss of time, but it forced them to disclose details of organisation, which should have been kept secret. Now a subordinate agent could be ordered to do what was required.

The oath of allegiance also put a stop, once and for all, to agents involving themselves in such subsidiary duties as the distri-bution of letters from Belgian soldiers at the Front; the circulation of *La Libre Belgique*, and other clandestine publications; and the assisting of Belgians of military age to escape across the frontier.

These extraneous activities not only often led to the arrest of agents, but invariably compromised the whole espionage organisation to which they belonged.

The militarisation also eased the minds of the many Belgians of military age enrolled in the 'White Lady'. These men, recruited from the most patriotic elements of the population, wanted to be sure that neither the Belgian authorities nor the public would criticise them after the war for not having crossed the frontier to join the Belgian Army. Finally, the fear of a post-war military court martial acted as an additional deterrent to those who were arrested. Betrayal was the principal source of information of the German Secret Police – German third-degree methods, and the use of stool-pigeons in the prisons taxed the loyalty of the prisoners to the limit of their endurance.

Not satisfied with the increased security which the militarisation had brought them, Dewé and Chauvin employed all their ingenuity and organising ability to consolidate the service, and to protect it still further against the German Secret Police.

All members of the 'White Lady' were instructed to use false names both in their reports, and in contacting other members of the service. Dewé became in turn van den Bosch, Gauthier, and Muraille; Chauvin assumed successively the names of Beaumont, Valdor, Granito, Bouchon, and Dumont; while Neujean was known as Petit.

To prevent discovery and arrest, the greatest ingenuity was employed in choosing and fitting out each of the two headquarters. The main one was a perfect rabbit warren. It had five exits – one into the front street; one into a back garden, from which access could be gained to a side street, by way of an alley; one to the roof through a skylight; and finally two, one on each floor, leading through very ordinary looking wall closets into the adjoining house, where an apparently harmless old couple lived, who, as far as their neighbours were concerned, never held any communication with the inmates of the house next door. At the reserve headquarters, in addition to several exits, there was a blind room without windows, which was specially useful on occasions when the council met late at night – the curfew laws, in operation in the occupied territories, required all lights to be extinguished by a certain hour. The 'White Lady' also had three houses in Liège which were used as hiding places for compromised agents.

The arrest of their colleague Father Des Onays, and the danger to which both of them had been exposed in their contact with frontier couriers, had taught Dewé and Chauvin a lesson. They now systematically removed all connecting links between themselves and their frontier posts. Frontier 'letter boxes' and couriers who knew their identity were retired, and new ones were recruited through suitable intermediaries. In doing this, they knew that they would still be exposed to many dangers, some unforeseen, others which they would have to face in the everyday execution of their duties; but, as chiefs of the 'White Lady', they realised that it was their duty not to incur unnecessary risks. On the other hand, they never shrank from undertaking a mission, however dangerous it might be, if they considered that they themselves were the best fitted to carry it out.

As a final precaution, the names and addresses of the three battalion 'letter boxes' were sent through to me in Holland in code permitting me to make direct contact with the battalions in the event of the 'White Lady' headquarters being seized.

Notwithstanding all these precautionary measures, and in spite of the guiding genius of Dewé and Chauvin, the 'White Lady' found itself engaged in a life and death struggle with the German Secret Police during the next eighteen months.

CHAPTER 7

THE HIRSON PLATOON

T HE EXPERIENCES AND adventures of the Hirson Platoon were representative of the thirty-eight platoons of the 'White Lady'. True, each kept watch over different areas, but their problems, their duties, their spy technique, and, finally, the dangers they encountered were the same. I have chosen to tell about this particular platoon, not because it provided more thrilling adventures than the others, but merely because, being one of the last units to be formed, its story can be told within the space of a single chapter.

It was towards the end of August 1917, after we had been in touch with the 'White Lady' about a month, that we received word of a young French refugee who was in hiding at the house of one of their agents in Liège. On the plea that they had given him important verbal information to communicate to us about their organisation, they requested that we make arrangements for his passage into Holland.

We were not very enthusiastic. We had already placed several frontier passages at the disposal of the 'White Lady'. We had provided them with a dictionary code which they could safely use. And we were anxious to abolish their system of sending delegates across the border into Holland. They were exposed to the danger of being caught, and the even greater danger – strange as it may seem – that they would divulge details of our organisation to the other Allied secret services, whose prying curiosity was as likely to attract the attention of the German Secret Police as any slip on the part of our agents. The 'White Lady' insisted, however; and so we sent in Charles Willekens, our most trusted frontier guide, to fetch him.

I was attracted to Edmond Amiable as soon as I saw him – a young man of about twenty, of medium height, trimly athletic, his frank eyes blazing with enthusiasm. In a few words, he gave me his story. He had intended entering the priesthood, and had already completed part of his novitiate when he felt the urge to escape from occupied territory in order to join the army and serve his country. He told of the difficulties in had encountered in making his way to Liège from Hirson, across the Franco-Belgian border. In Liège, through a Jesuit priest, he had come into contact with the 'White Lady'. I found in reality that he knew practically nothing about the existing organisation of the 'White Lady', but that the two chiefs, under the assumed names of Gauthier and Dumont, had discussed very thoroughly with him some of the problems which the militarisation involved, and on which they wanted my advice.

As I sat and listened to this young patriot, who had come from the very area the Allied secret service had in vain been trying to penetrate during the last two years, I conceived the idea of persuading him to return. It was the height of my ambition to establish a train-watching post on the Hirson–Mézières line, that important artery which ran parallel to the German battlefront, which increased in importance as the rumours of a big German offensive grew thicker. In occupied France, too, we would be tapping not only rest areas, but also regions used by the Germans for the massing of troops.

With the control of the Hirson–Mézières line giving us the transference of divisions from one sector of the Front to another, and with itinerant agents reporting troop concentrations in the different areas, we would be able to locate sectors chosen for attack, and would thus be in a position to supply information of vital importance to the Allies. Before our contact with the 'White Lady', we had urged our other organisations in the interior to penetrate into France, but the strict surveillance there, especially along the Franco-Belgian border, had checkmated all their efforts.

The finding of stationary agents was not difficult; the problem was the transmission of the reports. In Belgium, the ordinary activities of business and of life continued even in the presence of the Germans; in occupied France, trade and industry had been completely crippled, a great part of the civilian population had been deported, and those who remained had to obtain special permits to travel even 2 or 3 miles.

When I broached the subject to Amiable, he immediately consented. He insisted, however, that I get permission from his French authorities, so that on his return he could satisfy his father, a veteran of the Franco-German War, who had encouraged him to escape. General Bucabeille, the French military attaché at The Hague, readily complied with our wishes. He interviewed his young compatriot and returned him to us with an official blessing for the success of the undertaking.

As much as I should have preferred getting Amiable to start an independent service, with separate couriers right through to me in Holland, I knew this was impossible. In order to block off the area immediately behind their front line, the Germans had posted a cordon of sentries along the Franco-Belgian border, and were maintaining almost as strict surveillance there as they were along the Belgian–Dutch frontier. To penetrate this barrier, I knew it would require an organisation on the spot. I decided, therefore, to return Amiable unreservedly to the 'White Lady', and leave it to them to mount this new service in conjunction with their own.

Calling him No. A. 91, we placed him once again in the hands of our frontier guide, the trusted and undaunted Charles Willekens, and returned him to the address in Liège where we had picked him up.

Dewé and Chauvin threw themselves enthusiastically into the creation of this new service. For some time they had envisaged the formation of a company in the Chimay area, and Hirson would fit admirably into it as one of its four platoons.

Since not only the mounting of the Hirson Platoon, but that of a whole company was involved, Chauvin decided to accompany A. 91 on his mission.

On 29 August 1917, Chauvin and A. 91 arrived at battalion

headquarters in Namur. There Abbé Philippot, the Commander of the Second Battalion, to which the Chimay company was to be attached after formation, gave them a letter of introduction to Ghislain Hanotier, a friend of his, whom he knew he could trust.

Two days later, A. 91 and Chauvin, who had carefully hidden his identity under the name of Dumont, arrived in Chimay. While A. 91 left for Macon, a village some 2 miles from the Franco-Belgian border, Dumont went off to find Hanotier. This man, who had already served for two years in an old espionage service (the service Biscops, which eventually had lost contact with Holland), received Dumont with open arms. With his aid, Dumont in addition to a 'letter box' for Chimay, soon recruited two couriers – one between Chimay and the French frontier, the other between Chimay and the battalion 'letter box' in Namur.

In the meantime, A. 91, after several fruitless endeavours to find a guide to take Dumont and himself across the frontier, eventually addressed himself to Anatole Gobeaux, a man whom he had known since boyhood. Gobeaux, who between teaching in the Macon village school found time to run a sabot syndicate, belonged to one of those old families of Sambre-et-Meuse, whose patriotism and sense of honour are traditional. Brave, and determined, he had been a leader in every patriotic activity in the village from the first days of the occupation. It is not surprising, then, that when A. 91 told him that he was looking for someone to aid him in his mission, he replied: 'This someone is going to be me, Edmond. I am not going to allow anyone to deprive me of the honour of serving my country.'

I leave it to Gobeaux to tell of A. 91's, and Dumont's adventures at the frontier:

I could not help but be impressed by Dumont, who had now joined A. 91. His generosity and greatness of soul won my heart immediately. I was astounded at the calm manner with which, in a few words and without bravado, he outlined their plans.

Their objective was to reach Trélon, 7 kilometres distant, where A. 91's father lived. The distance was not great, but there was no necessity to stress the dangers they would have to encounter. A. 91 knew them only too well. The area was thickly wooded and in it were hidden innumerable German sentries, and Secret Police, aided by well-trained police dogs. If one were challenged, one had to halt, present one's permit to cross the frontier – granted only on exceptional occasions – and, finally, allow oneself to be rigorously searched. An attempt at escape meant almost certain death in the form of a sentry's bullet.

The Germans had good reason to guard this area. At Trélon was the Château de Merode, where the Kaiser often took up his quarters, and which was also the headquarters of one of the German armies. In addition, only 15 kilometres away, was Hirson, the centre pivot of the whole railway network immediately behind the German front; and there too was their general railway headquarters.

A way of crossing the frontier immediately suggested itself to me: 'X', the director of a small glass factory, just across the frontier, had a group permit which allowed him to take across the frontier daily twenty-five workmen, who lived in Belgium. All that was necessary was for my two friends to disguise themselves as workmen and join the group. But 'X''s patriotism, which he continually vaunted, was only a façade – he made us lose three valuable days by first of all consenting, and then showing the white feather.

One sole means now remained to me, and that was to entrust them to a friend of mine, Moreau, who lived at Baives, just across the frontier, and who slipped over occasionally to purchase necessities for his family. As luck would have it, Moreau put in an appearance the next day, and, as I had foreseen, he not only gladly agreed to act as their guide, but allowed himself to be enrolled in the 'White Lady' as their trans-frontier courier between Baives and Macon.

Dumont and A. 91 had a double risk to face. An ordinary inhabitant would have received a month's imprisonment for a first offence, if arrested trying to cross the frontier and he was not involved in any clandestine activity. But A. 91 had already been reported to the Secret Police as having fled the country; and it would have been impossible for Dumont, a Belgian from Liège, to explain his presence in the area. Knowing that they could not face an interrogation, they started on their hazardous journey across the French frontier on the night of 7 September.

Eight o'clock was sounding at the village church, when the three of them, dressed as workmen, got under way: A. 91 in a dirty pair of blue-jeans and a cap; Dumont in an old rain coat and a shabby felt hat. Guided by Moreau, who knew every path through the woods, they quickly gained the frontier. They advanced stealthily, a few yards at a time. With ears alert, straining at every sound, they expected each moment to be challenged by some hidden sentry; but so expertly did Moreau guide them that they saw no one. They pressed forward rapidly, anxious to get away from the frontier as fast as they could. The danger was by no means over, but they felt greatly relieved. On the outskirts of Trélon, Moreau left them to continue on their own. A. 91 was now near his home, and could be relied on to find the way.

Suddenly, as they came out of a clearing, the two men found themselves faced by several German soldiers. They were so close that it *was useless trying to run – they would have been mowed down. The only thing to do was to advance resolutely; they were away from the frontier, and most likely would be taken for ordinary inhabitants of the village. Their audacity and the casual air they assumed, worked; they were already about 30 yards past them, and had boldly entered a road leading to the village, when one of the soldiers, apparently as an afterthought, shouted, 'Halt!'*

Dumont and A. 91, pretending not to hear, hastened their steps. Again shouts of 'Halt!' 'Halt!' this time followed by the whiz of a bullet. As if by common accord, they threw themselves at the hedge bordering the road – A. 91 to the left, Dumont to the right. Dumont, emerging on the other side of the hedge, was seen by one of the soldiers, who had followed his manoeuvre. As the soldier made a dash for him, Dumont took to his heels. He was rapidly losing breath, when he fell headlong into a ditch which he had failed to see in the dark. Completely exhausted, he lay where he was. The soldier passed by without seeing him.

In the distance, Dumont heard a struggle going on, terminating a cry of triumph. Then silence. 'A. 91 has been caught,' passed through his mind. For an hour Dumont did not stir. Then a heavy rain started falling, and he resolved to make a move. His first thoughts were to reach the house of A. 91's father, but so convinced was he that A. 91 had been arrested that he dismissed the idea immediately – it would be the very spot where the Secret Police would be waiting for him. There seemed no alternative but to try and get back to Belgium.

Wandering through the night, aided by the obscurity and the rain, Dumont eventually reached Macon. It was in a pitiful condition, his face and hands torn by the underbrush, wet to the skin, covered with mud, and completely exhausted, that I found him at my front door at dawn. After a change of clothes, and a few hours' sleep, I drove him in a cart to Chimay, where together with Hanotier, we went over the night's adventures, and lamented the fate of A. 91.

What had happened to A. 91 during this time? When he passed through the fence, instead of running away from it as Dumont had done, he ran along it for about 50 yards, and there finding an opening, he pushed his way into the centre of the hedge. Here, afraid to move, he remained for at least three hours. At one time, he heard a group of soldiers, not 10 yards away from him, discussing what had happened to the two of them. It was not until the rain came that he found it safe to move. Eventually, groping his way across the fields, he reached his father's home at midnight.

Quickly, he explained to the surprised old man the crowded events of the evening. Anxiously, they waited for Dumont to arrive; and then as morning came, they gave up hope. Dumont had surely been arrested, was their only conclusion.

During the course of the day, A. 91 explained his mission to his father, himself a rugged veteran of former wars. The father nobly undertook to organise the Hirson Platoon. Much as his family would have liked him to remain at least for a few days, they counselled A. 91 to return to Belgium immediately – everyone in the village knew that he had left to join the French Army, via Holland, several months previously; it would have been suicidal to remain. On the next night, therefore, once again guided by Moreau, he regained my home in Macon without any further adventures. Great was his surprise and joy, when he heard of Dumont's safe return. It was a still more surprised Dumont, who greeted him, when A. 91 reached Chimay.

It was to the neighbouring village of Fourmies that Amiable Senior, who had assumed the name of 'Pierre', first went. Here lived

Felix Latouche ('Dominique'), a former railway employee of the Compagnie du Nord, with whom A. 91, when still a boy, had made friends. Apart from his ardent patriotism, Dominique had a private score to settle with the Germans: during the earlier stages of the occupation, they had forced him to remain for several months at his post on the railway, threatening deportation of his family and himself if he refused. He joyfully entered the services of the 'White Lady', when solicited by Pierre.

Dominique's cottage, right on the railway line, was admirably situated for watching the troop trains as they passed by, night and day; and here, the dream of the Allied secret services was at last realised. Aided by his wife, and his two little sisters, aged fourteen and thirteen years, Dominique mounted a train-watching post on the Hirson–Mézières line.

Everyone in this humble household did their share of watching. By day it was the two small girls, who, through a narrow slit in the heavily curtained windows, scrutinised the trains as they went by; at night it was Dominique and his wife. The composition of the trains was jotted down in terms of comestibles: beans for soldiers, chicory for horses, coffee for guns, and so on. The reports, in readiness for the courier, were hidden in the hollow handle of a kitchen broom, which was left innocently in its place in the corner. On 23 September, the Fourmies post, No. 201 in the service, started working, and from then on until the Armistice, not a single troop train was missed on this the most important railway artery behind the German front.

Pierre continued the difficult task of recruiting agents. The danger he ran can only be estimated by one who has been in the service. Even after narrowing down his list to the chosen few whom he considered capable and trustworthy, there always remained the risk of refusal, and the fear, not so much of betrayal, but of gossip reaching the ears of one of the many German stool-pigeons to be found in every village.

At Glageon, mid-way between Trélon and Fourmies, Pierre recruited his next agent, Crésillon, an employee at a sawmill forcibly kept in operation by the Germans. Adjoining the saw-mill was a German engineer park, where ladders to place over barbed-wire entanglements, trench floor-boards, mines to be used against tanks, and all kinds of trench material were manu-factured. At this park there was a continual coming and going of detachments, sent by their divisions to fetch supplies; and here it was that Crésillon kept watch. To his competent eye, the noting of regimental numbers, and the gleaning of military information became a routine performance; he was one of the principal members of the Hirson Platoon, who, later on in Feb-ruary 1918, sent us that sure indication that it was from the sector opposite this area that the Germans were to launch their great March offensive.

In addition to this valuable work, Crésillon also undertook the duties of 'letter box', and courier. The reports from Fourmies, Avesnes, and other areas were deposited at his house, and from here, regularly twice a week, he carried them half-way to Trélon to hand them over to Pierre. From Pierre, as we have already seen, Moreau carried them over the frontier to Gobeaux in Macon. Fearing that his constant meetings with Pierre, which generally took place during the luncheon hour, would attract attention, he eventually handed over his courier duties to his wife. In her pro-fession as midwife, she had an excuse to travel. The Germans never suspected, as she hurried out on her frequent calls, that the delivery of deadly spy reports, cunningly wrapped around the whale-bones of her corset, was her special vocation.

In the face of danger, illness, rain, and snow, the service went on night and day without a break. It was the couriers who had the most dangerous and the most arduous work. None showed a finer devotion to the patriotic cause they served than Eglantine Lefèvre. On the many occasions the Kaiser took up his quarters at the Château de Merode, near Trélon, and all the roads were ferociously guarded, and not even Crésillon's wife could circulate, it was Eglantine Lefèvre who carried the reports through at night by way of the fields and the woods. Her name is written down in the annals of the Hirson Platoon as having sacrificed her life in the execution of her duties. Stricken at the time of the Spanish influenza epidemic, she insisted on carrying the reports through to Trélon, even though she was running a high temperature and ached in every limb. She collapsed on reaching Pierre's house and died the next day.

The Hirson Platoon had now grown to some fifty-odd members. The Trélon-Glageon-Fourmies-Avesnes area was covered by an invisible network, which daily caught every German move; but in spite of Pierre's heroic efforts, Hirson itself still eluded his grasp. He had penetrated into the town; he had even succeeded in mounting train-watching posts there to control the important branch lines which converged at this centre; but he had been unable to find a courier to surmount the difficulties of the Hirson–Trélon route. It was Gobeaux who came to the rescue.

Knowing Pierre's problem, Gobeaux was naturally all attention when one day two Hirson workmen approached him with the object of planning an escape to join the French Army. Gobeaux was quick to suggest to them that they should join the army of the 'White Lady'. One of them, who took the service name of José, consented, and Gobeaux sent him back immediately to Hirson to mount a courier service between Hirson and Macon.

José, in spite of his willingness, was unable to find anyone to help him except his wife, and after making two journeys, covering the long distance alone, he gave up in despair. But Gobeaux, realising the importance of the Hirson reports, was not to be discouraged. Accompanied by an intimate friend of his, Delchambre, he set out for Hirson, early in January 1918, determined to solve the problem on the spot. Traversing the forest of St Michel, they managed to reach their destination. There they put fresh courage into José, and after many setbacks succeeded in enrolling two agents to act in a relay with him. They remained long enough to assure themselves that the Hirson train-watching posts had been definitely linked up with Pierre through the Glageon 'letter box'.

Jubilant at the success of their mission, the two of them started back on their return journey. They were approaching the frontier, when suddenly out of the night, they heard the traditional 'Halt!' There was only one thing to do – they took to their heels. But the two German soldiers who composed the patrol were young, and even though the darkness and the trees prevented use of their rifles, they could run. Gobeaux and his companion realised their only chance was to hide. Crouched behind a bush, they anxiously waited for the soldiers to pass. The soldiers, however, hearing no noise, started searching around. Gobeaux whispered quick instructions to Delchambre.

As the soldiers got within reach, the two jumped out on them, and made a grab for their rifles. Each grappled with his man; and, in hand-to-hand struggle which followed, Gobeaux, in trying to grab his man by the throat, stuck his thumb into his mouth. The German bit into the bone; but Gobeaux was a powerful man – with his free fist he knocked him senseless. Springing to Delchambre's aid, he dealt the other soldier a blow over the head with the butt-end of his rifle. Taking to their heels again, they managed to regain Macon in safety.

Gobeaux nursed a broken thumb for several weeks, but as he philosophically told me after the Armistice, 'The Hirson posts were well worth it.' What annoyed him most of all was that he had to remain in hiding until his thumb healed: for days, the Secret Police searched for a man with a lacerated thumb.

Such a direct fight with Secret Police or German soldiers was a rarity. It was confined to the frontier struggles at the two borders, where our agents, often poachers or smugglers, were quick with knife and gun. As a rule, it was hopeless to attempt physical resistance. The spy relied on his wits, and in this he was often more than a match for his German opponent.

The Hirson Platoon functioned until the end of the war without a single arrest – a truly remarkable achievement in the face of the strict German surveillance. Its success was largely due to the paternal guidance of Pierre. Their fervent patriotism, their trust in God, and the affection they had for each other, these were the influences that inspired them.

A remarkable feature not only of the Hirson Platoon, but of the whole 'White Lady' organisation was family co-operation. Husband, wife, children, even the dog (watching at the door), and often the furniture (a hiding place for compromising documents), each played a part.

Immediately after his return from Trélon, A. 91 went back to Liège with Chauvin. There for a period of six weeks, twice a week, he eagerly scanned the reports; he assisted Dewé and Chauvin in making the necessary criticisms, and watched with satisfaction the gradual extension of his father's platoon. He knew that it was supplying the Allies with the only information which came out of this vital area, and he was justly proud.

A. 91's three months' leave of absence, which General Bucabeille had granted him, was about to expire. Dewé and Chauvin reminded us of our promise to fetch him, and once again, on 24 November 1917, it was Charles Willekens who brought him safely into Holland. He had crossed the high-voltage electric wire three times – twice as a spy – in itself a heroic achievement.

After spending a day with him, plying him with eager questions, and listening to his detailed account of every incident that had occurred during his last eventful three months in the interior, I said goodbye and wished him good luck in his new adventure. Like Lawrence of Arabia, he was setting out as a seasoned veteran to become a cog in a machine – a recruit in the French Army. He was drafted into the 26th Battalion of the Chasseurs à Pied. After the war, he entered one of the religious orders.

CHAPTER 8

THE GERMAN SECRET POLICE
– THEIR METHODS AND
ORGANISATION

L ET US NOW look behind the scenes in the German camp to catch a glimpse of the forces arrayed against the 'White Lady'.

The German counter-espionage activities in the occupied territories were directed by the military authorities. There were two distinct groups: The *Geheimen Feldpolizei,* or Secret Field Police; and the Secret Police attached to the *Zentralpolizeistelle* or Central Police Bureau.

The Secret Field Police were the police of the German armies in the field, but as each army headquarters remained fixed for the greater part of the war, the various Secret Field Police units had definite areas to watch. Thus, for example, the Secret Field Police of the IVth German Army covered the Ghent sector; while those of the VIth Army had its sphere of action round Lille. In their aggregate these areas composed the *Etappengebiet*, or area immediately behind the German front; it also included most of Belgian Flanders. Although attached to their own army head-quarters, the various Secret Field Police units really took their orders from a central bureau that centralised their reports and ensured co-operation. The head of this bureau, the big chief of the whole Secret Field Police organisation, was *Feldpolizei-direktor* Bauer. His bureau was attached to German GHQ in Charleville.

The *Zentralpolizeistelle* had its headquarters at Brussels, and was attached to the staff of the German governor-general, von Bissing. The zone it covered was all that part of the occupied territory not controlled by the Secret Field Police, that is, all the back areas of Belgium, including the Belgian–Dutch bor-der. This Central Police Bureau, outside of its local attachment to the staff of the governor-general, was controlled by Colonel Nicolai, the director of all German military secret service activi-ties; his staff comprised Section IIIb, a section of the German GHQ staff. The head of the Central Police Bureau in Belgium was Captain Imhoff, who occupied himself chiefly with admin-istrative duties. The actual counter-espionage activities were directed by Captain Kohlmeier. Contrary to what might have been expected, it was this Central Police Bureau, and not the Secret Field Police, which was responsible for most of the spy arrests. The explanation of this is that both the border zone, and the headquarters of all the Allied spy organisations, fell within the area controlled by it.

The territory under the supervision of the Central Police Bureau was divided into four districts: the provinces of Antwerp, Limbourge, Namur, and Brabant, each in charge of a captain. These districts were in turn divided into a number of *Polizeistelle*, or Secret Police posts. The Secret Police posts at Liège, Brussels, and Antwerp were the ones with which the 'White Lady' generally came into conflict.

The chief of the *Polizeistelle* Lüttich (Liège) was Lieutenant Landwerlen, who was connected with the Lambrecht arrests, and about whom I shall have much to say later.

At Brussels there were three of these police posts: sections A, B, and C. Lieutenant Bergan, who together with Henri Pinkhoff was responsible for the arrest of Edith Cavell, was in charge of Section B.

In their drive on spies, the German Secret Police directed their attack along four channels: surveillance at the frontier; control of the population through severe police laws; surveillance in the interior of the occupied territories; and, finally, use of traitors.

By means of the high-voltage electric wire at the Belgian–Dutch frontier, and by the efficient surveillance which I have already described, spies were either caught at the border or were cut off from their base in Holland.

In the interior, by making compulsory the carrying of identity cards and the procuring of passes even for short journeys, the Secret Police not only hindered the transmission of reports, but acquired an effective means of controlling the inhabitants.

Random search of houses, sudden raids at railway stations, at cafes, and on the tram-cars, and often the blocking off of entire streets, frequently left a spy in their net. It was not even necessary to seize reports. Often a false identity card or the lack of a travelling pass started an investigation which enmeshed the spy.

A strict watch was kept at all military centres, and anyone acting at all suspiciously was immediately arrested; above all, houses which could possibly harbour train-watchers were kept under close observation.

But the Secret Police were clever enough to recognise that these measures alone would not suffice. The inhabitants soon learned to recognise even those agents who had been recruited from Germans who had lived for years in Belgium and France before the war, and who often passed for Belgians or Frenchmen. To overcome this disadvantage, and to avail themselves of a source of information which has been used since time immemorial, the Germans resorted to the use of stool-pigeons. It was the employment of these traitors, recruited from the dregs of the French and Belgian population, which accounted for at least 90 per cent of the arrests made. However small it was, every police post had its five or six informers who spied on their neighbours and collected that idle gossip, not harmfully meant, which often spelled death for the victim. Arrests were, of course, always made by the Secret Police, and the identity of these traitors was concealed as much as possible.

These stool-pigeons were successful in Belgium, but it was in Holland that they reaped their richest harvest. Here the Allied secret services, cut off from the interior and continually prodded by headquarters in England or France, were often tricked by these traitors who came to them with every possible proof that they had means of bringing information out of Belgium. This proof often was the very report the Germans had seized on some frontier courier, and which the stool-pigeon now used in order to get himself enrolled as a substitute courier. The tragic results can well be imagined.

Once the Secret Police had been given sufficient information to effect the arrest of a spy, they could carry on for themselves. They were past masters in the art of delayed arrest, that is, watching a suspect until all his contacts had been discovered. Not satisfied with arresting the spy, his house was also occupied, and anyone having the misfortune to call had to prove his innocence before he was released. If these measures failed to enmesh the entire organisation, third-degree methods were used on the prisoners: drugs, endless interrogation without sleep, and finally physical violence. Stool-pigeons were also frequently employed in the prisons. The unfortunate prisoner, worn out by mishandling, often fell an easy prey to these individuals disguised as fellow prisoners, priests, or nuns.

Since prison stool-pigeons were so frequently used by the Germans, it will be of interest to hear the story of one of them. Practically all were of French and Belgian nationality, but I cannot resist singling out the German, Hans G., for he was the most notorious one of them all.

One morning, towards the end of 1916, Lieutenant Bergan, in charge of the police post in Brussels, handed his assistant, Pinkhoff, an informer's report to investigate. Pinkhoff was not especially interested. He knew all these reports had to be followed up, but he would have preferred being put in charge of a more important case. Daulne, the Belgian chief of police at Aud-erghem, was accused of assisting refugees to escape into Holland. Probably some ex-convict trying to get even with the Belgian Police, is what passed through Pinkhoff's mind; he handed the investigation on to one of his minor agents.

Events, however, quickly took a surprising turn. The agent rushed back to Pinkhoff with the exciting information that not only was the report accurate, but that Daulne had in hiding in his house an escaped prisoner-of-war, a Russian officer, Count Jean Potoki. Pinkhoff immediately took charge, the house was put under observation, and Daulne and the Count were eventually arrested.

At the interrogation which ensued, Count Potoki, to Daulne's utter amazement, declared that he was Hans G., a deserter from the German Army, and that he had posed as a Russian to arouse Daulne's sympathy, and to secure a hiding place.

But to Pinkhoff, Count Potoki, a Russian officer of high rank, was of much greater interest than G, the deserter; and so, it was as the Count that the prisoner was charged, and it was still as the Count that he was convicted, and imprisoned in the Prison de St-Gilles in Brussels. Proof was soon forthcoming, however, that G was all that he had claimed to be – a German deserter, and the son of the station master at a small town close to Berlin. Pinkhoff, when called to account for the mistake, had a ready answer: 'You don't think I really thought he was a Russian, do you? Don't you see, he took Daulne in? He is going to be one of our stool-pigeons.' G demanded nothing better; he was once again in order with the German military authorities; and, above all, he had achieved his original objective: he had escaped service in the firing line.

Those Allied agents who were imprisoned in St-Gilles during the 1916–18 period will recognise the man if not the name: small, dark, thick-set, with high cheek-bones, aquiline nose, small moustache, and an aristocratic bearing. Several years spent as a waiter in Paris had given G a perfect command of the French language. In addition, therefore, to the role of Count Potoki, he often passed himself off as a Frenchman.

Sometimes he was introduced into a cell as a priest. Overflowing with sympathy, he eagerly listened to the confidences that were made him, and was always quick to intimate that he was willing to carry word, either by mouth or letter, to anyone who needed warning. Another variation was that of fellow prisoner. On these occasions, his passage to the cell would always be accompanied by the sound of blows, shrieks of pain, and by shouts of 'dirty spy' and other German imprecations. The cell door would open, and he would be thrown in a heap at the feet of his victim.

Some of the prisoners were taken in by him; others, acquainted with Secret Police methods, met his advances with insults, or simply refused to speak to him. His victims were many. So successful was he that there were times when he was even lent to the Secret Police in Antwerp. He was well paid. When he was instrumental in securing the arrest of a whole spy organisation, his blood money often ran as high as a thousand marks. Most of the credit, however, for G's work went to Pinkhoff. He was awarded the Iron Cross, and was eventually promoted to chief of the Secret Police in Bucharest.

It was not only stool-pigeons of the types I have already mentioned, who succeeded in tricking the Allied agents and secret

services. There were many members of the Secret Police who,
like Pinkhoff, could speak French fluently, and they too were
often successful in passing themselves off as Frenchmen or Belgians. B was a typical representative of this class.

An Alsatian by birth, B had lived for many years in Paris. He
spoke not only French but even the argot fluently. It is not surprising, then, to find him as M. 25 already enrolled before the war
in the German secret service. It was he who, in 1913, stole from
one of the forts of Verdun a new type of shell of secret construction which had just been introduced into the French Army. It
was a daring coup. While an accomplice attracted the attention
of the sentinel at the ammunition magazine, B made his entry
and got away with the prize. At the commencement of the war,
he was again sent on a mission to France, but, compromised in
connection with it, he was transferred to Brussels in 1915, and was
there attached to Police Section A under the direction of Lieutenant Schmitz. Working alternately under the assumed names of
Paul Forster and Paul Lefèvre, he soon proved himself one of the
best of the Secret Police in his section. Posing as a Belgian who
had extensive connections in Holland, he gained the confidence
of the Mayor of one of the large towns in occupied France, and
eventually received a mandate from him to make purchases in Holland for the municipality. Armed with an official letter from the
Mayor, to which the seal of the municipality had been attached,
and facilitated by a *visa* granted by the Germans, supposedly at
the request of the Mayor, B, alias Paul Lefèvre, set out for Holland. On arrival there his papers were an open sesame to several
of the Allied secret services. Of the arrests he was responsible for,
I shall tell in a later chapter.

This, then, is a brief outline of the German counter-espionage organisation in the occupied territories, as well as a general description of their methods and of a few of the characteristic types employed by them. Since it is outside the scope of this book, I have made no reference to the German secret service branch in Antwerp, which they used both as a spy school and as a base for the recruiting of many of the agents whom they sent into the Allied countries.

Between the two German counter-espionage services, a network was spread over the whole of the occupied territories – each village had its police post. In the aggregate there were several thousand secret agents attached to their payroll. If one adds to this number, the sentries spread along the Belgian–Dutch frontier, one readily realises the size of the German counter-espionage machine. It had to be large to watch and control several million inhabitants.

The German Secret Police were often efficient in making arrests; at other times, they blundered hopelessly. They were handicapped by the competition, and consequent lack of cooperation, between the various police posts. Each, in its endeavour to win credit for arrests, was inclined to keep clues to itself. This happened even among the three Secret Police sections in Brussels. Then, they were often tricked by double agents who, working for both sides at the same time, betrayed the one to the other. Their strength, the stool-pigeon recruited from among the inhabitants, was on occasions their weakness; information purchased at a price could not always be relied on.

In regard to the Secret Police methods, the types of agents they employed, and their treatment of prisoners, I offer no opinion. I have merely stated the facts. The reader can judge for himself. The Belgian and German points of view can never be reconciled, and I am not going to attempt the impossible.

The Germans point out that the Allied spies had enmeshed the German Army in the rear. Stringent action had, therefore, to be taken; and in war, any means are justifiable where spies are concerned. They further add that they had a problem to face, which none of the Allies had: they were in a hostile country, where each of the inhabitants was a potential spy; it would have been impossible for them to have exercised any form of spy control if their methods had not been harsh. The Belgians reply that the Germans had no right to invade a country which had committed no act of war, and whose only offence was that it happened to lie between Germany and France. Furthermore, they claim that on their own soil they had a perfect right to serve their country.

The German tribunals on the whole were fair, if one takes into consideration that they were military courts operating in lime of war. During the last two years of the war, I know of no case where an innocent person was shot as a spy. Theoretically, anyone caught communicating with the enemy could have been shot; actually, many of the spies who were caught were given prison sentences. It is true that many were shot who did far less harm than some of those who received prison terms. But the Germans did not always know the whole truth; they could only judge the evidence in their possession, and this as we have already seen was often only a fraction of what they might have gathered if they could have looked behind the scenes. Those who suffered the unfairest treatment were the many thousands of inhabitants who were arrested on the flimsiest suspicion, and then were often kept weeks, even months, in prison until they or their friends could prove their innocence.

CHAPTER 9

EXPLOITS OF THE CHIMAY COMPANY

AMID THE CONFLICTS with the Secret Police, the work of spying went on night and day. And in case the reader should lose sight of this, I must occasionally give him a glimpse of the spy at work. I shall, therefore, tell a few anecdotes about the Chimay company, which was the last of the nine 'White Lady' companies to be formed.

It was just before the time of the Hirson Platoon. The Allies were still without a train-watching post on the Hirson–Mézières line, and the French GHQ were desperately anxious to have reports on the German troop movements along this strategic artery. The Allied secret services in Holland had failed after many attempts. There was only one other possibility, and that was to drop a spy by parachute. Perhaps, by starting from the other end, working towards Holland, and linking up with the French secret service there, this difficult objective could be achieved.

Two men volunteered for the dangerous mission: a young non-commissioned officer, Maréchal des logis Pierre Aubijoux, who was to be the pilot, and the soldier Valtier, the man to be dropped.

It was in the early hours of the morning, when it was still dark, that Aubijoux and Valtier took off from a flying field near Jonchery. Valtier was to be dropped at Signy-l'Abbaye, near Rethel, his home village, where he would be immediately among friends whom he proposed to enrol as train-watchers and couriers in the projected spy organisation.

But night-flying in those days, without beacons and directional beams as guides, was at the best a risky undertaking. After flying for several hours, Aubijoux had to admit that he was completely lost; with a gasoline tank nearly empty, it was impossible to regain the French lines. There was no alternative but to make a forced landing. To add to their difficulties, dawn was just breaking and a heavy ground fog had come up. But luck was with them. They landed in a field, and though their plane crashed into a barbed-wire fence, they were unharmed. Dazed with their sudden landing, they were still recovering themselves when through the mist they saw two German soldiers rushing at them. In a flash Aubijoux had turned his machine gun against them. To set fire to the plane, and to make a dash for a wood that bordered the field, was the work of a few minutes. They did not look to see the effect of their fire, or if any more soldiers were coming.

The two men had no idea where they were. The wood, over-grown with bushes and underbrush, covered several acres. They realised that even if the two soldiers had been killed, there would probably be others who had heard the noise of their motors, and in any event the remains of the plane would shortly be discovered. The hunt would soon be on. A decision had to be taken. Wisely, they decided to remain where they were, within 100 yards of their plane. The audacity saved them; for after a hurried search of the wood, during which some of the men came within a few yards of where they lay hid among the bushes, they saw the soldiers hurry away. For two days and a night, without food and water, Aubijoux and Valtier remained in the wood. Just after dark on the second day, worn out and desperate, they decided to investigate a farmhouse they saw in the distance.

Peering through one of the windows into a dimly lit room, they saw the farmer and his family at their evening meal. Their sympathetic faces gave them courage to knock.

The farmer came to the door.

'We are the French aviators the Boches are looking for. Can you hide us?' Aubijoux anxiously asked.

One look convinced the farmer that they were genuine – their hunted hungry appearance could not be simulated. And then, as Aubijoux had rightly surmised, the Germans had already searched the house for them, the day before.

The farmer stood aside, and allowed the two men to enter.

Their immediate inquiry brought the information that they were at Bourlers, close to Chimay, at the farm of Gaston Lafontaine.

Lafontaine and his wife, courageous Belgians, had already

helped many French soldiers. They had hidden several during the retreat in 1914. For more than two years of the occupation they had received visits from the German Secret Police. They knew the risk they were running in hiding the two men.

Plans were immediately discussed, and Valtier, realising that they were among patriots, disclosed his secret mission. Lafontaine, anxious to help, promised to hide them in his loft, while he went off to consult with the nuns of the Congrégation Nancéenne de la Doctrine Chrétienne, at Chimay. Even though the Germans had installed a hospital in the convent, these nuns were taking an active part in every form of patriotic activity, and it was to them that everyone in the region turned for guidance and assistance.

Rose Lebrun, known in her order as Sœur Marie-Mélanie, understood the importance of Valtier's mission. The 'White Lady' was busy at this very moment mounting the Chimay company, and Sœur Marie-Mélanie had just been enrolled as a member of the service. She, therefore, sent Lafontaine off to consult with Grislain Hanotier, the sergeant in charge of her section.

Hanotier took quick action. He returned with Lafontaine to the farm. To him the solution was obvious. Valtier should leave the mounting of the train-watching posts at Hirson to him, and he and his companion should get across the border into Holland as soon as possible.

Valtier and Aubijoux demurred.

Hanotier countered with: 'What's the use? The Germans are still searching for you; and as long as you are in hiding, you cannot do any useful work.'

The two Frenchmen were eventually persuaded; and, having

furnished them with a guide, Hanotier duly started them on their way to the Dutch frontier.

But on the way Valtier suddenly saw matters in a different light. He had been given orders to mount a post on the Hirson–Mézières line; and it was his duty to remain until this had been done, even if it should cost him his life. The two of them, therefore, retraced their steps, and five days later to Lafontaine's astonishment they were again at his house. With resignation he accepted their argument, and bravely undertook to guide them through to Hirson.

Aubijoux and Valtier mounted their posts, and arranged a courier service for the reports to be brought through to Sœur Marie-Mélanie. This having been done, they were now willing to regain the French Army. So once again they set out for the Dutch border. But fortune does not always follow the brave – they were arrested at the Dutch border. Knowing nothing of their spy activities, and believing their story that they were French aviators who had been forced down behind the German lines by fog, the Germans treated them as prisoners-of-war, and sent them off to a prison camp in Germany.

The reports from Hirson came through for two weeks, and then the courier system broke down. In the meantime, however, the 'White Lady' had mounted their own train-watching posts on the Hirson–Mézières line; and from then until the Armistice, the Hirson Platoon, and the Chimay company – of which Hirson Platoon formed a part – carried on the work Valtier and Aubijoux had so valiantly begun.

It was a fine old type of Frenchman that Valtier had enrolled as his train-watcher in Hirson. When the 'White Lady' got through to him, he had an accumulation of a month's reports which he insisted should be sent through to Marshal Joffre personally, and to no one else. Valtier had certainly impressed on him the importance of the Hirson reports.

In other sectors close behind the Front both the British and the French continued to use aeroplanes for spy work. They generally confined themselves, however, to dropping parachutes, attached to which were baskets of carrier pigeons, and directions for their use. Many of these baskets fell into the hands of the patriotic inhabitants, who did not fail to release the pigeons with the information asked for.

The Congrégation Nancéenne de la Doctrine Chrétienne was a French Order, one of the many that had been expelled from France. The patriotism of these French nuns was the more intense because they were exiles. Established in Belgium, at Chimay just across the French border, they gladly and lovingly gave succour to their refugee compatriots fleeing from the fighting zone, or deported by the Germans. The German military hospital, which I have already mentioned, had been installed by force in their convent, with German doctors, nurses, and orderlies to care for the wounded. The nuns were, therefore, at liberty to serve their country, and to make full use of the fertile field which the German hospital placed in their midst presented for spying. Gobeaux, the captain of the Chimay company, and Hanotier, the sergeant of the section in whose area the convent fell, were quick to realise the value of the information that could be gathered by these patriotic sisters, and so with the consent of Marie-Hippolyte, the Mother Superior, they enrolled in the 'White Lady' two of the nuns – Sœur Marie-Mélanie, and Sœur Marie-Caroline.

There were no keener agents in the 'White Lady' than these two sisters of charity. Intelligent and resourceful, they knew how to make full use of their opportunities. It is true they were not called on to nurse the wounded, but the convalescing officers and soldiers, wandering around in the convent grounds, frequently tried to get into communication with them. They also had a small shop where they were permitted to sell postcards and other articles, and here the Germans were wont to gather.

These men all came from divisions in the front line, and the identification of these divisions in some definite sector of the Front was of enormous importance to British GHQ. One has only to examine the daily intelligence Bulletins issued both by the French and British GHQ to realise this. It was solely to gather information of this kind that lives were sacrificed almost daily in raids on the enemy's front-line trenches; and yet, these two sisters, quietly and unsuspected, achieved the same objective. Rarely did a report reach me from Chimay without one or two of these important identifications.

This was not the only utility of these two daring nuns. Their reports, picked up by the section courier, contained information covering every phase of German military activity. For example, there was the case of the officer of Prince Eitel Friedrich's staff, who was in the hospital with a broken leg, received from the fall of his horse. It was while lamenting that he was laid up for 'the big push' that he gave away that the great German offensive of March 1918 was to be launched in the Albert sector. He did not give the information in a sentence, nor even in a single day; but it was by carefully piecing together scraps of conversation spread over several days that the two astute nuns were able to arrive at a definite conclusion. This information was valuable corroborative evidence of what we had already deduced from our train-watching posts, and from the reports of the Hirson Platoon.

It was not only from the Germans that Sœur Marie-Mélanie, and Sœur Marie-Caroline garnered information; sometimes it was also from the refugees; and then, on many occasions, as will be seen from the following account, they often arrived at important deductions by combining information from both sources.

It was at the time that the German big gun had just started shelling Paris, and the Germans had been careful to fill their *communiqués* with the news. A gunner, wounded in the hand, was in the hospital, and was boasting about what the Germans would soon be doing when they had several hundred of these guns. Sœur Marie-Mélanie was immediately all attention. 'It hardly seems possible that they can shoot so far,' was her quiet reply. The gunner seeing no possible harm in this peaceful nun, quickly retorted that he himself had seen the gun in the Laon sector. This was a vague enough indication for the emplacement of a gun, but it was sufficient for the nimble-minded sister. It happened that three weeks previously, a French refugee from the village of Crépy-en-Laonnois had been given food and shelter at the convent. Eagerly questioned about the wholesale deportation of his village, he had attributed it to the fact the Germans were about to move artillery into the area.

'How do you know this?' Sœur Marie-Mélanie had asked him, knowing the importance of distinguishing fact from rumour.

'Well, they have laid down concrete gun-platforms and ammunition pits at Dandry's farm – at least that's what everyone thinks they are,' the refugee had replied.

Cleverly putting the two pieces of information together, Sœur Marie-Mélanie communicated her views to Hanotier; he passed it on to the captain of his company. Gobeaux, as we have already seen, was a man of quick decision. He decided to send a man to Dandry's farm. It was a dangerous undertaking – all the inhabitants had been deported. But it was precisely one of these deportees whom he persuaded to return. Travelling at night and hiding by day, the man was back on the third day. He had seen the monster gun. Three days later, I had the information in Holland.

From a spy in Germany, several weeks previously, we had already received full details of the trials on the coast of Heligoland which had been carried out with this high-angle-fire gun; and it was with exultation that I passed the report on to Colonel Oppenheim, the British military attaché at The Hague, whose duty it was to telegraph to British GHQ a daily résumé of all our reports.

There are many stories I might relate about Gobeaux. As captain of the Chimay company, he should really have protected himself as much as possible; but this was impossible for a man of his temperament. I might tell how he himself penetrated the cordon of sentries at the Bourlers aviation field, and was satisfied with nothing less than cutting off and sending me a sliver from one of the wooden tanks assembled there – because I had disbelieved his report that the Germans were using these tanks for camouflage purposes; or again I might relate how, at the Hôtel Godeau in Chimay, he stole the map-case of a German aviator – the case yielded several priceless maps on which were marked all the aviation fields behind a large section of the German

Western Front. (To mark them in this fashion was contrary to German Army regulations, but the aviator had transgressed for his own safety and convenience.) The story, however, that I am going to tell about Gobeaux is just a short one, but one which epitomises the coolness and resourcefulness of the man.

In the Chimay company there were four platoons: Hirson, Chimay, Charleroi, and one composed of couriers. Gobeaux was too well versed in spying to contact personally any but his principal agents. But, imbued with the military spirit of the 'White Lady', he felt it his duty to pass on a continual round of inspection, checking up, without their knowing it, the reports of the train-watchers, the itinerant spies and other agents in his area. As head of a syndicate of sabot makers, he had an excuse to travel around in his sector, visiting the members of this quaint industry – the manufacture of wooden shoes for the peasants of the countryside. (Most of the members made the shoes in their own homes, delivering them to syndicate headquarters in Chimay, where their sale was attended to.) But this excuse only held for occupied Belgium. Somehow he had to reach the area covered by the Hirson Platoon in France.

Gobeaux knew that if he kept slipping across the frontier, he would eventually be caught; so he cleverly bought a small strip of the Neumont Woods, just across the border, and there installed some of his sabot makers. He then had an excuse to get a pass. This was duly obtained from the *Kommandantur*, or German police post, at Trélon. The pass only read for the Neumont Woods, but getting across the frontier was half the battle – he could use his ingenuity to reach the rest of the Hirson area. One day, while on a visit to Pierre in Trélon, less sly than usual, he was arrested by one of the local Secret Police.

'Where are you going?' asked the plain-clothes man. 'Your pass?'

Gobeaux, who had already thought up a plan of action, showed his pass.

'This is no good – you are in Trélon. It's only valid for Neumont,' said the secret agent, holding the pass in his hand. 'You'll have to come along with me to the *Kommandantur*.' 'That's exactly where I was heading,' Gobeaux assured him. The plain-clothes man accompanied Gobeaux to the *Kommandantur*, and there explained to the lieutenant in charge, the circumstances of the arrest.

'Well, what do you want?' said the lieutenant, looking at Gobeaux suspiciously.

'It's about my pass,' replied Gobeaux, handing it to him. 'When I showed it to the sentry at the frontier, he said it wasn't valid – the rubber stamp is affixed in the wrong place.' The lieutenant examining the pass: 'The sentry is a fool.' 'That's possible, Lieutenant. You can tell him that; but I didn't dare dispute with him.'

The lieutenant, noticing that the pass had in fact been somewhat carelessly stamped, stamped it again, and handed it back to Gobeaux.

On many other occasions, Gobeaux's quick brain and brazen effrontery saved him from disaster.

CHAPTER 10

THE AFFAIR OF THE VILLA
DES HIRONDELLES

ABOUT THIS TIME a serious catastrophe befell the
'White Lady'; the best of planning could not have
averted it.

Chance, which cannot be gauged in advance, put the Secret
Police on their track. An anonymous letter, written by a jealous
relative who had never even heard of the 'White Lady' started
the train of events which ended so tragically.

Marcelle, the girl denounced in the letter, had left occupied
France without a passport, and had entered domestic service
in Liège. Thus far her planning was not at fault; but when she
set her cap at a rich man, who had money to leave, decidedly

she took a false step. Landwerlen, the lieutenant in charge of the Secret Police at Liège, was daily receiving such letters, and he did not attach special importance to this particular one; but he had two men who happened to be free, Wilhelm Muller and another agent, and so he sent them off to bring the girl in for questioning.

On their arrival at Wandre, where Reyman, Marcelle's employer, was living, Muller and his companion found no one at home. Inquiries among the neighbours brought them the information that Reyman might be at the Villa des Hirondelles, a house which he had rented to some tenants. The villa happened to be the secretariat of the 'White Lady' – the place where all their reports were typed out and prepared for transmission to Holland.

The 'White Lady' was prepared for a raid. The villa stood in its own grounds on the banks of the Meuse, and in the rear, out of sight of the front door, a boat was moored, furnished with oars all set for an escape down the river. In the villa there were twenty-eight guns, and 10,000 rounds of ammunition; the front windows were heavily shuttered, and a strong oak door barred the front entrance. One person, forewarned, could have held a dozen Secret Police at bay until all compromising documents had been destroyed, and the other inmates of the villa had escaped. But luck for once was against the 'White Lady'.

The two plain-clothes men had just reached the thick hedge which enclosed the villa, when they met, face to face, two of the 'White Lady' couriers coming out – they had just deposited their reports at the villa. Muller gruffly demanded: 'Who lives here?'

Completely taken aback, the couriers, Franchimont, and van

den Berg, made no reply. Muller, immediately sensing there was something wrong, pulled out his gun, and ordered them to follow him.

In the interior of the villa there were four persons: Madame Goessels, who was in charge of the secretariat; Rosa, a servant who worked by the day, and who cleaned up the villa twice a week; and in a back room, from whose windows they could easily have escaped to the boat, there were two 'White Lady' agents, Louis and Antony Collard, who had just arrived from Belgian Luxembourg and were stopping for the night. The stenographers happened to be away. Of the whole group, Madame Goessels, a buxom woman of about thirty-five years of age, endowed with extraordinary vitality, was the dominant character. Engaged in every form of patriotic activity since the beginning of the war, she was experienced in Secret Police methods, and so far had proved more than a match for them.

Muller knocked at the door. The voice of Madame Goessels was heard asking 'Who's there?' Muller, experienced at his work, stuck his gun into Franchimont's side, and in a whisper ordered him to reply.

Madame Goessels, hearing the voice of one whom she had just let out of the villa, was completely disarmed. She opened the door. In a glance, she took in the situation.

The reports which Franchimont and van den Berg had brought, had been hidden in a sofa, forced down between the seat and one of the sides; but Madame Goessels knew that the two Collards were in their room, copying out some information which they had just brought back from Luxembourg. She had just left their room and had seen the reports spread out on a table. Her one thought was to warn them. But how? Their door was closed. To gain time, she stood in the doorway, and from there, in as loud a voice as possible, she answered Muller's questions:

'Does Monsieur Reyman live here?'

'No. You are at the house of Madame Goessels.'

'Have you ever been arrested?'

'No. Neither by you, nor by the Belgians.'

'You are Mademoiselle Marcelle?'

'No, I am Madame Goessels.'

'You are French?'

'No, I am a Belgian.'

But Muller was suspicious. Franchimont and van den Berg were young men. Perhaps she was hiding refugees here, and so pushing her aside, he and his companion entered to search the villa.

Unfortunately, the two Collard brothers heard nothing of this dialogue, so engrossed were they in their work; it was only when they heard footsteps outside their door that they realised something was wrong. Both of them had pocketbooks on their person containing incriminating papers. Antony had the presence of mind to throw his out of the window; but Louis was caught unawares. In any case, spread on the table were the reports, and these the Germans immediately seized.

While this was going on, Madame Goessels slipped upstairs – she had a plan. Quickly grasping a gun, she stuck it in her blouse, and waited on the landing for one of the Secret Police to mount; she knew the other would remain below to guard the prisoners. It was Muller who appeared. 'Trying to hide something?' he said as he went into her bedroom to make a search. This was the opportunity she was waiting for. Quickly she closed the door from the outside, and tried to turn the key. But Muller was too quick for her; he wrenched the door open covering her with his gun. The search of the villa was now continued, and with the additional discovery of the guns and the ammunition the Secret Police thought they had all the evidence they needed.

Handcuffed and tied together with some rope which they found in the villa, the prisoners were taken to the police post at Wandre; from there Muller telephoned for reinforcements. These were not long in coming, and the prisoners were taken off to the Liège police post for questioning. While Muller and his companion were away making their report, the prisoners were confined in a room under the guard of a German soldier. Madame Goessels was quick to seize her opportunity. Already, she had a defence planned, and to each in a few short sentences, she whispered their part.

To Franchimont: 'I am your mistress. You have often visited me at the villa. You know nothing about my activities.'

To van den Berg: 'You are Franchimont's friend. You dropped in on a casual visit.'

To the two Collards: 'You are two of my lodgers. I don't know who you are, nor anything about your activities. Remember your oath as a soldier. Reveal nothing.'

Her own defence had also been decided on. She would explain the guns and ammunition by claiming that she had planned on aiding refugees to cross the frontier, and that the guns were intended for them.

After they had waited for an hour, Landwerlen was ready to put them through a preliminary interrogation. Each told the story they had agreed on. In addition, the two Collards explained the reports in their possession by stating that having decided to cross the frontier, they had compiled the reports with the intention of selling them to an espionage service in Holland. They had a twofold reason for putting up this defence. First of all, it would divert attention away from the 'White Lady'; secondly, according to German law at that time, a spy could not be executed unless it had definitely been proved that he had either directly or indirectly communicated with the enemy – the intention to do so was not sufficient. The first interrogation completed, the prisoners were removed to the prison of St Leonard.

The Secret Police believed Franchimont's and van den Berg's story, and released them shortly afterwards. But the two Collards were doomed from the start. Many of the reports were in code, which in itself was evidence of a spy organisation, and, in addition, the information contained in Louis' pocketbook hopelessly compromised them. As regards Madame Goessels, Landwerlen was convinced she was culpable of espionage, and although he had no direct proof, he was determined to trap her in some way.

Through their counter-espionage section, the 'White Lady' had immediately been informed of the arrests; within two days on 10 March 1918, through agents Fauquenot and Creusen, they were already in touch with two of the prisoners. The two Collards were in solitary confinement and could not be reached. Fauquenot's first message, written in code, warned them of the reports hidden in the sofa:

Have spoken to Franchimont. He was arrested on the 8th. He says one can count on him. He is accused of espionage. The affair is complicated on account of the false identity cards; the Germans want to know where they come from. He speaks of documents in the sofa. Do you know what he is talking about? They found nothing on van den Berg. Muller is doing the interrogating. They undressed one of the Collard brothers yesterday and thrashed him with a cane. Let us know what you want us to ask them.

Reyman had an excuse to enter the villa, he was the owner; and it was he who not only rescued the reports from the sofa, but found Antony Collard's pocketbook still lying where he had thrown it.

The two Collards, young men, twenty-one and twenty years of age, were born in the beautiful little village of Tintigny, in the valley of the Semois, at the southern tip of Belgian Luxembourg. Here, far from large towns, they had lived a peaceful life in a happy home of seven children. Stirred by the call of their country, they had come to Liège in September 1917, to escape across the border to join the Belgian Army, and it was here that the 'White Lady' contacted them.

It was not difficult to persuade these two young patriots to return to Tintigny to organise an espionage group in their area. They were completely successful, and at the time of their arrest they had not only covered the whole of the Virton section with a spy network and had mounted a train-watching post at Longuyon on the important Longuyon–Sedan line just across the border in occupied France, but they had also started a penetration into the Grand Duchy of Luxembourg. In addition to this role as organisers, they had also acted as couriers linking up the Virton section with Liège.

It was for this reason that their arrest immediately severed all connection between the 'White Lady' and the Virton section. Not only were there no means of collecting the reports, but it was impossible for the 'White Lady' to warn the members of the group what had happened. The situation was all the more tragic because several of their names were written down in the papers contained in Louis Collard's pocketbook. The Germans were quick to act, and the arrest of Collard Senior, the young men's father, Monsieur and Madame Bastin, and Abbé Arnould – all of the Virton area – followed in quick succession.

The Secret Police now had a group of seven prisoners in St Leonard. They were sure they could tear sufficient information out of them to put them on the track of the main organisation. But as the weeks went by, they had to admit defeat. The four newly arrested members knew nothing about the 'White Lady' organisation. Madame Goessels kept repeating the same refugee story, until they got tired of questioning her; and the Collard brothers remained heroic in their silence. Every third-degree method was tried; and not even 'V' the most successful stool-pigeon in St Leonard, who after the war was condemned by the French to Devil's Island, was able to move the two martyred brothers to betrayal.

With the arrests of Collard Senior, a widower, and of the Bastins, two families of small children were left at home without parents. Marie-Thérèse, a girl of eighteen, the oldest of the five remaining Collard children, not knowing what had happened to their father and brothers, was left in a state of torment. Franticly, she ran to the German police post at Florenville. There they refused to give her any information. Eventually, in despair she set out to see her cousin Duchesnes in Namur, accompanied by Irene Bastin, a girl of the same age. Perhaps, he could give her some news. Duchesnes sent the two young girls to Liège, and there, through mutual friends, they managed to get into touch with a member of the 'White Lady'.

The 'White Lady' gave the two young girls what comfort it could, and immediately took steps to care for the children of the two families. At the same time, through Marie-Thérèse, they received enough indications to re-establish connexions with the unarrested members of the Virton section, and to set them working again. Marie-Thérèse and Irene Bastin were enrolled as members of the 'White Lady', and themselves undertook to make the necessary contact between the 'White Lady' courier and the agents in their area. The following is the letter which the 'White Lady''s courier brought back on returning from his first trip:

The mission which you honoured us with was easy to accomplish. On our return, we found that a faithful and devoted agent had already reorganised the service. All we had to do was to help with the second part. As for the Abbé you spoke about, we enrolled him in the service through the intermediary of Pol. Leopold is very happy, and, as you have no doubt found out for yourself, is very zealous.

If you have orders to give us, send them along. We are entirely at your disposal.

We are happier every day that you have chosen us to continue the work of our dear parents. Please accept our sincere thanks, and respectful mark of our friendship.

MARTHE AND MADELEINE VAILLY [their two service names]
19 July 1918.

When this letter was written Marie-Thérèse had not yet heard the tragic news of what had happened at Liège the day before.

Shortly after this the Secret Police discovered that the two young girls had been to Namur and Liège. They were imprisoned for several weeks; and it was only when the Secret Police realised that they could obtain no information from them that they were released.

In the meanwhile the investigations of the Secret Police in Liège had come to an end. There was no more information to be obtained. The prisoners were put on trial. Becker, the member of the Secret Police who had done most of the investigating, was the chief witness for the prosecution. The military prosecuting attorney demanded the following sentences: against Madame Goessels, and Louis and Antony Collard, the death penalty; against the father, Léon Collard, twelve years' hard labour; against Abbé Arnould, fifteen years' hard labour; against Joseph Bastin, ten years' hard labour; against Madame Bastin, two years' hard labour. Two German lawyers represented the prisoners. They confined themselves chiefly to pleading for a diminution of the penalties demanded.

Judgment was rendered on 2 July 1918. Louis and Antony Collard, Abbé Arnould, and Madame Goessels were condemned to death; the others to various terms of hard labour. The sentences of Madame Goessels and Abbé Arnould were eventually changed by the governor-general to hard labour for life.

Louis and Antony Collard were shot at the Citadel of the Chartreuse at Liège, on 18 July 1918.

Nothing can be sadder than the last farewell visit to their father. They were brought together in the office of the director of the prison. The father subsequently wrote:

My children pronounced with affection the names of each one of the family. It seemed as if they were more preoccupied with the lot of the others than they were with their own. With precision they made known to me their last wishes.

At the end of the room, near a table, were seated the director of the prison, and some German officers. Two doors opened out on to the corridor. Soldiers stood posted at them, immobile, and respectful.

At the signal for the separation, my children threw themselves on their knees: 'Father, give us your last blessing.'

I blessed them, and then prostrated myself in turn: 'You also, my children, before you die, bless your old father.'

We were all three on our knees.

Another signal was given. I embraced my sons. They went off, without shedding a tear, holding their heads high, and leaving me a last word of consolation and affection.

They had already left me, when I realised my cruel situation: I would never see them again. I precipitated myself out of the room. The soldiers allowed me to pass. I saw Louis and Antony about to turn the corner of the corridor. They saw me, and with a cry 'We'll meet in heaven,' they disappeared from sight.

But the cup of grief of the aged father had not yet been filled: two years later, Marie-Thérèse followed her brothers to the grave.

After the war, both the British and the Belgian governments bestowed on Louis and Antony Collard, posthumously, the same high decorations which they had conferred on Dieudonné Lambrecht.

In rendering homage to the two Collard brothers, we must remember Madame Goessels. Her nimble mind had saved the lives of two members of the service; in doing it, she had not hesitated to pretend a relationship with Franchimont which was completely at variance with her character. She could have revealed more about the 'White Lady' than any of those who had been arrested; she, too, remained heroic in her silence.

The 'White Lady' had weathered the storm, but Dewé and Chauvin had had many anxious moments. The Secret Police never knew how close they came to arresting them. Following up the clue that Rosa, the maid, also did part time work for a Mademoiselle Weimerskirch, the Secret Police decided to search her house. When they arrived, Dewé and Chauvin were in a back room. As the Secret Police came in at the front door, Dewé and Chauvin left precipitately at the rear.

CHAPTER 11

LÉON TRULIN – YOUNGEST SPY SHOT DURING THE WAR

LILLE WAS NOT only occupied by the enemy but it was right in the firing line. From the British lines the outskirts of the town were plainly visible, and buildings occupied by the Germans were a constant target for the British heavy batteries. But the British shells often missed their mark, and although the centre of the town was not bombarded whole sections of the suburbs lay in ruins. Had the town been smaller, it would have been evacuated; with 200,000 inhabitants this was not possible.

So the civilian population of Lille remained as eyewitnesses to the busy German military activities in this important centre.

Heavy batteries were dotted around in the area; troops destined for the various sectors of the Front detrained there daily; several aviation fields were located close by; and, finally, warehouses filled with shells and other war material were to be found in various parts of the town. In short, it was a field where even the most amateur spy would have had no difficulty in preparing a daily report of intense interest to the Allies.

If the Allied secret services were intent on recruiting spies in the area, the Germans were equally determined to prevent them. In addition to having an army of Secret Police patrolling the region, the Germans did everything within their power to intimidate the inhabitants. No person was allowed out of doors between 6 p.m. and 6 a.m.; passes were required to travel from one commune to another; the Mayor was forced to deposit a sum of 5,000,000 francs, and to hand over five hostages, interchangeable every three days, as guarantees against hostile acts undertaken by the population; the severest sentences were imposed for the most minor offences. And, finally, since the town was in occupied France, it was blocked off from Belgium by an efficient frontier patrol and a cordon of sentries.

It was in this town that Léon Trulin, a young Belgian, seventeen years of age, found himself at the outbreak of the war. His family, consisting of a widowed mother and nine young children, had moved there from Ath, in Belgium, four years previously. One can imagine what effect the thunder of the guns night and day, and the ceaseless excitement and turmoil of the war had on a boy of his age.

Keenly alert to the bustling activity, Léon and his friends among the boys of the neighbourhood watched with youthful curiosity the heavy guns as they rumbled through the town; and, just because it was forbidden, it became their special game to discover the eventual emplacements. With a cunning superior to that of any adult, they found means to avoid the vigilance of the German sentries. The aviation fields, too, were special centres of attraction. But it was the ridge to the east of the town, looking down on the British lines, that was their favourite objective. Here, crouched among the ruins, they eagerly discussed means of escaping across the border to join their respective armies.

Léon had already sounded his mother; he knew it was useless trying to argue further with her. He was the eldest son, and her solicitude for his safety could not be overcome; and so, one night, he disappeared from his home, leaving behind him the following message (one can excuse the youthful subterfuge; he knew a farewell scene would break his mother's heart):

DEAR MOTHER,

I was detected taking photographs of the trenches. I threw my camera into a ditch. I am being followed. I am leaving to defend my country. May God protect me! Dear Mother, have courage. Burn this paper.

– LÉON

In this fashion Léon entered upon a life of constant peril. He was to undergo the greatest hardships. An abandoned ruin or the damp woods were often to be his only shelter.

Coming from the north of France, he traversed Belgium, collecting military information as he went along. He knew the value of it; he would hand it over to the recruiting officer on his arrival in Folkestone. Near the Dutch frontier he fell in with a group of refugees, and together with them, on 5 July 1915, successfully evading the German sentries, he crossed the electric wire into Holland.

Disembarking at Folkestone, in England, he hastened to the Belgian consulate. A disappointment awaited him: he was unable to pass the medical examination.

Léon was not dismayed. A rifle had been found too heavy for his frail shoulders, but he knew there were other ways of serving his country. The walls of Lille had been placarded with the names of spies who had been shot. There must have been others who had escaped. He, too, would be a spy. He showed the Belgian consul the information he had collected en route, and requested to be put in touch with a secret service organisation.

B's headquarters happened to be conveniently near, and so it was there that Léon was sent. Handing over his report to Monthaye, a Belgian attached to B's staff, Léon eagerly offered his services. Rapidly glancing at the report, Monthaye found it of interest, but it only dealt with those parts of Belgium through which Léon had passed, and this area was already covered by other spies. Of far greater importance was the fact that the boy had come from Lille, from which the service had been cut off for weeks. Pulling out a large scale map of the town, Monthaye beckoned Léon to his side. Quick to orientate himself, the young Belgian pointed out all he knew. It was difficult to discern who was the more excited: Monthaye, because of the priceless information he was jotting down; or Léon, because he realised from the interest evidenced that his services would be accepted.

Léon spent a week in Folkestone, during which time he was rapidly put through a course of training. He was taught how to distinguish between German units by the marks on their uniforms; photographs and sketches of different calibre guns were shown him; and, finally, he was given additional objectives to those on which he had already concentrated. A sum of money was handed to him for expenses, and he was promised that if he came back with a good report he would be put in touch with B's organisation in Holland, and would be enrolled as a permanent agent.

It was as a prescript that Léon returned to Lille. Unfortunately, he had sent his mother a letter from Holland to announce his safe arrival; this no doubt had been read by the German censor, and Monthaye had warned him not to go near his home. He went, therefore, to the house of Raymond Derain, his closest friend.

Raymond, a boy of his own age, listened with tense interest and excitement to the details of his friend's mission. He, too, wished to serve his country; it was not difficult to win his support. Together the two boys set about accomplishing the special mission on which Léon had been sent: they drew up a lengthy report on the forts of Lille, showing the repair work which had been done since their destruction by the French during the retreat at the commencement of the war. It was work which required the greatest skill and audacity, but with the help of a pair of field-glasses which Raymond discovered at home, and with the aid of a small boy of fifteen, who courageously penetrated some of the fortifications, they carried out the task.

On 26 July, Léon was back in Folkestone with the information. Monthaye was both surprised at his quick return, and at the efficiency with which the plans and reports had been drawn up. He was taken in to see B, who congratulated him on his splendid accomplishment. A few days later, Léon found himself back in Holland, where he was put in touch with Carlot, one of B's head agents.

After the war, Léon Trulin's notes were found at the Belgian consulate, in Flushing, where he had deposited them for safe keeping prior to his return to the occupied territories. The following extract gives us a clear indication of the instructions which he received from Carlot:

Léon 143 will return to Belgium, and will pass through Deynze. He will establish train-watching posts at Deynze, Ingelmunster, Courtrai, Mouscron and, if possible, at Tourcoing.

He will report on the troops in the different areas; their identification, the condition they are in, and their depots. He will establish a chain of couriers between Menin, Courtrai, Deurne, and St Laurent in such a way that a report from Menin will reach Flushing in two days.

Train-watching reports will be sent at least twice a week. Léon 143 will be paid for his reports on the troops of occupation from 10 to 40 francs, according to the value of the information; a bonus of 100 francs will be allotted him for the creation of each new train-watching post, to be paid after it has functioned two weeks; an additional bonus of from 25 to 50 francs every two weeks, according to the importance of the line, will be paid him for each post during the period it functions.

Train-watchers will receive from 8 to 10 francs per day of twenty-four hours; as for the couriers, they will be paid 110 francs for each

batch of reports if they reach Flushing within two days, 100 francs
for three days, and after that 5 per cent less for each day late.

The payments will be made to Léon 143 on his return to Holland,
or to any delegate he may appoint, but only on results obtained. He
will furnish us with receipts from his agents for each sum paid them.

On his return to Holland, Léon 143 will give us the name and
description of each agent, and if possible their photographs. In addi-
tion, he will indicate the function of each in the service, and the
payments each is getting; he will procure from each a declaration
that he or she will work exclusively for our service.

These notes should at once dispel all ideas that the Allied agents
in the occupied territories received large sums of money for their
services. Léon was authorised to pay his train-watchers from 7
to 10 francs per day for twenty-four hours' service; actually, this
meant about 5 francs, for a train-watcher could not possibly
work efficiently more than twelve hours per day.

In addition, it must be borne in mind that these agents had
to live. The salaries they obtained, it can be seen, barely covered
their living expenses.

The instructions about receipts, names of agents, and photographs are typical of the methods employed by some of the
Allied agents in Holland. In their endeavour to prove their own
honesty in the distribution of funds, they entirely lost sight of the
dangers to which they were exposing the agents in the interior.
A report containing this information, falling into the hands of
the Germans, would have meant a death warrant for the agents
involved. The accuracy of a report, and the dangers incurred
in securing the information contained in it, should have been

a sufficient guarantee of honesty – not only of the agents in the interior, but of those in Holland.

Looking at a map, and taking into consideration that all the areas mentioned were in the Etappengebiet, the most strictly controlled part of the occupied territories, one realises immediately what an enormous task had been assigned to Léon. Even for a man of mature years with large resources at his disposal, and a wide circle of friends, the undertaking would have presented infinite difficulties and dangers. How could a young boy of eighteen possibly overcome them?

Too young to win the confidence of older people, Léon turned to his youthful companions. On his return to Lille, he called them together; some were only fourteen years of age, the oldest was eighteen. Meeting in one of the many abandoned houses of the quarter, one can see him impressing on his youthful followers the importance of his mission, and one can picture the enthusiasm with which each one undertook to carry out the duties assigned to him.

The young band, with the limited means at their disposal, did their bit as patriotically and as bravely as any soldier in the firing line. Often their ruses, their tricks, and their camouflages were carried to boyish extremes – but were successful, and for two months, regularly twice a week, B received a report covering everything of military importance occurring in the Lille region. Sometimes it was Léon himself who carried the reports through to Holland, each time braving the electric wire and the perils of the frontier; on other occasions, it was Camille, a friend of Léon's residing at Tournai.

The train-watching posts had not yet been mounted. This

part of the programme, outlined by Carlot, had been beyond the boy's power. Realising this, Léon had wisely confined himself to making the reports from the Lille area as complete as possible. Rut the inevitable happened.

One day, on approaching too near a new gun emplacement, one of his companions was arrested by the Secret Police. Léon was not greatly disturbed. He thought the boy would be able to find a satisfactory excuse. But on the next day events took an alarming turn. Raymond Derain, greatly agitated, sought Léon out in his hiding place. Raymond's sister had fortunately been able to reach him before he returned home: the Secret Police were in their house; they had inquired after both him and Léon Trulin; she had overheard the conversation, and had slipped out of the back door to warn him.

There was only one thing to do, and that was to flee. Remaining in hiding for the rest of the day and night, Raymond and Léon set out for the Dutch frontier at dawn the next morning, carrying with them the last batch of reports which they had just collected.

Léon realised that he had to get across the border at all costs. He knew that he was hopelessly compromised both by the letter he had written his mother from Holland and by his arrested comrade, whom he was convinced had betrayed them. Fortunately, he knew the way. Travelling mostly at night, and hiding by day, they eventually reached the Dutch frontier to the north of Antwerp, on the night of 3 October 1915.

At this period, the Germans had not yet added a buried wire to the electric fence. Generally, by digging underneath the fence, the refugees escaped into Holland. Léon and Raymond Derain were stealthily digging their way through, when suddenly there

was a cry of 'Wer da!' The searchlights were turned on. Léon
and Raymond were in plain view. Several shots rang out. Sentries came running up.

They were trapped. Léon's immediate care was to get rid
of the reports. Grasping his pocketbook, he hurled it as far as
he could into Dutch territory. But the Secret Police were no
respecters of neutrality (later they were to arrest Fauquenot and
Creusen on Dutch soil). Léon, to his horror, saw a member of
the Secret Police cross over and pick up the compromising evidence. Raymond Derain made a desperate attempt to escape,
but a vicious bayonet thrust in his thigh swiftly brought him
down. In the morning they were taken to Antwerp, where they
were confined in the prison des Béguines.

On 12 October they were transferred to Lille, where they were
not surprised to find the rest of their band in prison. As they
had surmised, their comrade had betrayed them.

The prisoners were quickly brought up for trial. In the face of
the overwhelming evidence, it was clemency alone that they could
hope for. Against Léon Trulin the following charges were filed:

- Military espionage.
- The recruitment of five members.
- Possessing a pocketbook that contained:
  - *The reports of the five members from 20 to 27 September.*
  - *Thirty-three photographs of trenches.*
  - *Plans of aviation fields, munitions depots, and trenches.*
- Attempting to cross the Dutch frontier.
- Having made several illegal journeys to Holland and
  England.

On 7 November the following judgment was rendered by the court martial: Léon Trulin, eighteen years of age, was condemned to death; Raymond Derain (eighteen years of age), and Marcel G. (fifteen years of age) were both condemned to hard labour for life; Lucien D., Marcel L., and André H., all under eighteen, were sentenced to fifteen years' hard labour. The man who betrayed them was acquitted.

Léon's mother was prostrated with grief. Too ill to leave her bed, she was unable to be present at the one and only interview which the Germans permitted, the day before the execution. It was Léon's three little sisters who came to say farewell to him. He received them with calmness and dignity. It was he who extended comfort and tried to dry their tears. Returning to his cell, he wrote the following letter – touching in its simplicity:

> *I am dying for my country without regret. I grieve for my dear mother, my sisters, and my brothers, who are suffering for what they are not to blame.*
>
> *I embrace my poor mother with all my heart. I hope God will preserve her to watch over her other children who are so dear to her. I embrace also: Emile, Edgard, Edmond, Adolphe, Eva, Céline, René, and Angèle, also Alida and her children, and my other relatives, and friends. I forgive the Germans. I did my duty, but they have been very hard on me.*
>
> *Dear mother, I hope you will forgive me before I die. I shall face death without weakening. – LÉON TRULIN.*

A postscript was attached to this letter; in it Léon bequeathed to his mother, his sisters, and his brothers, various small souvenirs which belonged to him at home.

He was executed at dawn on 8 November. Refusing to have his eyes bandaged, he faced the firing-squad unflinchingly as he had promised in his letter.

Léon Trulin was the youngest spy shot on the Western Front.

Today, if one passes a small grey house in the rue aux Gades, in Lille, one will notice a large white marble plate on its wall, bearing the following inscription:

IN THIS HOUSE WAS BORN, 2 JUNE 1897,
LÉON TRULIN,
SHOT BY THE GERMANS AT LILLE,
8 NOVEMBER 1915,
FOR SERVICES RENDERED TO HIS COUNTRY.
THOSE WHO PASS BY, REMEMBER THIS HERO.

The lot of Raymond Derain was no less sad. Three years of prison life left their mark. Released in Germany at the time of the Armistice, he died at Strasbourg towards the end of November 1918 before he could reach his parents who were waiting to welcome him home.

There were many young agents employed in the Allied secret services during the war, but the service Léon 143, or Léon Turpin as it was sometimes called, was the only secret service organisation composed entirely of minors. There were many Allied spies, but none was braver than Léon Trulin.

CHAPTER 12

THE BISCOPS SERVICE

WHAT I HAVE already written must have indicated that some of the spy's greatest dangers came from note-books and stool-pigeons. Those who employed note-books often thought they were safe in using codes, false names or abbreviations, but they forgot that these secret notes would call for an immediate explanation if they fell into the hands of the Secret Police, and that German third-degree methods, if given a definite objective, had been known to break the strongest will.

Not only did the guilty suffer, but the innocent were often involved. Any person whose name was found in the possession of a spy was immediately arrested; they remained in prison until they had proved their innocence. To illustrate my point, even though it may be a digression from the main objective of this chapter, I shall tell, very briefly, the tragic story of Sister Xavéria.

Sister Xavéria's brother was Alexandre Franck, the friend and companion of Backelmans (both of these men were eventually arrested by the Germans and shot as spies). One day, quite by accident, she met Backelmans on the street-car. Surprised to see him, for she knew that together with her brother he had left for England at the beginning of the war, she had 101 questions to ask; but she had arrived at her destination and had to take leave without all the information she wanted. When she got back to the convent she decided to get into touch with Backelmans again. She sent him a note asking him to call on her, and not being sure that he knew her convent name, she signed the message 'Sister of Alex'.

In the meantime, Backelmans had been arrested, and his tell-tale memorandum book was in the possession of the Secret Police. In it Backelmans had noted down the name of Sister Xavéria as a reminder to tell Franck about the encounter. To make matters worse, the innocent Sister's note fell into the hands of the Secret Police.

Here was a person whose name not only figured in Backelmans' note-book, but who used a false name. Sister Xavéria was promptly arrested and, in spite of her protests, was confined for weeks in prison. At the trial, the German Prosecuting Attorney demanded a sentence of ten years' hard labour; it was only the skill of her Belgian lawyer which eventually secured her acquittal.

We will now see how a foolish entry in a memorandum book led to the breaking up of the Biscops Service, which, although in no way to be compared with the 'White Lady' in size or importance, ranked next to it.

An Antwerp oculist, Dr 'X', a member of the Biscops Service, was arrested as a suspect in an affair which had nothing to do with his espionage activities; in fact, the worthy doctor was entirely innocent of the charges which had been levelled against him. The Secret Police had already realised their mistake, and were about to release him when they noticed in a memorandum book, which they had seized on him, the date of a rendezvous with 'W'. The Secret Police wanted to know who 'W' was.

The doctor, having forgotten about the entry, was taken completely unawares. Disconcerted because 'W' stood for the name of the Biscops' 'letter box' in Brussels, and not being able to think fast enough, he took refuge in refusing to answer. The Germans concluded that he had something to hide. They threatened to keep him in prison until the point had been cleared up. The doctor was taken back to his cell, and there found a companion installed in it. It was the stool-pigeon, Delacour.

The stool-pigeon told an appropriate story which completely won the confidence of his victim who, in turn, feeling in need of sympathy, gave an account of what had happened to him. In the course of his story he not only revealed that 'W' was Mademoiselle Marguerite Walraevens, residing at 128 rue Medori at Brussels, but that having had difficulty in finding the number, he had chalked a 'W' on the wall next to the door.

It was Captain Goldschmidt, in charge of Secret Police Bureau 'A' at Brussels, who undertook the investigation. He sent his agent, Jean Burtard, to the indicated address. There, finding the 'W' marked on the wall, Burtard was convinced the information was correct. Ringing the bell, he asked to see Mademoiselle Walraevens. With all the cunning which we have seen him employ in ensnaring his other victims, he tried to win her confidence by giving himself out to be a courier from one of the Allied secret services in Holland. But Marguerite Walraevens was on her guard; she knew of the doctor's arrest; besides, Burtard appeared suspect to her; and so with a show of righteous indignation, she conducted him to the door. Taking no chances, she immediately burned all compromising papers in her possession; and when Burtard returned a few minutes later with reinforcements to arrest the inmates of the house and to make a thorough search, he found the ashes still warm in the hearth.

The Secret Police, as usual, took possession of Mademoiselle Walraevens's house and arrested everyone who presented himself there. In this way, they not only caught several members of the Biscops Service, but also arrested a woman courier, when she arrived to deposit her reports.

Stool-pigeons were once again called in to play their roles. Time and again, the reader has seen them at work, and has no doubt wondered how it was possible that prisoners, whose lives were at stake, could have been so foolish as to compromise themselves with strangers, however trustworthy they might have appeared. But those who have been worn out by endless interrogations and third-degree methods, and who have been kept in solitary confinement for days, even months, need human sympathy, and someone to talk with. The stool-pigeons were invariably compatriots who claimed to be in the same cruel situation that they were in; the prisoners felt that surely they could be trusted. In many cases, they were actually fellow prisoners, whom the Secret Police by threatening with the death sentence had forced to work for them.

Louise de Bettignies was betrayed by a woman who was arrested in the Cavell affair; and now in the Biscops investigation, unbelievable as it may seem, the Secret Police employed the woman 'Z' whose husband had actually been shot by the Germans for espionage. To save her own skin, she proceeded to betray her fellow prisoners.

Having won the confidence of one of the principal members arrested – whom I shall call 'Spelier', for although criminally indiscreet he acted in good faith – the woman 'Z' cunningly laid her trap. She volunteered the information that she had means of communicating with the outside through her daughter, who had permission to come and see her once a week. 'Spelier', anxious to warn Léon Deboucq, the chief of the Biscops Service, as to what had happened in Brussels, wrote a letter to him, and communicated his address in Charleroi to the woman.

The letter, of course, was handed over to Goldschmidt who, after photographing it, sent three members of the Secret Police off to Charleroi to arrest Léon Deboucq. When they arrived at Deboucq's house, in the early hours of the morning of 16 September 1917, the whole family was away at Mass. The governess, Emilie Fenasse, was the only one at home. Declaring themselves as members of the Secret Police, the three agents took possession of the house, and sat down to wait for the return of the family. They did not notice, however, that Emilie Fenasse had turned on the porch light. This was a warning signal which Deboucq had arranged. When Deboucq turned the corner into the street where his house was located, he immediately noticed the light. Sending his family home, he precipitously fled to Brussels.

By allowing Deboucq to slip through their fingers, the Secret

Police had momentarily lost the thread of the organisation. Marguerite Walraevens, 'Spelier', and the other members of the Biscops Service who had been arrested in Brussels only represented a small section of it. Deboucq had been clever enough to organise his service on the basis of separate and independent nests; the sections at Malines, Namur, Charleroi, Mons, Maubeuge, Valenciennes, Tournai, and in Belgian Luxembourg still remained intact.

Deboucq, a man of about forty, an engineer by profession, extremely intelligent and resourceful, was neither a coward nor a man who would give in easily. Although his wife and one of his daughters had been arrested, he was determined to get his service working again, and to re-establish the connections with Holland, which had been severed by the arrest of Marguerite Walraevens. From his hiding place in Brussels, at the house of his aunt, Anna Verhegge, an old lady of seventy, he started spinning the thread again. He found a new 'letter box' in Brussels, in the person of Madame Descamps, another lady well advanced in years; and at Turnhout, close to the Dutch frontier, he enrolled Abbé Dierckx as a relay 'letter box.' All that now remained was to connect up these 'letter boxes' with a trans-frontier courier.

In his search for a frontier passage, one of his agents, Abbé Amceaux, of Namur, put him in touch with Dewé, Chauvin, and Neujean, of whom Abbé Anceaux had heard through a Namur priest, one of the 'White Lady''s agents. Deboucq travelled to Liège and there met the three men, who were presented to him under the false names of Gauthier, Bouchon, and Petit.

The 'White Lady', which was hiding Deboucq at this time, realised that he was now compromised from two distinct directions – the Walraevens group, and through Siquet. Wisely the organisation decided, for its own safety as well as his, that it would have to get him out of the country at all costs. A frontier guide was found who took Deboucq through the high-voltage electric wire into safety.

Had Deboucq been able to come to the War Office service, all would have been well, for we had a number of reserve frontier passages which we could have placed at his disposal. But instead, on his arrival in Holland, he reported immediately to B's representative, for it was to this group of the British GHQ service that the Biscops organisation belonged.

The two 'letter boxes' at Brussels and Turnhout being intact, Deboucq and the B. Service immediately attempted to establish connection with them. At this period, the B. Service had just organised a new frontier passage on the Dutch–Belgian frontier, opposite Turnhout. The helpers at this frontier passage consisted of smugglers, who were working in conjunction with some German soldiers on frontier duty. I am sure neither the representative, nor Deboucq, knew that these German soldiers were involved in the combination, otherwise they would never have risked sending through this frontier passage messages which contained the names and addresses of two members of the Biscops Service.

Strange to say, however, the German soldier who was handed the messages enclosed in a shaving-stick, faithfully carried out his part of the undertaking. He carried the shaving-stick to a man called Verschueren, residing between the frontier and Turnhout, and requested him to carry it farther to Abbé Dierckx, at Turnhout. Verschueren, alarmed at having these instructions handed to him by a German soldier, refused to accept the shaving-stick; and the soldier, not knowing what to do with it, buried it. Shortly afterwards the group of German soldiers smuggling at the frontier were caught; it was then that the soldier in question told the Secret Police about the shaving-stick which he had buried.

It was dug up. In it were found two rolls, each the size of a cigarette, one was marked Turnhout, the other Brussels. In the Turnhout roll, Abbé Dierckx was requested to get in touch with the man whom Deboucq had nominated to succeed him as chief of the Biscops Service; this man was referred to as the 'White Negro' and Abbé Dierckx was informed that he could contact him by presenting himself at the house of Anna Verhegge, 44 rue Philippe de Champagne, in Brussels. The Brussels roll was addressed to the 'White Negro'. In it he was told to start the Biscops Service functioning again, and that he could communicate with Holland through Abbé Dierckx, whom the representative had obviously intended connecting up to the frontier passage by way of Verschueren.

Goldschmidt of the Secret Police Bureau 'A' once again took the investigation in hand. Abbé Dierckx was immediately arrested. The German secret agent Coulon (the man who had arrested Parente), armed with the Brussels roll, which Gold-schmidt had previously photographed, and disguised as Abbé Dierckx, was sent to call on Anna Verhegge.

The old lady could not help but have confidence in him, for she had never seen the real Abbé Dierckx; besides, on the roll which Coulon showed her, she recognised the handwriting of her nephew. She confessed that she could not put Coulon in touch with the 'White Negro'; but she knew someone who probably could, and so she sent him to Madame Descamps, the Brussels 'letter box'.

Coulon was a French subject, and so was Madame Descamps. The old lady, whose hearing and eyesight were already impaired by age, had complete confidence in him; in fact, she took quite a liking to this priest who hailed from her own country. She regretted, however, that she did not know the identity of the 'White Negro', but she assured Coulon that he could get in touch with him through her nephew, Father Bormans, at Charleroi, to whom she hastened to give him a letter of introduction.

Immediately after Coulon's visit, a friend of Father Bormans happened to call at the house, and as he was returning to Charleroi that same evening, Madame Descamps gave him a verbal message for her nephew to the effect that a priest with a communication from Holland was on his way to see him. When, therefore, Coulon arrived in the guise of an ordinary civilian, instead of that of a priest, Father Bormans was immediately suspicious; as soon as Coulon broached the subject of espionage, he showed him the door.

Coulon, who probably had not felt sufficiently sure of himself to parade in clerical dress before a real priest, returned to Brussels somewhat crestfallen. However, he soon devised a suitable story to tell Madame Descamps: he explained that having come from a town so close to the frontier he was a natural object of suspicion to the Secret Police, and having no excuse to go to Charleroi, he had gone there in disguise. The old lady apologised for her nephew's lack of faith, and promising to take the matter in hand herself, post haste, she sent Bormans a letter explaining matters, and asking him to arrange a meeting in Brussels between the 'White Negro' and Abbé Dierckx; to the letter she joined the Brussels roll, which Coulon had brought back with him.

The 'White Negro', impressed by the undoubted authenticity of Deboucq's message from Holland, lightly dismissed Father Bormans's suspicions; and accompanied by his daughter, proceeded to keep the appointment which in the meantime had been arranged at Madame Descamps's house.

Coulon was the first to arrive at her house. Chatting amiably with the old lady, he waited for his victim to arrive. The bell rang. Madame Descamps hastened to the door to usher in the 'White Negro' of whom she had heard so much, and who by now had thoroughly aroused her curiosity and interest. In triumph she returned with him and his daughter to introduce them to Abbé Dierckx. No sooner had the 'White Negro' acknowledged his identity, when to her blank amazement, Coulon pulled out his gun, and arrested the three of them.

On searching Madame Descamps's house, the Secret Police had a surprise in store for them. They discovered a number of spy reports belonging to an entirely different service, one attached to the cereal company in Holland (the cover used by the second of the British GHQ), the one directed by Major Wallinger. This patriotic old lady, in spite of her age, had for over a year been an active member of the Wallinger Service. For this service, she had also been playing the role of 'letter box'.

The usual traps were mounted in the houses of Anna Verhegge, Madame Descamps, and in that of the 'White Negro', whose real name was François Pevenasse, a druggist at Charleroi. One arrest led to another until about forty members of the Biscops Service, including Abbé Anceaux of Namur, were arrested. A number of Wallinger agents were also caught in the net.

Once again Stöber had a major spy trial on his hands. With elaborate detail a chart was displayed in the court room; it looked like a transcription of a page of ancient history. The different Biscops train-watching posts, couriers, 'letter boxes', and head agents were shown in a diagram, and opposite each name, the service name was shown. Deboucq was Diogenes; Pevenasse had two service names, the 'White Negro' and Demosthenes; Abbé Anceaux was Horace; and so on. The trial took its normal course; the Secret Police were in possession of all the evidence, and it was easy for them to reconstruct the role of each agent.

Stöber demanded seven sentences of death and secured five: Marguerite Walraevens, Abbé Anceaux, and three others. The governor-general commuted all these death sentences, however, to hard labour for life. The other prisoners were also given long prison sentences with hard labour. On the whole, all the prisoners were lucky – scores of spies had been executed in Belgium on far less evidence.

This was practically the end of the Biscops Service, or the service of the Sacré Cœur as it was sometimes known. It had functioned for more than a year before the Brussels arrests, and with its twenty-odd train-watching posts, it had rendered the Allies inestimable services. Deboucq was both a brave and a clever organiser. He was not to blame for the downfall of the service. The arrest of Marguerite Walraevens was due to pure chance; and it was the B. Service, and not he, who was responsible for the choosing of the Turnhout frontier passage that proved so disastrous. Had Deboucq been given a safe means of communicating across the frontier, his service would probably have continued until the Armistice.

The Biscops Service is also of special interest, because on several occasions, it crossed the path of the 'White Lady'. The explanation of this is perfectly simple. Both services had a large number of priests enrolled in it, and both of them largely recruited their members from the Belgian intelligentsia. Unselfishly, and at a great risk to themselves, the 'White Lady' helped the Biscops Service in ways which I have already indicated.

CHAPTER 13

THE CONNEUX FLYING SQUAD

T HE 'WHITE LADY' was always extending itself. And with
each step farther afield the safeguarding of the organisation as a whole became more difficult. It was only by
strictly adhering to the principle of independent nests that it was
possible to keep the service intact. Even though plans for new
extensions were often submitted to headquarters in Liège for examination and action, their execution was never entrusted to existing
units. A special and separate 'flying squad' was created in the area
from which the development was to take place, and the flying squad
was charged with organising the new platoon. Only after this new
platoon had been working for some time, and had deposited its
reports regularly at its 'letter box', was this 'letter box' connected
up to one of the existing courier platoons of the 'White Lady'.

At this time there were three of these flying squads in existence – one at Tournai, one at Arlon, and the other at Conneux. From Tournai, Lille and Douai, in the northern part of occupied France, were reached. From Arlon, the Grand Duchy of Luxembourg was penetrated. Here a train-watching post was mounted on the vitally important Trier–Luxembourg line, which together with the 'White Lady''s post on the Aachen–Herbesthal–Liège line enabled us to control all traffic westward out of Germany to points on the Western Front between Verdun and the sea. Finally, it was intended that the Conneux Flying Squad should push down into occupied France in the direction of Charleville and Sedan. It was two young girls who planted the 'White Lady''s flag in Charleville, and because I have their modest report before me, I am going to let them tell the story, after I have made a few introductory remarks.

To the south of Namur, in the provinces of Namur and Luxembourg, there stretches the chateau country of Belgium. Here, living on their estates abounding in fish and game, one finds chiefly the families that compose the aristocracy of Belgium. Among these families, the 'White Lady' had many staunch supporters, notably the de Moffarts, the de Villermonts, the de Radiguès de Chennevières, and the de l'Epines. It was here that the Conneux Flying Squad was organised. Its objective, Charleville, was not only the headquarters of the German Crown Prince, but it was also an important railway centre. It was on the strategic line Trier–Luxembourg–Sedan–Charleville–Mézières–Hirson; and, in addition, leading from it were the branch lines to Rethel, and Givet.

The families I have mentioned had friends in Charleville, but they had been out of touch since the war; even so a friend was not always one who was willing to risk his life as a spy. It was only by sounding them out personally that a suitable chief could be found to organise the Charleville platoon. A delegate had, therefore, to be sent across the border. Two young girls, Baroness Clémie de l'Epine, and Marie-Antoinette, the daughter of the Marquise de Radiguès de Chennevière, volunteered for the job. The 'White Lady' wisely allowed them to undertake the mission: they knew that because of their age they would have a better chance of getting through than the older agents; and if they were caught, they might escape with a less severe sentence. They also had the advantage of being personally known to the people they intended to solicit; there would be no need for them to carry any incriminating written messages. Although considerably worried, the families of the two girls patriotically gave their consent.

Clémie de l'Epine's family had an estate at Gedinne on the French border. Using this as a base, the two young girls started to organise their expedition.

It was no simple matter to get across the frontier. A barbed-wire fence, 10 ft high, a relic of pre-war days, separated Belgium from France in the Gedinne area, and along this fence, with the help of sentries and Secret Police, the Germans kept a strict surveillance – to prevent the passage of spy reports, all circulation between occupied France and Belgium was forbidden. It was necessary, therefore, to find an experienced guide to take them through to Charleville; in their search for one, they naturally addressed themselves to some of the many potato smugglers in the area.

I will now let Clémie de l'Epine continue the story. With true modesty, she has confined her youthful report to a bare recitation of the facts, and has not attempted in any way to stress the importance of her mission, or the value of the results achieved. These two young girls were, however, completely successful; and the Charleville platoon, which grew out of their efforts, sent us the first reports that the Allies had received from this area since the early stages of the war:

It was necessary to find a trustworthy guide. After a search of several days during which we received several set-backs, the one being afraid, the other saying it was too far, we finally, with the aid of Lucien Voltèche, one of our foresters, found the man we wanted – a smuggler, a big strapping fellow, about twenty years of age, with a determined though friendly face, who answered to the name of Georges. For 100 francs he was willing to conduct us to Charleville, and back.

We hastily put some provisions in a sack, and at one o'clock in the afternoon, we were on our way to Charleville. In appearance we strongly resembled the women of Seraing – bare-headed, and wrapped in dirty, threadbare, hooded cloaks, which we had borrowed for the occasion. We followed each other in Indian file, Georges leading, carrying half a sack of potatoes on his back.

We arrived at a small farm, and Georges, to his disgust punctuated with appropriate remarks, had just noticed that half his potatoes had escaped, when suddenly from nowhere we heard a gruff command, 'Halt!' Two members of the Secret Police emerged from behind some bushes, and demanded our identity cards. We had nothing to fear – we were in Belgium. But for Georges it was different: there were the potatoes.

He was taken out of sight by the two plain-clothes men. We waited. An hour went by. Was he coming back? Would we have to return and start finding a fresh guide all over again? These were our thoughts, when we saw him approaching us. He was free, but minus his potatoes. Once again we were en route.

We now started climbing the wooded slopes of a steep hill, zig-zagging to avoid open spaces. After half an hour of climbing, we were in sight of the barbed wire, about 10 ft high, strands close together. But it was not here that we were to pass. We skirted the fence for some distance, until finally Georges gave a grunt of satisfaction. It was still there – some broken strands, a hole conveniently made by some smugglers, and through it we went. We were in France. Still the woods. We followed a goat track which took us down into the valley. It was now getting dark. In the distance, we saw the village of Monthermé. Soon we were in the village, and, as we entered it, we took on the casual air of one of the villagers. Georges had friends in the village, and we were to spend the night.

We arrived at a cottage. Before entering it, Georges asked our names. On the spot we christened ourselves: Marie-Antoinette became Antoinette Duval, and I, Henriette Dhust. Georges pushed the door open.

Scene: A workwoman in a light print dress, standing over a stove in a dingy room which was kitchen and living-room. 'Where are the potatoes?' she asked gruffly. Georges explained and we took his part. When things had calmed down, Georges took the woman over to a corner, evidently to explain our presence, for she bade us welcome, and did her best to make us comfortable. After we had had a cup of brown liquid which passed for coffee – but we were glad to get anything – she showed us to a room; it contained the only bed in the house. There were no sheets, and so we went to bed in our clothes.

It was still dark when Georges woke us; at four o'clock we were on our way. Again the woods, we climbed several hills, and finally descended into the valley of the Meuse. At a cottage on the water's edge, we found a friend of Georges', who after a parley, lent us his boat. While we anxiously scanned the river up and down, Georges rowed us across; and on reaching the opposite bank he hid the boat under the overhanging branches of a tree, ready for our return journey.

We were glad to reach the friendly shelter of the woods again. With our arms held out in front of us to ward off low branches and to push aside the bushes, we continued our march. It had rained overnight, and soon our shoes were wet through, our cloaks sodden. Suddenly we heard voices. False alarm! It was some woodcutters. From them we learned that there was a sentry ahead, and so we made a detour to avoid him.

Like Christopher Columbus about to discover the New World, we found ourselves on the outskirts of Charleville. But for our entry we had to look respectable, and so with our fingers we straightened each other's hair, while our friend, for this is what Georges had become by now, cleaned our shoes with a handful of grass. Finally, almost presentable, we prepared to make our entry into the town. But gone were our smiling faces. Down there, 50 yards ahead of us were two soldiers. Rouf! We were through the door of the nearest house, nearly upsetting a woman holding a baby. We apologised profusely, and explained our sudden entry; but evidently she was used to this kind of irruption, for she didn't seem at all surprised.

We promptly realised how foolish we had been – our sudden bolt might have attracted the attention we wished to avoid. Charleville was full of soldiers, and the only chance of escaping detection was to put on a bold face, and pass as one of the inhabitants. But our unannounced entry had its utility; we borrowed a small girl, who had entered from an adjoining room to see what the commotion was about, and under her guidance we set out to find the house of Abbé Bierry, the friend on whom all our hopes were pinned. At his house, on hearing that he was at home, we dismissed Georges, fixing a rendezvous for eight o'clock, the same evening. It was now nine o'clock, and we had a whole day in which to accomplish our plans.

The venerable Abbé was surprised at our visit. He anxiously inquired after our families; and then, adjusting his spectacles, he gave us a look as much as to say, 'Well, what's it all about?' Glad of the opening, we immediately plunged into our plans. Instead of showing us the door, which he might well have done for broaching such a compromising subject, to our relief, he immediately understood the situation, and the importance of our mission. He regretted that owing to his duties he could not play an active role himself, but Monsieur Dommelier, the editor of the local newspaper, certainly would – he had often expressed a desire for just such an opportunity. He would go and fetch Monsieur Dommelier.

Monsieur Dommelier was all that he had been described. His only regret was that we had not got in touch with him sooner. He thought that we should call into consultation Monsieur Grafetiaux and his wife, proprietors of a large pharmacy; they were patriots, intimate friends of his, and he knew they would wish to participate.

Thanking the Abbé for having started us off on the right road, we adjourned to the pharmacy, and there in the back sitting-room, after Madame Grafetiaux had kindly provided us with a change of clothing, we held a council of war. After spending several hours discussing plans, and going over instructions for the train-watchers, and the itinerant agents, we finally settled on the following organisation: Monsieur Dommelier was to be the chief of the Charleville

Platoon, and Madame Grafetiaux was to be his assistant. Between them they were to find the necessary agents to mount four train-watching posts at Charleville to control all troop movements passing through in the directions of Sedan, Rethel, Hirson, and Givet. In addition, they were to enrol itinerant agents to report on all German divisions moving in and out of the region. For courier from Charleville to Gedinne, it was decided that a certain Paul Martin was the man indicated for the job – to their knowledge he had guided several refugees across the frontier, and was a man with the necessary determination and courage. It was arranged that Martin, or whomever they could find as courier, should carry the first batch of reports through to Lucien Voltèche, our forester at Gedinne; and that he would indicate some hiding place in the woods between Gedinne and Monthermé, where thereafter the reports could be deposited and picked up. On our return, we would arrange for a courier from Gedinne to Conneux.

By this time it was already six o'clock. Madame Grafetiaux prepared a good dinner to fortify us for the road; and at eight o'clock we met Georges outside the Abbé's house. Our newfound friends accompanied us to the outskirts of the town, and there, after many fervent handshakes, and mutual wishes of 'Good Luck!' we took leave of them. Once again we were en route. We were tired, but we had the satisfaction of knowing that our mission had been entirely successful.

The first part of the return journey, as far as Breaux, was over a different route; to avoid the woods outside of Charleville, through which Georges was afraid he would not find his way in the dark, they followed the course of the Meuse instead, and passed through Nouzon. Georges brought his two young charges back in safety, though not without several exciting moments (one when they waded into the Meuse to escape the notice of a detachment of troops; another, when Georges failed to locate immediately the place where he had hidden the boat). The 60-odd miles from Gedinne to Charleville and back was accomplished in forty-seven hours – an incredible feat for two young girls travelling on foot across country, and through thick woods.

It was some time before the first reports came through. The recruiting of agents took longer than Dommelier and Madame Grafetiaux had expected. But eventually we received them in Holland. There could have been no better proof of their value than the telegram of congratulations which came back immediately from British GHQ.

The reports came through regularly for a month, and then the same old trouble, the courier service broke down. Lucien Voltèche had gone twice to the cache in the woods, and had found no reports. This was all the 'White Lady' knew. Clémie and Marie-Antoinette immediately volunteered to make a second expedition to Charleville, and once again they set out for Gedinne to secure the services of Georges.

Chance modified their plans. On arrival at the family estate, they found an aviation unit installed there. Ever anxious to obtain military information, they made friends with one of the non-commissioned officers. Details of the latest German fighting plane was their objective, but their thoughts were quickly diverted when they discovered that he was leaving for Charleville the next day to bring back supplies with one of his unit's covered motor lorries. The opportunity was too good to lose, and so with all the guile they could summon up, and using the pretext that they wished to visit a relative, they begged him to hide them in the truck.

Thinking that it was merely a youthful escapade, and, no doubt, not insensible to their charms, the good fellow – as Clémie herself described him – willingly took the risk. It was rash of the non-commissioned officer, if he had been caught it would have meant a court martial; but he knew, as well as did our valiant young friends, that the interior of a military vehicle was the very last place the Secret Police would search for them. He dropped them off at a secluded spot outside of Charleville, and it was there that they met him again the next day.

The journey was safely accomplished and so was their mission. Monsieur Crépel, the Mayor of Nouzon, was a friend of the Grafetiauxs, and as he had to come to Charleville frequently on business for his commune, he was persuaded to act as courier from Charleville to Nouzon. The courier service from Nouzon to Gedinne was undertaken by Lucien Voltèche, and so communications were once again established. They remained intact from then until the Armistice.

CHAPTER 14

SIEGBURG – PRISON
FOR WOMEN

THE PERCENTAGE OF women condemned to death
was not as great as that of the men. Close to 300 men
were shot as spies in the occupied territories. But in the
prison sentences, no discrimination was shown. For the women
life imprisonment with hard labour was the order of the day.

Prior to their trial, all prisoners were confined in the local prisons in Belgium and occupied France. I have already described
the prison regime, and have also told in detail about the stool-
pigeons and the third-degree methods employed. Once they had
been sentenced, they were transferred, almost without exception, to some prison in Germany; and in the case of the women,

it was to Siegburg that they were almost invariably sent (some were also confined in the prisons at Delizch and at Sagan).

The town of Siegburg, situated in the valley of the Rhine, about two hours from Bonn, is a typical Rhineland town, dominated by a ridge of hills whose fertile slopes are covered with vineyards. In the lower end of the town, we find the prison, composed of two T-shaped buildings, one for men, the other for women, surrounded and separated from each other by high prison walls.

The director of both the male and female sections of the prison was one whom I shall call von G., a retired Prussian officer. Having been wounded during the early stages of the war, he seemed to have a grudge against the political prisoners. He was a martinet, and did not have enough generosity to understand that though they had harmed the Germans, they had committed no moral offence against Society. He insisted on an iron discipline, and for the least offence punished the political prisoners with the utmost severity.

On the walls of the cells the following warning was posted: 'You are now a prisoner. Your window is barred, your door is locked, the colour of your clothing indicates that you have lost your liberty. God has not wished that you continue to abuse it for the purpose of sinning against His laws and those of man. He has brought you here to expiate your crimes. Therefore, bow down under the all-powerful hand of God, bow down under the iron regulations of this prison. If you do not obey willingly, your spirit will be broken. But if you accept humbly the punishment which has been inflicted upon you, the fruit of your submission will be a humbled heart, and a tranquil conscience. God wishes this to be so.'

That was his creed and he carried it into effect. He was

universally hated by everyone, even by the German personnel, who felt that they, too, were being watched as von G. went round on his daily tour of inspection. He was arrested by the British when the army of occupation reached the Rhine, but, fortunately for him, he managed to escape.

Frau R., the directress of the female section of the prison, had secured her appointment through influence in higher quarters. The widow of a former army officer, and a woman of some refinement, she seemed at times to have some compassion for the tragic lot of the women under her charge; but any generous impulse by which she might have been moved was never put into effect, for she was completely under the domination of von G., of whom she was in mortal fear.

The prisoner on arrival was taken to the office for an examination of her commitment papers and the establishing of her identity. After this she was taken to the bath house where, in the presence of the 'Housemother', she was forced to undress and take a bath. Her clothing was then removed, and she was given her prison outfit.

The prison dress was brown for those sentenced to hard labour, and grey for the others. It consisted of a blouse, and a skirt reaching down to the ankles, both of which were made of a rough woollen material. To this was added a blue and white cotton neckerchief, a white apron, blue and white cotton stockings and sandals. Underclothing was of cotton. This prison uniform remained obligatory until 1917 when, on account of the shortage of clothing, the prisoners were allowed to wear the clothes with which they had entered the prison. If, however, they used this privilege, they were forced to pay for their laundry.

The cells, arranged in three tiers on both sides of a large gallery from which all the doors could be seen at a glance, were 12 ft long, 8 ft wide and 9 ft high. Each contained a small table and an iron bed on which a straw mattress in three sections was placed. Opposite the door was a small barred window, one section of which could be opened with an iron key in possession of the wardress. The windows were only opened for a stated period during the day; however, the prisoners soon learned to open them clandestinely at night with a wooden key of their own manufacture. The heavy cell door contained a peephole, but had to be opened completely to pass food to the prisoners.

An oil lamp, attached to the whitewashed wall, was allowed to be lit for an hour during the winter; but on Sundays and holidays, even this privilege was withdrawn. Lights were extinguished before the evening meal, and it was only by touch that the bowl of thin gruel could be reached. These long hours of darkness, which during the winter often lasted fifteen hours, had a most depressing effect on the prisoners.

At seven o'clock a bell announced that it was the hour to rise. The doors were opened by the wardresses, and the prisoners put out their water jugs and their sanitary buckets. Fifteen minutes later, these were ready to be taken in again. At eight o'clock, 100 grams of black bread and a cup of hot black unsweetened liquid, which passed for coffee, were handed in. Except for two promenade periods in the courtyard, one in the morning and one in the afternoon, each of forty-five minutes' duration, the prisoners were kept busy in their cells from the morning until the evening meal. Those who were expert with the needle were allowed to make garments; the others were provided with machines with which they stamped out men's trouser buttons. Sunday was a day of rest. Mass was celebrated at nine o'clock, vespers at one-thirty.

The principal meal of the day was a vegetable soup, served at 11.30 a.m. This was nourishing, but the vegetables were so badly washed that insects often floated on the liquid; hence the name 'bug soup' by which it came to be known. Before 1917, a few pieces of meat were occasionally discovered in this soup; but after this period, meat was never seen again. At four o'clock, the prisoners received another cup of black coffee, together with 75 grams of black bread. The final meal, consisting of a bowl of thin gruel, was passed in at six o'clock. The cell doors were then locked, and under no circumstances were they opened again until seven o'clock the next morning.

The food was entirely insufficient to sustain the prisoners, and as food became scarce in Germany, what was offered the prisoners became worse and worse. In the bread, potato meal was used; and in the soup, beetroot became the exclusive vegetable. During March 1917 packets of food started reaching the prisoners from France. It was a godsend. They were allowed to receive 4 lbs of biscuits a week. It was time, for many of the younger prisoners, some of whom were only fifteen years of age, were suffering terribly from hunger. The most pitiful cases, however, were the unfortunate mothers who had given birth to children in the prison, and were not getting enough nourishment to nurse them.

If births occurred at night, they often took place without any assistance. Mothers were permitted to keep their babies for nine months. After this, the infants were either put in a home in Siegburg, or were given out to some German nurse.

On one Sunday a month, the mother was allowed to have the child brought to her; the leave-taking was heart-rending, and it was especially sad for the mother to perceive that her baby was gradually forgetting her.

Bad as the food was, it was the lack of medical care, and the insanitary conditions in the prison, which caused the greatest suffering. I have already mentioned the bucket. Those who became ill were required to report sick to the prison doctor. In a long file, outside his office, they could be viewed each morning waiting to see him. The care they received, however, was almost nil. Doctor 'Get Out', for this is what the prisoners called him, either prescribed nothing, or gave the same pills for a dozen varied ailments. Some of the prisoners had such little faith in the prison doctor that they were discovered dead in their cells without having approached him. Dysentery, typhoid, and tuberculosis ravaged the prison. A large percentage of the 300 prisoners died within its walls. Prisoners were not even spared the sad task of having to carry the coffins out of the cells.

The number of victims would have been even greater had it not been for the devotion of some of the prisoners, such as Léonie Vanhutte, who were allowed to nurse their companions. Léonie Vanhutte herself contracted typhoid and nearly died.

The case of Louise de Bettignies was typical of the harsh treatment meted out to the prisoners. Having discovered that her companions were engaged in assembling shell fuses without knowing what they were intended for, she encouraged them to refuse the work. For this, she was thrown into a special cell for recalcitrant prisoners. These cells, smaller than the others, contained no furniture other than a narrow wooden plank, which served as a bed. The meagre food ration was also reduced. But von G. relied on the cold to break her spirit. Even though it was mid-winter and the cells were unheated, he removed her blankets and took away from her the woollen underwear which she had brought to the prison, substituting in their place the regulation cotton ones.

Shivering in her cell, Louise contracted pneumonia. For days she hovered between life and death. Eventually she recovered, but her health remained permanently shattered. Shortly afterward, a small tumour appeared in one of her breasts. As it grew at an alarming pace, she was forced to consult the doctor. He quickly diagnosed the malignant growth and urged an immediate operation. Having no faith in him, however, and knowing that the small prison infirmary was not equipped for a major operation of this kind, she asked for permission to be transferred to a clinic in Bonn.

Von G. was adamant. Louise was a prisoner and had no rights. For a time she held out against him; but, finally, realising that she had no alternative, she signed the paper giving the prison doctor the right to operate. The operation, as she had feared, was unsuccessful. It was only when she was dying that von G. eventually granted permission for her to be transferred to a hospital in Cologne. There she died 17 September 1918.

After the Armistice, with full military ceremonial her remains, draped with the French flag and placed on a gun-carriage, were escorted through the streets of Cologne to the railway station, en route to her last resting-place in Lille. General Degoutte and General Simon, representatives of the French and British armies of the Rhine, marched in the funeral procession. This was Louise de Bettignies, the valiant patriot, whom von G. had treated as a criminal.

No one can adequately portray the tragic lives of these women prisoners. Even worse than the prison treatment was the mental agony they had to endure not knowing what was happening to those who were dear to them.

In spite of all their suffering, not one of these brave women, from the Princess de Croy down to the humblest peasant, regretted having served her country. Those who survived returned home at the Armistice, happy that their sacrifice had not been in vain.

CHAPTER 15

DESERTERS AND A DAME

FROM TIME TO time, German deserters were crossing the frontier into Holland. Our frontier agents reported this; the Dutch papers also occasionally made reference to it. I was so busy, however, organising our services in Belgium that at first I could not give much attention to it. Besides, how was I to get hold of them? I certainly wasn't going to compromise our frontier agents by having them lead deserters in uniform to me.

One day, walking on the Blaak, I came face to face with two deserters. Their tattered uniforms and their drawn faces told me their story: they were down and out, wandering around like stray dogs, ready to be pounced upon by the Dutch authorities as vagrants, and sent off to the concentration camp at Alkmaar, which they hated almost as much as being in the German Army.

I boldly accosted them, and told them to come and see me at the office. I had no fear of compromising myself. By now, both the Germans and Dutch knew what I was doing; the former were powerless to prevent my activities, and it was the policy of the latter not to interfere with me.

For the price of a suit of clothes apiece, and a few loose gulden in their pockets, the means of making them look respectable and obtain work, they gave me full details of their regiment, their division, the place and date at which they had left them; and, on a large map, one of a complete set for the Western and Eastern Fronts, I marked off battery emplacements, regimental and divisional headquarters, and other objectives for our artillery and aeroplanes. Colonel Oppenheim was delighted with the information.

To get more deserters, I offered a reward to the ones I had interrogated, for each deserter they brought me. My plan worked admirably; somehow or other, each deserter crossing the frontier gravitated to his companions, who passed him on to me. I am sure I missed very few.

Most of these men deserted from leave trains on their way back to the Front. The Herbesthal–Liège line passed within sight of the Dutch frontier, and I suppose the temptation was too great for some of the poor devils. These men were of interest, for it was important to know exactly what part of the line each division held; but the most valuable ones were those who deserted from trains carrying their divisions from east to west, or vice versa. Train-watchers gave the movements, but since the German troops no longer wore their regimental numbers, they could not identify the divisions.

172

I can still hear the shout of satisfaction from Colonel Oppenheim, when, after our posts had reported the passage of two divisions going east into Germany through Liège, I announced to him that I had just interrogated two deserters, and knew conclusively that it was the 8th Corps. Two weeks later, he sent me a copy of a telegram from GHQ, which read: 'Congratulations 8th Corps identified by prisoners on the Russian Front.' It was such telegrams, received from time to time, that kept us keyed to the greatest enthusiasm.

Sometimes a deserter would try to give me wrong information, and sometimes the German secret service in Holland deliberately sent me fake deserters. But armed with detail maps of the eastern and western battle fronts which gave the last location of each German division in line, as established by prisoners, and also having in my possession the army Brown Book,[1] which gave the regimental numbers of the units in each division with the names of divisional commanders and a mass of other information, I knew enough to be able to trap any deserter immediately whenever I found him telling lies. They soon passed the word around that I was not to be fooled.

Once, I will admit, the German secret service had both Colonel Oppenheim and myself worried. To some extent, we were deceived. One morning, on entering one of the cubicles in which I interrogated deserters and other suspects so as to keep them isolated from the main office, I found myself to my surprise facing a Turk in semi-uniform. In fluent French, he informed me

---

1   A publication by British GHQ containing all known information about the German Army.

that he had deserted at Trier from a Turkish division, which was on its way by rail from the Dardanelles to the Western Front.

I was at a loss. I knew nothing about the Turkish Army; I had no Brown Book on it; I had no maps of the Turkish Front. I knew that considerable re-grouping had been going on; German divisions had appeared on the Italian Front in support of the Austrians, and heavy Austrian howitzer batteries had been located on the Western Front. Colonel Oppenheim had sent me a 'blue slip': 'Be on the look-out for the appearance of Austrian troops.' I suspected the Turk, even though he made a good impression and had a good story, complete in every detail, even as to his place of entrainment, and the route his train had followed. If it was true, here was information of the greatest importance; and yet, if it were false, and I reported it, I knew I should be laughed at.

I reported my views to Colonel Oppenheim, and asked him if he would like to see the man. To my relief, he agreed. He was unable to break down the man's story, and, under the circumstances, did the only thing he could do: he telegraphed the information. The man was paid, and the Germans probably had a good laugh. No Turkish division ever appeared on the Western Front. Months later, I ran into our man peddling carpets on the streets of Rotterdam. As I looked at him closely, I could swear I saw him smile.

I didn't mind this continual crossing of swords with the German secret service; it added zest to our work.

We now pulled off one of the biggest secret service scoops of the war. On entering one of the cubicles in response to word from our doorman that there was a deserter to see me, I found a young anæmic-looking fellow, who nervously pulled a package out from under his coat. 'What is this worth to you?' said he, as he pulled a book out of the wrapping. 'It is the latest edition of the German field post directory. Two days ago I removed it from the Düsseldorf post office, where I was working.'

I was undoubtedly a comical sight, for blank amazement must have been clearly written on my face. I grasped the book, not believing my ears, and hardly trusting my eyes. I am sure that my hand shook as I thumbed its pages. Here was a complete list of every unit in the German Army. It was of vital importance to the Allies to know what new regiments, batteries, aeroplane flights, and other units were being formed from time to time; knowing this, they could make an exact estimate of the strength of the German Army. In addition, there in the most authentic form was the location on the Eastern and Western Fronts of each of the German field posts. This meant that we had the code by means of which we could tell, from intercepted post cards and letters, the exact place where all the regiments or units indicated in the addresses were located.

I made a dash for my Brown Book. Incomplete as it was, I knew it was sufficient to enable me to check up the authenticity of this field post directory. Hastily, by means of my battle-front maps, and by some intercepted post cards, I checked up the location of those regiments whose position in the front line had been established by captured prisoners. Hurriedly I searched in the book for the mention of the new regiments of the 600 series; I had just had some deserters from infantry regiment 606, not listed in the Brown Book, and at the time I was afraid that, encouraged by their success with the Turk, the German Service was again trying a joke on me.

Everything tallied. The book was undoubtedly genuine. No monetary value could be put on the volume; it was priceless. An army of spies could not have gathered the data it contained. It made our Brown Book look silly, and yet the Brown Book represented the sum total of our information about the German Army gained during more than three years of spy activity, and from the interrogation of several hundred thousand German prisoners of war captured by both the French and British armies. By adroit negotiation and by handing us for examination a torn-out page instead of the whole directory, the deserter could have demanded and received a fabulous sum for it; instead, he meekly accepted £100, the first sum I offered him.

I often wondered afterwards what happened to these German deserters, who sold their country for a mess of pottage. I confess I hated interrogating them. They were such poor devils, without a country, without money, without work, and without friends in a foreign country. Perhaps I kept them from the concentration camp, and helped them to get work. I hope I did. At least, I salved my conscience by thinking so. Anyhow, I had to do it; it was war.

Of all the many German deserters who passed through my hands, Heinrich Feldmann made the best impression. I felt that he was giving me information, not just to get a few gulden, but because he had a genuine grievance against the German authorities. There was no mistaking his sincerity and his real grief when he told me about his wife and three children in Berlin: how for months they had lived on nothing but turnips and watery potatoes; how white and emaciated he had found them on returning home on leave; and how he had sworn he would desert to Holland, obtain work, and send them money to buy a few of the bare necessities of life. He declared that he had a greater responsibility towards his family than to the Kaiser and the military clique who were driving Germany to its ruin.

When, therefore, Colonel Oppenheim asked me to check up on certain of the new regiments and batteries which we had found mentioned in the field post directory, it was quite natural that I should think of Feldmann. Knowing where he was working, I sent a confidential agent to arrange a secret meeting with him. Feldmann was surprised at the sudden precautions, and he was evidently curious to know what I had in mind.

I outlined to him briefly what I wanted him to do, explaining that he would be well paid, and that here was an opportunity for him to help his family. I admitted that it was obviously a dangerous mission, as, of course, he was perfectly aware, but that I could diminish the danger by supplying him with the necessary papers 'proving' that he was unfit for military service. He hesitated, but when I showed him the perfect specimens of our engraver's art, including a pass permitting its bearer to travel on the German railways, he accepted. He recognised that he had a sporting chance of success.

In a week I had coached him in the sort of information I required, and he was ready to pass the frontier. With a handshake and wishes for his good luck, he departed, having in his possession the address of our secret agent in Sittard, who had been warned of his coming, and who had received instructions to take him across the border into Aachen. Once there, it was up to Feldmann to continue on his own.

Our Sittard agent, who belonged to a band of smugglers

operating there, reported that the journey to Aachen had been successfully accomplished. We sat back and waited. Three weeks elapsed. Then one morning I got a telegram from Roermond, addressed to one of our confidential agents in Rotterdam. 'Please send eight more bags this evening Johannes.' This was a code message, which meant that Fleischer had returned, and would meet me at 8 p.m. at the same place as before.

He brought back information of the greatest value to us. He had visited several training camps, and had secured, not only confirmation of the formation of several new regiments, such as those of the 600 and 700 series, but also details of the formation and tactics of the special storm troops, *sturmtruppen* which the Germans were to use so successfully in their great offensive in March 1918. He reported that these *sturmtruppen*, made up of picked veterans, were being formed into units and drilled in the training centres in Germany and behind the Front. They were to be used as spearheads to make gaps in the enemy's front line, through which the less-experienced troops would then be poured. This was the German 'infiltration' process, which the Allies had to combat later on, and with which the war *communiques* were filled after the launching of the German offensive.

In addition, Feldmann gave a valuable description of economic conditions in Germany, and brought back with him samples of cards, composed of coupons for each day in the month, which entitled the German citizen to specific daily quantities of bread, fat, and other foods; he also supplied us with a variety of *ersatz* products, the substitutes for coffee and other foodstuffs which the Germans were using. He confirmed what we already knew, that starvation conditions were rapidly developing in Germany, but maintained that, spurred on by the Austrian successes against the Italians, and by the collapse of Russia and the subsequent signing of the peace of Brest Litovsk, the German people still hoped for victory in the great offensive, which they all knew their High Command was preparing on the Western Front.

Feldmann was now set a new and much more difficult task. We were extremely anxious to establish a train-watching post at Trier. We were getting all the troop movements coming out of Germany on the Aachen–Herbesthal–Liège line, but the other main artery through Trier was unwatched. If we could mount a post here, we would be catching every troop movement out of Germany to the Western Front between Verdun and the sea. Success would mean a magnificent achievement.

Feldmann was afraid. He could not have been more sceptical of success than I was. Again and again I had failed in the attempt. We never had been able to mount a train-watching post in Germany itself. It was obviously a far different affair working with Germans in Germany, than with Belgians or the French in the occupied territory. In the one case, we only had money as the incentive; in the other, we had patriotism. Again, it was harder to spy in Germany because the agent was continually surrounded by neighbours who would give him away if they saw anything suspicious. Finally, a train-watcher, having to remain at his post, had to rely on a courier. It was chiefly at this that the German agents balked. We had had many successful ones, like Fleischer, working alone; but they steadily refused to put their lives in the hands of a compatriot worker.

However, Feldmann finally accepted the mission, and returned to Germany. We never saw him again. Whether the fairly large sum which I gave him for organisation purposes was too great a temptation, or whether he was caught and shot, I do not know. I have a suspicion that having found out that the papers we gave him were such perfect forgeries that they could pass muster with the Germans, and having saved a fairly large sum of money, he returned to his family in Berlin. He realised that their existence depended on him, and he probably thought we had set him an impossible task. They were obviously his greatest and only consideration in life, and as he had refused to sacrifice them for his Kaiser, we could not expect him to sacrifice them for us.

Another brave and arresting figure comes back to my mind. I knew him as 'The Dane'. What his name was, or where he came from, I do not know, although I met him several times. Slight of build, fair, with blue eyes, he looked the reserved, well-bred Scandinavian of cultured and professional interests. He certainly did not look the arch-spy that he was. When I came to know him better, however, I realised why he was so successful. He was a marine engineer of exceptional quality; he was a man without nerves, always cool and collected; nothing escaped his austerely competent eye; and he was possessed of an astounding memory for the minutest detail of marine construction.

I read his reports from time to time and marvelled at them. In my opinion, he was undoubtedly by far the most valuable agent the Allies ever had working in Germany. To the chief in England belonged the credit of finding him; at least, I believe so. He became the solitary agent in Germany that our naval section in Holland possessed, but he was all they needed. He covered every shipbuilding yard and every Zeppelin shed in Germany. I can only give a very general survey of his activities, as his reports dealt chiefly with naval matters which were handled by the naval section. But he rendered such outstanding services to our military section as well as his own, and his reports were so brilliant, that I am sure the reader will be interested in the meagre details I can offer.

The key to his success was that he made the Germans believe that he was working for them against us. As a representative of a Danish shipbuilding yard, which was supplying the Germans from time to time with tugboats and marine equipment, he was allowed to travel freely to Kiel, Wilhelmshaven, Hamburg, Bremen, Emden, Lübeck, Flensburg, and other shipbuilding centres. His capable and affable management of company affairs caused such a sea of orders that they were unable to meet the demands. His popularity with German clients and their trust in his apparently candid nature were unbounded. When in due time he applied for a pass to proceed through Germany to Holland it was readily granted, especially in view of his suggestion to the German authorities that he could buy much needed raw material there, and also tugboats and other small craft, which could be purchased as if by his Danish company, but in reality for supply to Germany. He was so successful with his purchases in Holland that regularly, once every three weeks, he was permitted to make the trip.

Little did the Germans know that it was we who were largely responsible for the Dane's success. T, because of his shipping connections, was able to give him valuable information as to where he could purchase material, and secure an odd tugboat now and then; and since in the natural course of affairs the British authorities would have protested or prevented such purchases as he made, our lack of action enabled him to return to Germany and ingratiate himself by boasting how successful he had been in covering up his purchases from the British. In this way, he became *persona grata* with the German authorities, and by bringing back small presents in the way of clothing, foodstuffs, and luxuries which were then unobtainable in Germany, he was able to ingratiate himself with the heads of the shipbuilding yards, and with other German officials.

With his extraordinary memory, he was able to sit down, when in Holland, and write out page after page of reports, giving an exact description of the ships which were under construction or repair, and supplying us with the invaluable naval information on which the admiralty relied absolutely. Every battleship and cruiser has a distinctive silhouette which is as individual as that of a human being. The silhouettes of all the pre-war German warships were known to us, and in these the Dane was so thoroughly drilled that at a distance of several miles he rarely made a mistake in identifying the larger of them.

From him we got full engineering details of the submarines which the Germans were turning out as fast as they could in order to put over their unrestricted submarine warfare campaign. We learned of the number under construction, the repairs which were being made, and, what was very important, the number which were missing. In the Allied defence against submarines, with the use of depth bombs, mines and gunfire, it was often difficult to tell whether these enemy craft had been sunk or had submerged of their own accord.

Long before the *Deutschland*, the German merchant submarine, was ready for its trip to America, we had received a full description of it from the Dane. From him we also knew of the commerce raiders, which were then being fitted out. He reported the successful return of the *Moewe* when we thought it was still at large. Through him the British Admiralty got exact details of the German losses at Jutland, and also a minute account of the damage done to some of the ships which returned. In a battle of this description, fought during periods of fog and darkness, it was impossible to make an accurate estimate of losses from direct observation during the action.

A check was kept on all Zeppelin hangars, and here again an account was given of damage done to the ships during their raids on England.

His most sensational report was a detailed description of the big high-angle-fire guns, which several months later fired their 300-lb shells at Paris from the forest of St Gobain, a distance of 75 miles. Full particulars of the trials which were carried out with these guns firing out to sea from the coast of Heligoland were given by the Dane. The actual damage done by these guns on Paris was relatively insignificant, considering the expense incurred. I believe the total casualties were only about 200. The guns were expected to be chiefly effective as a cause of shock and alarm, the mystery of their position and operation being kept up as long as possible. On the mind of the general public the almost magic quality of the great new guns' power did produce something like panic, but once again the secret service had destroyed for GHQ the element of surprise planned by the Germans. I have often wondered whether the High Command had placed any faith at first in this particular report of the Dane, the facts seemed at the time so incredible.

In addition to these technical details which he brought us, he was able to give us valuable information about political and economic conditions in Germany. Because he was in contact with high officials and officers in Germany, he brought us back the point of view of the men who really knew what was going on, not the opinion of the man in the street, who was told what the German High Command wanted him to believe.

The greatest danger that the Dane ran was in his contact with us, as he never carried any incriminating materials whatever – notes, lists, letters, even special papers or inks – when he was in Germany. With him we employed the same methods that I used in meeting all our agents working in enemy territory. We kept several houses in Rotterdam and in The Hague, which we were continually changing. To reach these places from the office we employed every trick conceivable, such as never going there on foot from the office, never driving up to the door, doubling back on our tracks, and sliding into a doorway to see if we were being followed. As far as possible, we always met these agents at night, not only to avoid recognition, but to prevent the taking of photographs, in which the Germans were expert. A photograph of a man going into a house owned by us was sufficient evidence in the eyes of the Germans for his immediate execution, if they caught him in Germany or the occupied territory.

As soon as the Dane arrived in Holland, he called us by telephone, announcing his arrival under an assumed name known to us. Then we fixed a time of meeting at one of our houses, A, B, C, D, the addresses of which, corresponding to these alphabetical letters, were known to him. In this way all danger arriving from a possible overheard telephone message was removed. One of the girls at the telephone exchange might have been in German pay, or the Germans might have tapped our wire, as he once successfully did with theirs until a Dutch telephone linesman discovered it.

On his arrival in the house, the Dane immediately got down to the writing of his report, which he did in German, and this occupied sometimes three or four hours. One by one the German shipbuilding yards, such as Blohm and Voss at Hamburg, the Vulkan Yard at Bredow near Stettin, the Schichau Works at Elbing and Danzig, the Weser company at Bremen, the Germania Werft, and the Danziger Werft were gone over, and a description was given of the ships on every single slip in these yards, until every shipbuilding yard in Germany was covered.

When I first saw him write out his reports without any notes, in a calm and matter-of-fact manner, I felt convinced he was faking some of them, but I soon learned to respect his statements, when time after time, later on, we received verification of details which he had reported. As soon as his reports were completed, they were rushed to our office on the Boompjes for translating, coding, and cabling to London. The Dane generally remained over in Holland for two or three days, sufficient time for the admiralty to cable back any questions on his reports which they wished answered, or to acquaint him with details of information which they wanted him to secure on his return to Germany.

The Dane continued his work to the very date of the Armistice. He was paid huge sums, far in excess of any of our other agents; and as he was the father of a family, and apparently of high moral character, I am sure he saved his money, which was amply sufficient for him to retire on. In his villa in Denmark today, none of his neighbours suspect, I am sure, the great role this reserved and observant gentleman played during the war. But it was those very characteristics, with a memory truly phenomenal, that made him undoubtedly a master spy.

CHAPTER 16

SURPRISES OF THE COAST PATROL – THE WIRELESS TORPEDO BOAT

T O THE GERMANS the coast of Belgium was of enormous importance, for it supplied them with bases from which their submarines and torpedo boats could sally forth to prey on Allied shipping. These bases were located at the harbours of Ostend, Zeebrugge, and Blankenberghe, and of these the first two were by far the most important, since they were connected by canals to Bruges, where the lighter craft could retire in case of Allied attack, or where submarines could be assembled from parts sent from Germany. Realising the value of the

Flanders Coast to her, Germany did everything within her power to make it impregnable by studding it with heavy gun batteries, and by supplementing them with a vast number of aircraft which were also used for raids on England.

It was our duty in Holland to complete the work of aeroplane reconnaissance by supplying the admiralty with all possible information about the location of the various coastal batteries and aerodromes. We had four sources of information: spies, German deserters, Belgian refugees, and our own direct observation. The Dutch frontier was only 7 miles distant from Zeebrugge, and so with a good telescope, even on a fairly misty day, it was possible to watch the German activities at this small artificial port.

For the duration of the war one of our experts kept daily watch with a powerful telescope from Kadzand in Holland, the nearest point of approach, on all points between Zeebrugge and the frontier. He reported the coming and going of the twenty-odd submarines and torpedo boats stationed at Zeebrugge, and activities of the mine layers and dredgers operating there. This was of great value to the admiralty, which thus came to know the exact strength of the enemy, in small craft, at this base; and by knowing the direction of departure and return of the submarines and torpedo boats, the British patrol boats were able to be in wait successfully for them.

The position of the batteries could only be approximately located by our frontier agent, and then only when they went through target practice, as they were all carefully camouflaged. Their rough locations were valuable, however, as they helped us to check up on the reports from refugees and deserters, especially the latter, and also supplied GHQ and the admiralty with objectives for aeroplane reconnaissance and subsequent bombardment.

By far the most valuable information we obtained about the coastal batteries came from two deserters from the German Marine Corps, which for the duration of the war permanently occupied the Flanders Coast. One morning to my delight, I found them waiting for me in one of our office cubicles. Our frontier agent, near Kadzand, had seen them crossing the frontier, and contrary to instructions had himself conducted them to me in Rotterdam. Interviewing them in separate cubicles, I was able to check the story of the one against that of the other, and then compare their joint information with what we already knew. Their reports were undoubtedly genuine. In addition to giving me several new battery positions, they gave me valuable information about the calibre of the guns and their range: most of them were from 6 to 15 inches, and some had a range of over 20,000 yards. I was told that the Kaiser Wilhelm battery, which was constructed with the aid of Russian prisoners of war, had a range of 23 miles. From them I learned also for the first time the German names of the different batteries, such as the Kaiser Wilhelm, the Goeben, Deutschland, Cecilia, Tirpitz, and Hindenburg.

But what thrilled me most of all, one of them solved a baffling mystery which had worried us for a long time. Our frontier agent at Kadzand had on several occasions reported seaplane manoeuvres at Zeebrugge in conjunction with what seemed to him a fast motor boat, in which, strange to say, he could never see a steersman. At first I paid no attention to these reports, attributing the phenomenon to faulty observation, but he was so insistent about his guideless motor boat that eventually I became concerned. The two deserters, as if agreed between themselves, professed at first to know nothing about the matter. The sight of a hundred-guilder note, however, started the one talking, and to my constant query: 'What are the Germans doing with those motor boat and seaplane manoeuvres at Zeebrugge?' he suddenly amazed me by replying: 'The boats are guided by wireless from the seaplanes.'

I was now all excitement. Gradually I got the rest of the story out of him. The motor boats, fitted with torpedoes in their bows, were set in motion from the shore, propelled by an ordinary motor, and were guided to their objective by wireless, transmitted from observing seaplanes. They were intended as a surprise for the next visit of the British monitors, which periodically appeared off the coast to bombard the German base and batteries. Here was startling information, which I lost no time in telegraphing. The admiralty immediately sent back a telegram of congratulations, and a bid for further information! A few weeks later, the Germans had a chance to use their guideless boats against the monitors, but to their chagrin, provisions had been made to render them harmless. Once more the secret service had exercised one of its prime functions: it had destroyed the element of surprise.

Owing to the fact that most of the Belgian inhabitants had been driven from the coast either by the destruction of their homes by bombardment from the sea and air, or through deportation by the Germans, there were very few of them left in this area. For this reason it was well nigh impossible to introduce a spy into the zone. We had to content ourselves with the reports brought us by Belgian boatmen navigating the canals between Bruges and Holland. The information was old by the time it got to us, but since most of the coastal batteries were permanently imbedded in concrete and, therefore, did not change position, time was not an important factor. This information concerning the coast defences was picked up by the boatmen from occasional refugees from the coast, who still found their way to Bruges.

What interested us most of all, however, in these boatmen's reports, was the German activities in Bruges itself. Bruges, situated at the apex of a triangle, whose sides were the canals connecting her with Zeebrugge and Ostend, and the base the Zeebrugge–Ostend coastal strip, was the centre from which both Ostend and Zeebrugge, especially the latter, were fed. Bruges itself could accommodate about thirty submarines and an equal number of torpedo boats. We had to watch not only the number of the enemy craft in the harbour, but what was more important, the number which were being built. Some were assembled from parts sent from Germany; others were constructed in the shipbuilding yards at Antwerp, of which those of the Cockerell Works were the most important.

Aeroplane reconnaissance, air photographs, German deserters, our Bruges boatmen spies, and the unceasing watching of Moresco, our frontier agent at Kadzand, supplied the admiralty with all the information they required. On a large-scale map in Rotterdam we marked each battery emplacement and aerodrome as they were reported. With enthusiasm we watched the numbers gradually grow until we had located about 150 guns between Ostend and the Dutch frontier, and on the Zeebrugge mole. I would be surprised if there was a single battery or aerodrome on the coast which was not known to us. It was the accurate information, coupled with the wonderful bravery of the men, and the brilliant direction of Admiral Sir Roger Keyes and the officers under him, which permitted the successful raids on Zeebrugge and Ostend, culminating in the blocking up of these two harbours, and the destruction of the German submarine bases on the Flanders Coast, which had been for such a long time a menace to both the Allied shipping and the British lines of communication.

In addition to watching Zeebrugge, we also kept the Scheldt under close observation, to prevent the steamers which were laid up in Antwerp from slipping out to their home ports in Germany, where they could be fitted out as commerce raiders or employed for some useful purpose. In Antwerp disuse was turning them into derelicts. German warships would, of course, have been interned as they had to pass through Dutch waters, but ordinary merchantmen were free to steam down the Scheldt past Flushing, and by keeping within the 3-mile limit along the Dutch Coast, they were out of danger; from there they had a very short distance to go to be safe in a German port such as Emden.

When, therefore, our Antwerp agents reported that some of the ships, which had lain idle for more than two years, were getting up steam, we were naturally on the watch, and the admiralty was immediately informed. Our patience was soon rewarded, for two ships were reported steaming down the Scheldt. Under cover of the night, they got as far as Flushing, but in the early hours of the morning, as they were trailing along the Dutch Coast, they found the British patrol boats waiting to sink them. They were so close in that many of the British shells fell on Dutch soil.

Whether or not these ships were in Dutch territorial waters when they were sunk, I do not know. The matter was hushed up. The *Nieuwe Rotterdamsche Courant* reported the bare facts, and no comments were made. The Dutch government, pursuing its policy of keeping out of the war at all costs, was often embarrassed by both sides. Their brilliant Foreign Affairs Minister, a master of diplomacy, steered them successfully through many difficult situations, and doubtless this was one of them.

A few days afterwards, returning from London where I had been urgently called to consult with C, I was met at Harwich by a flag lieutenant, who informed me that the convoy would not be leaving for three hours, and that Admiral L. wanted me to have lunch with him on board his flagship. Leaving the diplomatic bags on shore under guard – on this occasion I had been asked by the Foreign Office to act as King's messenger to The Hague – I gladly accepted the invitation.

I was immediately put at my ease by the Admiral, who had under him submarines, torpedo boats, and lighter craft which were stationed there: one of the most important commands in the navy. His chief interest in me was the information I could give him about the two ships which had been sunk. 'What do the Dutch think about it?' said he, with a twinkle in his eye. I told him all I knew.

CHAPTER 17

ESPIONAGE, COUNTER-ESPIONAGE AND SPY HYSTERIA

THE ORDINARY PUBLIC has no conception of secret service. The beautiful female spy is not an essential to every secret service coup – she rarely figured in our wartime services – for every Gabrielle Petit or Louise de Bettignies, the two brave Allied agents who paid the supreme penalty for their devotion to duty, there were a hundred male spies, less glamorous but just as efficient; nor is drugging or the rifling of safes and strong-boxes a common practice. Physical violence is an exception, and so also is the carrying of firearms or any other weapon, even as a means of defence.

The spies who have been shot and whose cases have attracted the greatest publicity have not always been great spies. The penalty for spying during the war was, in most cases, death. Some of the victims had succeeded in procuring information of the greatest value and had inflicted material damage on the enemy; others were caught and shot before they had been able to do any harm. Yet often those in the latter category received the most attention from the press. Mata Hari, for instance, was not one of the great spies of the war: I don't think she was actually successful in conveying much information to the Germans, but she is known to the whole world because she was a woman born in romantic circumstances, because she was a dancer, and because she died bravely before the firing squad at Vincennes, dressed in her best clothes, with a pair of long white gloves in her hands, which she drew on calmly as she awaited the fatal command.

The spy hysteria during the war was another example of the public's lack of knowledge. At the outbreak of hostilities many pre-war German spies did remain in the belligerent countries with instructions to carry on, but their number was grossly exaggerated, and violent precautionary measures were taken by local military authorities (often as ill-informed as the public) which resulted in a great number of innocent people being shot. Even in far-off South Africa, General Delarey was mistaken for a spy and shot at night by a sentry, when the general's chauffeur, not hearing the challenge, failed to stop. This took place close to Johannesburg, hundreds of miles from the nearest German colony, in a situation where, if a spy had existed it would have been very improbable that he would be dashing around in a car at night.

I shall never forget what havoc the rumour of a lurking spy caused in my own brigade during our first week in France. So unnerved did those in command become that sentries were posted in each gunpit with orders to shoot anyone who did not stop when challenged. During that same night one of the gunners, coming out of his billet half asleep to relieve himself, was killed by a sentry. The sentries were removed, and that was the last we heard of the phantom German spy.

True it is that when an army is retreating in its own country, it often leaves spies behind to report on the enemy's movements. In open warfare, they can return to their own lines, or even communicate for a short while by means of a hidden telephone wire, or pigeons, or for a few hours by means of a portable wireless set or some signalling apparatus. But once the belligerents have settled down to stationary trench warfare, with a continuous line of barbed wire entanglements between them, it is more than unlikely that any system of spy reports can exist directly across the battlefront lines. It would have surprised me greatly to have been told of a single authentic case in the Great War where a German spy was caught within a couple of miles of the front lines. Even if a spy had been there, he would have been useless without means of communication. Working from Holland, I knew how difficult it was to get a regular courier to penetrate close to the German front line, and yet I was directing agents of French and Belgian nationality working in their own country. Within the actual firing zone, they would not only have had to secure military uniforms, but also – at least on some occasions – have had to live in contact with the soldiers, for on both sides during the last two years of the war practically every front sector was entirely freed of civilian population by enforced evacuation. Yet spies were a constant subject of talk and of precaution among those in command in the firing zone.

Of a similar order was the general belief that German spies were signalling to submarines or other craft out to sea. Boy Scouts were even sent out in some parts of England to watch for signal flashes at night; this, however, as well as other fantastic means of communication, was soon proved a bogey after the first few months of the war. The only participation of submarines in spying was that they probably landed one or two spies on the west coast of Ireland.

However, though all this war hysteria came from lack of knowledge on the part of the public, or from a tendency to credit the 'wonderful' Germans with secret service tricks even more fantastic than those invented by the writers of fiction, on one point at least the public had correct information: before the war the Germans undoubtedly had the finest secret service in the world. It is certain that there was very little they did not know about pre-war Allied armies and navies.

This service of theirs was organised with characteristic German thoroughness; it worked in direct contact with their Foreign Office and with the general staffs of their army and navy, who used it often to obtain all required information of a secret nature which they could not obtain through diplomatic or other regular channels; its agents were all picked men and women, who went through a special course of training before they were sent out into the field. Some were permanently fixed in a definite country; others, using Berlin as a base, were sent abroad on special missions. Graves, the German spy who was arrested in

England just before the war in an attempt to get specifications and details of the new British 14-inch naval guns, at that time under construction at Beardmore's in Glasgow, was a typical example of the well trained, intelligent German spy. He would never have been caught had it not been for the carelessness [or was it betrayal?] of the German secret service, who misaddressed a letter sent to him.

Men of this type were not chosen at random or given *carte blanche* as to their activities, but dispatched to secure specific data. They were picked to obtain such varied information as the design of a new engine of war, details of training, equipment, and strength of a foreign army, plans of fortifications and even topographical sketches of certain sectors of a country, or perhaps plates for the printing of accurate maps of a country in which at some future date they might be called upon to conduct a campaign. Thus, for example, at the commencement of the war, the German war maps of Belgium were far more accurate than those possessed by the British – a matter of prime importance in modern warfare, where most artillery fire is indirect, preliminary angles and ranges being measured off on a map. The gun platforms which were laid down before the war in France and Belgium by German spies, or under their supervision, although greatly exaggerated in number, were no myth, but an actual fact.

Once the war began, however, the permanent German agents in France – and especially in Great Britain – were gradually cut off from their base by the efficient control exercised at the various ports of exit and entry, and by the watchful eye of the censor's department, which was instrumental in catching quite a number of spies. Every trick involving the use of invisible inks or chemicals, which the Germans were very fond of using, or the employment of codes in connection with letters, telegrams, or newspaper advertisements, was uncovered. One of the most crafty schemes to be defeated was the method by which the German agents received and concealed their supplies of invisible inks and chemicals. Handkerchiefs or apparently innocent supplies of extra clothing were impregnated with the material, and when ink was needed the cloth was soaked in water and wrung out. Such inks were used not only between the lines of an ordinary letter, but under the postage stamps, and on the inside, or even under the gummed parts, of envelopes.

A last precaution against German espionage was to delay letters and telegrams to neutral countries so long that any information they might have contained became worthless for any military or naval use. Even parcels were held, for it had been discovered that the German agents conveyed brief reports by a code method of long and short stitches, or some other stitching device, used on the garments or other cloth articles enclosed, and by sending packages of a shape secretly agreed upon, or wrapped in coloured paper which had a meaning for the colleague to whom it was addressed.

At length, for the transmission of their information, the Germans came to rely almost entirely on Germans with forged neutral passports, or on neutrals, a certain number of whom were allowed to travel to and from the allied countries. This was proved by the number of spies of this category who were shot.

It was no easy matter for a neutral to get to England. The sailors of neutral ships were not allowed to land, and visas were granted only to those neutrals who had pressing business to transact and whose *bona fides*, antecedents, and sympathies were known. In each neutral country there was an efficient counter-espionage organisation, and it would have surprised many an individual to have seen the accurate information obtained about him before a visa was accorded. The British counter-espionage organisation, located in T's office in Rotterdam under the direction of de Mestre, was typical. No visa was granted to a Dutch subject until the applicant had been checked over by de Mestre himself. The name of every neutral who was suspected of trading with the enemy, or of being pro-German, was inserted in the British Black List, which was in the hands of all consular or passport officers. Inclusion in this list meant automatic barring from England. As to the traveller's purposes, and the usual commercial information, it was not only obtained through recognised business channels, such as the banks, but in many cases the applicant was watched for a long time by our agents. Every movement was followed; I often laughed over the indiscretions of some of the individuals – in the hands of their wives the information would have been devastating.

Whether any of these individuals of neutral nationality ever used the diplomatic dispatch-bags of one or another of the neutral countries, I do not know, and it would have been almost impossible to find out. I know, however, that Mata Hari was suspected of this. It was a danger we had to face, but about which we could not do very much. The probable procedure in such a case would be that Smith, a citizen of Slavonia, would have a personal friend at his country's embassy in London to whom he would hand a letter addressed to Jones, possibly a common friend in their home country. At the opening of the diplomatic bag, which of course was immune from censorship, the letter would be found and automatically posted and this procedure could then be repeated in the reverse direction. It is unlikely that a diplomatic representative would lend himself wittingly to the transmission of a spy's report, but he might do it to oblige a pretty woman, or a friend, who would, of course, assure him that the only motive was to avoid the embarrassment of having some official in the British censor's office read one's private affairs.

In addition to these activities, de Mestre's agents also kept watch on all known German agents in Holland. Through their movements and contacts, we often got valuable clues as to who were transmitting reports to the Germans. Old Haas and his niece were de Mestre's best agents; no one could possibly have suspected this old man, or his unobtrusive niece, as being sleuths in British pay. In appearance they were so colourless that even in a small gathering they would have attracted no attention; in addition, they were good linguists, intelligent, observant, and endowed with unlimited patience – qualities which made them invaluable as CE agents.

Finally, the various counter-espionage organisations in the different neutral countries were able to check up on any individual reported as being suspect by the chief in England, or about whom information was required – for example, the person to whom a suspicious letter had been addressed. It was surprising how often a spy was caught by some small slip. I remember a case where the British censor became suspicious of a letter addressed to a man in Holland. De Mestre traced the address to a German agent. In the letter, which was, of course, written from a fictitious address in England, a message was included asking for all letters to be sent in future to a street number up in the 2000s. A check of the London streets soon showed that there were only two or three streets with such high numbers. An investigation was undertaken, which promptly led to the arrest of the German agent who was acting as a letter box.

As will readily be understood the German secret service had tremendous difficulties to face during the war. Communication across the sea (a far more effective barrier than any high voltage wire), a highly efficient censor's department, hawk-eyed passport control officers at the various ports, unceasing watching on the part of the Allied CE agents, and the absence of willing spies of their own or of allied nationality operating in their own country or in occupied territory, were obstacles greater than those I had to contend with.

From Berlin the old pre-war German secret service continued to function. It, too, had spread itself, and although it continued to send out agents direct from Berlin, many of them were recruited by its branches, which it established in neutral countries, and in the occupied territories.

The difficulty of communication was not its only problem; it had to face both a scarcity of agents and a falling-off of efficiency as compared with those of its pre-war service. No longer, could it pick its men, train them, and send them where it wished. It had to accept anyone who could fulfil the prime function of either being able to get in or out of a belligerent country, or who had some means of communication. The result was that many of its wartime agents were inefficient, careless, and stupid. Lody, who was caught during the early stages of the war, was a typical example. Arriving in England, armed with an American passport, he was able to enter the country undetected among the crowd of Belgian refugees who were then flocking into England. Carelessly worded telegrams which he sent out to a neutral country promptly gave him away. He was followed continuously for a couple of weeks in an attempt to link him up with other agents, and, when this proved futile, he was finally arrested in Ireland. In his possession the Irish police found a mass of entirely unnecessary incriminating documents which were conclusive evidence against him. However stupid he may have been, he faced death bravely, earning the unstinted admiration of everyone who came in contact with him during the few days he was confined to the Tower of London before he was shot.

The German secret service probably obtained its most valuable information either through influential neutrals living in the Allied countries, or through traitors whom they occasionally were able to bribe by means of large sums of money. People of the type of Bolo Pasha and his accomplices in France, although comparatively rare, were the most dangerous because they were the least suspected, and often had access to information which no neutral or other agent could reach.

From Holland I naturally came more in contact with the Belgian branch of the German secret service than with any of the others, though even here it was only on rare occasions. The German counter-espionage service, whose job it was to prevent spying in Belgium and with whom I was continually crossing swords, was entirely separated from the German secret service proper, whose sole function was to send agents into the Allied countries or recruit them in the countries themselves, and collect the information they secured.

The Belgian branch of the German CE service, or Secret Police, had its headquarters at a house located in the rue Berlaimont, in Brussels. In my narrative I have already described its activities; its agents dogged us at every turn, and earned our respect and admiration. During the earlier stages of the war, it was under the direction of a man called Bergan, who was formerly at the head of the German counter-espionage service in Düsseldorf. Bergan was the guiding genius whose task it was to combat each move we made, and at the same time keep watch on several million Belgian inhabitants. Strange to say, Bergan could not speak a word of French, and so in his actual contact with the Belgians, he was very dependent on his assistant R, a former German agent, who had operated in France before the war under the guise of a butcher. Little had the Parisians known, when they bought their meat from this red-cheeked, rotund individual, that he was in German pay.

The German secret service in Belgium, distinct from the German counter-espionage organisations previously described, was under the direction of a mysterious woman, known as Fräulein Doktor, and under a dozen other names. She was said to be the daughter of a noble family whose influence had secured for her the appointment. The truth about her is that she won her appointment by merit. Her real name was Elsbeth Schragmüller. At the outbreak of the war, she had just taken her degree of Doctor of Philosophy at the University of Freiburg. Inspired by a desire to serve her country she made repeated applications for enrolment in the German secret service. Eventually during the early weeks of the war she was sent to Brussels where she was put to work reading confiscated letters written to Belgian civilians by relatives in the field. So brilliantly did she acquit herself in intelligence work that she won the commendation of General von Beseler, chief of staff of the corps besieging Antwerp, and shortly thereafter Colonel Nicolai, chief of Section IIIb of the general staff in charge of military intelligence, put her in charge of the German spy-training school in Antwerp. She was a good-looking, buxom woman, with the disposition of a tiger. From her headquarters in Antwerp she dispatched many an agent into England and France. It was said of her that she sent into a trap any agents who had played her false and whom she wished to get rid of. So confident of this were the British authorities in the case of one of her spies, whom they arrested immediately on his landing in England, that they merely imprisoned him for the duration of the war. Her policy was to make her agents so thoroughly afraid of her that fear of vengeance would deter them from treachery. Most of the information we had about her came from a Belgian who managed for a short while to enlist himself in her service. His report, in the form of a memorandum from C, was one of the first communications I read on entering the secret service.

In spite of Fräulein Doktor's efforts and those of headquarters in Berlin, it was quite evident from the questionnaires issued to their agents, which fell into our hands from time to time as the war progressed, that the Germans were getting very little information out of England; the result was that they gradually concentrated their efforts on Russia, and probably on the United States, where the activities of Captain Boy-Ed and his satellites were fully unmasked.

This very deflection from their chief aim served them well,

for it revived the belief in the omnipresence and omniscience of German power, and renewed the spy hysteria which had been an indirectly useful weapon earlier in the war. In future wars new inventions will have to be reckoned with; but not to be overlooked in importance will be the extraordinary effect of the psychology of fear and its eminently useful weapon, the dread of a net of spies.

CHAPTER 18

'40 OB'

WAR HAD BEEN declared between Germany and England but a few hours when a group of trawlers sailed from the east coast of England in the direction of Emden, the German port at the mouth of the Ems River where the Dutch coast joins that of Germany. To any German coastal patrol boat which might have spotted them, they were just some of the many fishing boats operating in the area. A boarding party would have revealed that they were manned chiefly by cable experts. Under the cover of darkness and mist, slipping silently between the Dutch islands in the vicinity, they grappled for the German deep-sea cables. Covered with mud and seaweed these cables were eventually hauled up on deck; and one after another they were cut and allowed to sink back into the depths.

It was a brilliant coup, conceived and executed by a young naval officer who, disguised as a fisherman, had mapped out the area several months before the war and had planned every step which had now been so successfully carried out.

After fruitlessly trying to get through on their cables, the Germans at length realised what had happened. To communicate with the outside world only two channels were now left open to them: cables owned by neutral countries, and wireless communication through the air. The ether soon buzzed with German coded wireless messages, not only to their diplomatic representatives in neutral countries, but also to those of their warships cut off in distant parts of the globe by the outbreak of hostilities.

The French immediately suggested jamming the German wireless, but the British had a craftier plan. They decided instead to intercept the messages and to use them to their own advantage. The idea was excellent. But how was this to be done? It was obvious that somehow or other the German codes had to be stolen or acquired, or some master mind had to be found who, by methods of cryptography, could break the multiple and intricate ciphers which were being used. The director of naval intelligence at the admiralty, to whom the task was assigned, quickly realised that both methods had to be used.

It is true that the art of cryptography can be developed by constant practice, but it also requires a special flair. Whence, at short notice, was the British Admiralty going to recruit the necessary personnel, and above all where was the man to be found who had sufficient experience to direct such a service? Chance favoured the British. In the admiralty itself was a man who, as a hobby, had made a life study of cryptography. This man was Sir

210

Alfred Ewing, director of naval education, a noted scientist; and it was to him that Admiral Sir Henry Oliver, director of naval intelligence at the outbreak of the war, turned.

Sir Alfred eagerly accepted the assignment. Starting with a staff of five men, he patiently trained them and then added to their number until eventually he had a band of fifty assistants – mathematicians, linguists, and, later, secret ink chemists. Space for Sir Alfred and his staff was found in the Old Admiralty Building in Room 40, and to keep the nature of the organisation secret it was always referred to as '40 OB' (Old Building).

Ewing's appointment was one of the most judicious ever made at the admiralty. While battles raged at the Front and at sea, this frail, slightly-built man, with his enormous head, bushy eyebrows and dark piercing eyes, tranquilly seated in his peaceful office at the admiralty listening attentively, learned through intercepted and decoded messages what the next moves of the enemy would be. Even though the Germans constantly invented new codes or combined existing ones, he and the men working under him were always able to solve their mystery.

The existence of the British cryptographic service was one of the most jealously guarded secrets of the war. Even some of the British Cabinet ministers did not know of its existence, and many a member of the admiralty never heard of it until long afterwards. But those who were in the know realised that it contributed largely to the ultimate victory of the Allies. The public for the first time heard of it in 1925 when Sir Alfred Ewing caused a sensation by referring to it in an address which he gave at the University of Edinburgh. Shortly afterwards, Lord Balfour made the following declaration: 'The country owes "40 OB" an immense debt of gratitude, a debt which, for the moment at least, cannot be paid. Secrecy was an essential part of the work and never was a secret better guarded.'

There are hundreds of code and cipher systems, some of which are simple, others so complex as to tax the uttermost ingenuity of the cryptographer. Some are based on a verse or prose passage, or on an intricate combination of numbers, others are as elementary as the prearranged interchange of the letters of the alphabet. Some require the use of ponderous code books; others, in order to prevent their falling into the hands of the enemy, can be committed to memory. The skilled cryptographer must take most of these in his stride.

Cryptography alone, however, could not possibly unravel the secrets of all the German coded messages which crowded both the air and other channels of communication. In the case of a simple code, it was possible for an expert to find the key by studying the words or letters which kept repeating themselves; but in the case of the big German codes, which generally had four or five figure numbers, corresponding to a list of different words and phrases, supplemented by some fixed dictionary to supply words missing from the list, it was necessary to have a copy of the actual code.

The dictionary part was worked by slips having numbers so spaced that they fitted opposite the words on each page; the number of the page was obtained by adding it on to the front or the back of the code number. Thus, for example, if the word 'jeopardy' occurred on page 63, and when putting the slip on this page the number 534 came opposite this word, then the code number for jeopardy would be either 63534, or 53463. This could be made more complicated by multiplying this number by a common factor, or adding a fixed sum. As the numbers on the slip were changed continually, and as there are hundreds of dictionaries of all sizes and editions in existence, this dictionary code was undecipherable without a key.

As many of the German coded messages were based on the larger codes, '40 OB' could therefore never have achieved its brilliant success had not many of these codes, by some means or other, fallen into the hands of the British. The difficult task of acquiring them devolved on the British naval intelligence service.

In October 1914, Captain W. R. Hall, who later was knighted and promoted to the rank of admiral, took over from Admiral Sir Henry Oliver the direction of the naval intelligence service. Sir Reginald, or 'Blinker' Hall, as he was affectionately known to his intimates, was splendidly endowed for this work. The following estimate of him made by Walter Hines Page, the American ambassador in London, in a confidential letter to President Wilson in 1917, was no exaggeration:

> *Hall is one genius that the war has developed. Neither in fiction nor in fact can you find any such man to match him. Of the wonderful things that I know he has done there are several that it would take an exciting volume to tell. The man is a genius – a clear case of genius. All other secret service men are amateurs by comparison … I shall never meet another man like him: that were too much to expect.*

Apart from Hall's intimate experience and knowledge of everything pertaining to secret service, he was an uncanny judge of character. One glance was sufficient for him to sum a man up.

It was thus that he immediately gauged the qualities of Ewing, chosen by his predecessor, and promptly gave him *carte blanche* in the running of '40 OB'. The rest of his staff were chosen and handled with equal perception. He also had a remarkable ability in cross-examination, which proved the downfall of many a suspected German spy who was snared in the net he laid for him. However watertight their story, as Horst von der Goltz and others found when they had to face him in 1915, he intuitively picked out the flaws in their alibis or defences. 'He can see through your very immortal soul. What eyes the man has got!' was the despairing remark of one of his victims. But it was the acquiring of German codes which was Sir Reginald's special vocation. Under his expert guidance and planning some were stolen by his daring agents; some were recovered from sunken German submarines and warships; others were captured by the British forces in various parts of the world. Although the British diplomatic and fighting services knew nothing about '40 OB' yet, as if attracted by a magnet, all information acquired by them pertaining to German codes found its way to Hall. His net was spun so finely that nothing missed him. To illustrate his methods we will tell how three of the many codes which fell into his hands were obtained.

A few hours after the German occupation of Brussels, the powerful wireless station at the Belgian capital had been converted to German use. As the intercepted messages started coming in to '40 OB', it became immediately evident to Sir Alfred Ewing that the Germans at the Brussels station were making extensive use of one of their large diplomatic codes. Many of the messages defied the efforts of some of his best cryptographers.

British agents, recruited from among the Belgians who remained behind in the occupied territory, were sending a steady stream of spy reports through to Holland. Here, then, was as good a field as any in which to attempt to secure possession of one of the larger German codes. H. 523, one of the best of the British agents, was charged with the mission. Careful observation and inquiry by him yielded results. He discovered that the German coding staff was located in the Kommandantur in Brussels and that it was composed of four coding clerks, one of whom was an Austrian, Alexander Soll, a brilliant young engineer, born in a suburb of London, whose father had moved with him to Brussels several years before the war. Immediately after the occupation of Belgium, the German and Austrian authorities had called to the colours all their nationals of military age residing in the territory, and young Soll had been one of them. His knowledge of the French language and of Brussels had won for him an assignment in the German counter-espionage service, and from there, in the course of time, he had been transferred as a coding clerk to the Kommandantur.

On receipt of agent H. 523's report, the British secret service was quick to seize on the point that Soll was born in London. A check-up of aliens registered in his suburb revealed that Soll had a relative still living there, that she was employed in an English family, and that, as in the case of so many Austrians, she was violently anti-German. It was not difficult, therefore, to persuade her to write a letter to her brother on fine tissue paper urging him to aid the British by securing for them the code. Her letter was handed to H. 523 on one of his periodical trips across the frontier into Holland.

To approach Soll directly was a dangerous and delicate undertaking, but H. 523 was skilled in the right methods of approach. After winning Soll's confidence by giving him news of his relative, H. 523 finally handed him her letter. At first Soll was afraid, but after considerable persuasion he eventually fell in with H. 523's plans. Soll's first thought was to steal the code, but H. 523 quickly pointed out to him that this would defeat their object, as the Germans would immediately change it. And so Soll set about the laborious task of secretly copying the code during his hours of service. This took him several months, since he could only do the copying during the odd moments he was left alone in the coding room during the luncheon hour. Finally, however, in April 1915 the task was completed. But to H. 523's dismay Soll refused to give him the code. He insisted instead on escaping across the frontier with it to Holland. In vain H. 523 pleaded with him that his flight would arouse the suspicion of the Germans that the code had been copied. But Soll was adamant; he had just received confidential information that he was about to be transferred to the Front; and from the firing line, above all, he wished to escape. Therefore, early in April 1915 on a moonless night, the two of them set out for the Belgian–Dutch frontier.

It was the period just after the Germans had completed their formidable barrier along the Belgian–Dutch border to prevent the passage of spy reports and to put a stop to the flow of refugees escaping across the border to join the Belgian Army. A high-voltage electric fence, 8 ft high, sentries every 100 yards, searchlights, police dogs, a horde of secret service Police, and mounted patrols covered the length of the frontier. Arriving near the border, Soll began to regret his decision. The danger was as real as being in the trenches. He was now glad to get rid of the compromising copy of the code by handing it to H. 523.

Equipped with india-rubber gloves and socks to enable them to cross the high-tension electric fence, the two men crouched in the long grass, awaiting the moment when the sentry near them would reach the point on his beat farthest away from them. But their wait was cut short, a police dog started barking, the alarm was given, the searchlights were switched on, and the sentry started shooting. H. 523, experienced in crossing the high-voltage electric fence, made a dash for the border and succeeded in getting across, but Soll turned back and tried to escape. H. 523 brought the code to Colonel Oppenheim, the British military attaché at The Hague; and in due course it was forwarded to Sir Reginald Hall. What happened to Soll will ever remain one of the mysteries of the war.

Soll's father, who lived with him in Brussels, never heard of his son again. He was convinced that his son got across the frontier; and when after the Armistice he failed to return home, he accused the British of making away with him to prevent the Germans finding out that the British had a copy of the code.

After the war, while in charge of the secret service section of the British intelligence commission, whose function it was to liquidate all the British spy services which had operated behind the German Western Front in occupied Belgium and north-eastern France, I came across some evidence to show that Alexander Soll had been kept in solitary confinement in the Namur prison, that he was tried by court-martial, found guilty of being a deserter from military service, and shot. My informant was a former German soldier who had served during the war as a warder at the prison. This man, born in Silesia, acquired Polish nationality by the Peace Treaty, and remained in Belgium after the Armistice. I am inclined to believe the warder's story – he had no reason to invent it – but Soll's father refused to accept it. To him it was just another ruse of the British to keep the truth away from him. On the other hand, if the Germans did shoot Alexander Soll, why did they not notify his father? And why after the war, when the father made inquiry in Berlin, did the German authorities inform him that they had no record of his son's execution?

Whatever the solution to the mystery, and whatever suspicions the Germans may have had, it is evident that they were not aware that the British had secured a copy of the code, for, except for a few minor variations, it remained unchanged and in active use until the end of the war.

For the story of the second code we must now switch to another part of the world. One of the principal sources of oil supply for the British fleet was the oil wells of the Anglo-Persian company in Persia. These oil wells, situated several hundred miles inland, were connected to the Persian Gulf by a pipeline. The protection of this vital artery of supply became a supreme necessity. The task was a difficult one, owing to the length of the pipeline and the barren nature of the country through which it ran. The whole length of it could not be guarded at the same time, and the surveillance had to be entrusted to mounted patrols. Not only had these patrols to watch out for marauding bands of Turks and Kurds, who knew the terrain much better than the British, but Persia itself was a hotbed of German intrigue; and, as was the case in other neutral countries, it was overrun by German agents, who, in most cases, were directed by some German official enjoying diplomatic immunity.

Von K— the German consul at Shiraz, was specially active, and of this fact the British intelligence service was fully aware. In fact, so well were they posted as to his activities, and so closely was he watched, that the British knew several days ahead of time of a raid on the pipeline he planned to carry out with the help of Kurdish irregulars.

The date and the locality of the raid being known, an ambush was laid for Von K— and his band of Kurds. It was a surprised German consul who found himself surrounded and forced to surrender before more than a shot or two had been fired. Pleased as the British were with their haul, they were even more delighted and surprised when they discovered an important German code in the possession of Von K—. So sure had he been of success that with characteristic German thoroughness, he had brought the code along with him. He had wished to lose no time in sending through to the Turkish lines, for wireless transmission to Berlin, a coded message announcing the details of his coup.

The code was promptly forwarded to Sir Reginald Hall. It was the German code number 13040. It proved later to be one of the biggest scoops of the war.

Even though the Germans heard of the capture of Von K—, it never dawned on them that he could have been so foolish and indiscreet as to have permitted the code to fall into the hands of the British.

Several codes were also recovered from German warships sunk by the British Navy. Of these the code from the cruiser *Madgeburg* was one of the most important. Within a few minutes after a British torpedo struck her, she went to the bottom, and only a handful of the crew were saved. Days afterwards a British torpedo boat patrolling the area sighted a floating body. It turned out to be the commander of the *Magdeburg*. Buttoned securely in his tunic was the code book. Some of the survivors later testified that when last they saw their commander, he was standing on deck with the code book clasped in his hands.

Such, then, was the organisation which Hall had brought to perfection. Not only was there '40 OB', which was capable of mastering every German cipher, but also Sir Reginald's network spread throughout the world, which was able to acquire by theft or capture every important German code. This combination of skilled cryptographers and the actual possession of the large German codes enabled Sir Reginald and his organisation to decipher every German coded message which came into their possession.

To pick up the German wireless messages, receiving stations were erected at Lowestoft, Lerwick, Murcar, and York. These stations not only sufficed to intercept the messages for dispatch to '40 OB', but they served also as radio goniometric stations to furnish bearings for triangulating the position of any German vessel using its wireless.

Not satisfied with intercepting every German wireless message which flashed through the air, agents were actively employed in all neutral countries to secure copies of coded telegrams and cables sent out by German diplomatic representatives over neutral telegraph and cable lines.

Long before the war Germany had seen the necessity of establishing a complete wireless system throughout the world. In accordance with this plan she had in 1911 erected a wireless station at Sayville, Long Island. This foresight had permitted her throughout the first two months of the war to have untrammelled wireless communication with her representatives in the United States. But in September 1914 the United States government seized the station, realising that it was being used to direct movements of German commerce raiders still at sea and was thereby infringing American neutrality. At the same time a censorship was enforced and the sending of coded messages was prohibited.

German ingenuity, however, soon found a means of evasion. Receiving the incoming messages sent out every morning at 3 a.m. from the powerful German station at Nauen, near Berlin, was simple. Many of the interned German ships, although forced to take down their regular antennæ, re-rigged them in funnels or other places of concealment. Several secret receiving stations were also erected in private homes. The sending of messages, however, was more difficult. One method was to use prearranged key phrases embedded in apparently innocent commercial telegrams; but for messages important enough to demand the use of one of their large codes they availed themselves chiefly of neutral channels, especially those provided by Sweden. The Swedish Foreign Office was notoriously pro-German, and German messages were frequently put in Swedish cipher and sent to Swedish ministers in other countries for delivery to their German colleagues. Incredible though it may seem, Germany also occasionally beguiled the state department on one pretext or another into forwarding her messages.

The British network of agents in the neutral countries picked up most of these cables, however; and even those forwarded through the state department were intercepted in London, as the cable lines from the United States to Europe passed through the British Isles. In Holland, one of the British agents was specially assigned to procure through secret connections of his in the Dutch telegraph office, copies of all telegrams sent to Berlin by the German minister at The Hague. Such a telegram, intercepted by a British agent in neutral Chile and decoded by '40 OB', gave the British Admiralty the information that Admiral von Spee and his squadron were about to sail from Valparaiso for the Falkland Islands. This permitted the admiralty to draft the plan which led to the sinking of von Spee's ships by Admiral Sturdee. Proof of the efficiency of the British network was that a telegram which was sent through four different routes to von Eckhardt, the German minister to Mexico, was picked up by the British in each case.

By 1916 over 2,000 coded messages were coming into '40 OB' daily, and not one failed to be decoded. Relying upon the secrecy of their codes, the Germans were amazingly loquacious. They filled the air with the most secret information concerning their army, navy, and diplomatic service, and all this '40 OB' grasped out of the ether. In addition most of the German messages sent over neutral cables were also intercepted. The result was that the British had as accurate information about German affairs as the Germans themselves. To cite a few instances: the movements of German warships were known in the cases of each of the principal naval engagements; and in the case of the Battle of the Dogger Bank, the British knew twenty-four hours ahead of time which German warships had left port and the

times of their departures; track was kept of all German submarines, and a map was kept on the wall in '40 OB' showing the
position of each one as revealed by its wireless messages;
the admiralty was warned well in advance about each Zeppelin raid; the activities of Sir Roger Casement in Germany were
flashed freely back and forth between Berlin and von Bernstorffi
in Washington, and the British knew the exact day he embarked
by submarine for the west coast of Ireland, and thus were able
to lie in wait for him. The German confidence in their codes
also cost their intelligence services dear: the names and activities of dozens of their spies were revealed in their messages,
and this was the cause of many a sensational arrest.

Not until after the war did the Germans realise that all their
coded messages had been an open book to the British and consequently to all the Allies. They continued to use most of their
larger codes throughout the war, and even when changes were
made, these were transmitted by wireless in the old code; con-
scquently '40 OB' was able to listen in and make note of these
changes. Even the precautionary measures they adopted were
exploited by '40 OB'. For example, whenever a Zeppelin started
out on a raid over England, it left the regular naval code behind,
and instead took along with it a special code, prefixed 'HVB'
This was in case it was shot down. Preliminary to a raid, each
Zeppelin taking part in it radioed 'HVB alone on board'; this was
sufficient indication to '40 OB' that a raid was about to take place.

But it would be unfair to Sir Reginald Hall if we blamed the
Germans entirely for their blind confidence in their codes. Great
credit is due him for the tricks he invented to keep the Germans
in the dark. Again and again during the war he was puzzled how

to make use of his information without betraying the existence of '40 OB'. His ingenuity in this was almost as great as the skill of his organisation in intercepting and decoding the messages. Even in communicating information to British staff officers of the army and navy, the source was always carefully camouflaged.

Many ingenious ruses were employed by Sir Reginald to mislead the Germans. From action taken by the British on information contained in the German coded messages, it eventually became obvious to the Germans that there was a serious leak somewhere. At all costs Hall had to dispel any suspicion among the Germans that their codes were compromised, or could be deciphered by an organisation such as '40 OB'. Two of his agents, both of French nationality, played an important role in this work of deception. One of them was an attaché at the French embassy in a neutral country, the other was a member of the French secret service. Both of them posed as traitors and succeeded in winning the confidence of the Germans. Apart from giving the Germans information which the Allies could afford to let them know, they would occasionally startle the Germans by giving them information about the most secret German plans gleaned by Hall either through '40 OB' or from one of his spies in Germany. On one occasion the bogus traitors informed the Germans that Sir Roger Casement had embarked on a German submarine and was on his way to the west coast of Ireland. (Hall knew that the submarine was at sea and could not be stopped.) In reply to the frantic demands of the Germans as to the source of the information, all the two informants could offer was that it was a most jealously guarded secret, but that they had been able to discover that the information came from a high official in Germany who was in the pay of one of the Allies. Since Hall's two agents were located in two different neutral countries and played their parts with infinite astuteness, the Germans considered the information supplied by the one as a corroboration of that of the other. Desperately the German counter-espionage service attempted to locate the arch-traitor, and as time went on offered a fabulous reward for information which would lead to his arrest. In the meantime, Hall and '40 OB' calmly continued to extract Germany's most intimate and vital secrets from her coded messages which flowed back and forth between Berlin and the outside world.

CHAPTER 19

SPY FROM THE SKY

I T WAS JUST before the big March offensive of the Germans, in 1918. The Allied High Command had every indication that the Germans were about to make their last and supreme effort, but until the offensive actually broke loose, they could never be sure where the main attack was to be.

The Germans were masters in the art of concealing their plans, and with the network of railways behind their front, they could quickly displace troops from one sector to another.

The back areas were of great interest to the Allied Command, and we were urged to obtain the fullest possible information about them. Our agents in the Hirson and Valenciennes areas of France, and those around Arlon, Maubeuge, Givet, and the rest of Belgium, did their part nobly, but in spite of all our efforts,

227

we were unable to penetrate into the Grand Duchy of Luxembourg. The inhabitants of the Grand Duchy, although they had very strong Belgian and French sympathies, are Teutonic in origin, and so there was a sufficiently large barrier between the Grand Duchy and Belgium to prevent our expanding our Belgian organisation into it. As it happened, our agents round Fourmies, Hirson, Avesnes, and Aulnoye reported brilliantly the real concentration of the enemy's troops, for it was opposite this area that the big German offensive was launched; still, an uncontrolled area such as the Grand Duchy was always a source of alarm, since anything might be happening there. It can, therefore, be readily understood why British GHQ decided upon direct action.

A plan was accordingly hit upon to drop a man armed with a basket of carrier pigeons into the area by parachute from a plane, at night. The dropping of the man presented no special difficulty; planes often crossed the enemy lines at night on bombing raids. But to find the right man was a problem. First of all, he had to be a Luxemburger, for only a Luxemburger could speak the Low German dialect of the people in the Grand Duchy; and secondly, he had to know the country well, and have friends who could hide him if necessary. It had also to be a man who would volunteer to undertake the mission. The man was found, however, by the British intelligence service in France, and the mission was successfully carried out.

After the Armistice, in Brussels, I met S, the hero of this story. In fact, we saw quite a lot of each other; frequently we dined together at the Savoy. He had a stock of interesting stories about the Belgian Congo, where he had spent many years, but he would not tell me at first what piqued my interest the most: how it had come about that he, a subject of the Grand Duchy, was wearing the uniform of a major in the British Army, and how he had won the much coveted Distinguished Service Order, which, during the war, was only given for bravery or special service in the field. From a fellow British officer I got the bare details of his story, which eventually over a few drinks S told me in full.

For several years before the war, S had occupied a post as engineer of one of the mines in the Congo. As the war went on, he saw most of his Belgian colleagues leave, one by one, to join the Belgian Army, until he finally felt the urge himself. Having been so long in the Congo, and coming as he did from the Grand Duchy with its strong Belgian sympathies, he never gave a thought to the possibility that the Belgian authorities in Folkestone would refuse to enrol him in the Belgian Army. But so they did. Determined to get to France, he applied to the British authorities, who, realising how useful he would be in their intelligence service, immediately gave him a commission as Lieutenant in the army. It was here that they found him in their search for a Luxemburger. He had been disappointed at not getting into the actual fighting line, and here was action at last. He joyfully accepted.

He fully realised the danger of the undertaking. The aeroplane flight across the enemy front, and the actual drop by parachute, was nothing compared to the risk he ran of discovery, which would have meant his instant execution by the Germans. He had no idea where he would land in the dark; it might be on the top of a house, or in an enemy camp. Even after successful landing, the parachute had to be destroyed, a hiding place for the pigeons had to be found, and he had to scout around over a large area to get the information so urgently needed by GHQ.

During the months he had already been in the intelligence service, his time had been spent chiefly in interrogating captured prisoners of war; so he was already sufficiently well grounded in intelligence work, in the organisation of the German Army, and in the distinguishing marks of the different units which comprised a German division, to be able to undertake the mission without further training. His job was explained to him in a few minutes: he had to cover as much of the Grand Duchy as he could in as short a time as possible, and report on the number of troops, and, if possible, the identity of the division and regiments which he found in the area.

A pilot was chosen who had participated in several aeroplane raids on objectives in the Grand Duchy, and who knew the country comparatively well. S was instructed in the use of a parachute, and also in the method of attaching messages to the pigeons, but by far the most important task was to indicate to the pilot on a large scale map exactly where he wished to be dropped. If he could reach his father's house on the outskirts of Ettelbrück before daylight, he knew he would be safe, for there he could deposit his pigeons, and using his father's house as a base, he could scour the country.

As soon as it was dark, on a night when there was no moon, the adventure was begun. Taking off from an aerodrome near Albert, S and the pilot had to cover about 150 miles, and in the darkness of the night, all that the pilot had to guide him was his compass and his instruments. Flying at a great altitude, no interference was met with from German planes, and after a flight of about two hours, the pilot touched his passenger; it was time to get going. With his basket containing twenty of the best army pigeons strapped to him, S went over the side.

Luck was with him; he landed in a field, severely shaken up but unhurt. Some 50 yards away he discovered a hedge, and in this he hid both the parachute and the pigeons. He now cursed the darkness of the night, for although in possession of a flashlight, he dared not make use of it. Setting out at right angles to the hedge in search of a road, he crossed another hedge, and suddenly found himself on a good macadam road. After following it for about half a mile, he came to crossroads and a signpost. To his joy, he discovered that he was about 20 miles from Ettelbrück. He now knew exactly where he was, for this was his home district every inch of which was known to him. Back once again he retraced his steps to get the birds, and then he struck out on the hazardous journey to his father's house.

It was 10.30 p.m. by his wrist watch; he had ample time to cover the distance before daylight. At least a dozen times he left the road suddenly to hide from an approaching cart or people on foot; he was glad by this time of the friendly darkness. The 20-mile tramp was the most terrifying part of the whole undertaking, he told me. The parachute jump he had accepted stoically; once he had undertaken the mission, he knew he had to go through with it, just as a soldier feels, when he goes over the top in an attack, that there is no alternative. But walking along the road with the incriminating pigeons was different; every sound alarmed him, and he knew, contrary to what he had felt while he was in the air, that he was now sole master of his own destiny: getting to his father's house depended on his ingenuity alone.

Eventually, with worn-out nerves, he reached his father's home at about three o'clock in the morning. As he stood before the house, he suddenly felt alarmed; he hadn't heard from his father for several months; perhaps he had moved, and there were German troops quartered there. Hastily he hid his pigeons, and grasping his revolver, he knocked on the window of what used to be his father's bedroom. After a while, to his relief, the familiar grey head appeared through the window. With a cry of astonishment, the father recognised his son, and within a few seconds he was in the house.

The father, like the son, was pro-Allies, and though there were some remonstrances from the mother, a hiding place was soon found in the attic for the pigeons, and two were immediately sent off to announce his safe arrival.

S realised that the greatest danger he ran was in his own home district, where everyone either thought he was still in the Congo, or had heard that he had joined the Allied forces. He, therefore, persuaded his father to cover his own district, while he, after remaining in the house all day, got out of the area as fast as he could, under cover of darkness.

Within a week, amply supplied with funds, he was able to cover the area comprising the Grand Duchy. Three divisions were discovered at rest, one at Wiltz, and the other two at Bettingen and Petange. As this was the normal number to be found in these areas, he was able to report to GHQ that there was no concentration of troops in the Grand Duchy, and this was all they wanted to know. A hazardous and desperate experience for a single negative statement – but the value of the statement was as great as the agent's daring. To ensure his reports reaching GHQ, three pigeons were sent off with the same messages, two of which, he subsequently discovered, arrived safely. After sending these messages off, S went into hiding in the town of Luxembourg, and there he stayed the few remaining months until the Armistice.

He rejoined the British Army after the Armistice. He was congratulated by the chief of staff, promoted to the rank of major, and decorated with the much-coveted Distinguished Service Order. This was the story of the small, sandy-haired, tropic-dried Luxemburger, weighing scarcely more than 9 stone. I wouldn't have believed it of this mild-mannered reticent man, if I had not had corroborative evidence from a fellow officer, and if I had not seen with my own eyes his major's crown and the ribbon of the DSO.

CHAPTER 20

AN ASTOUNDING PROPOSITION FROM THE HAMBURG SOLDIERS' COUNCIL – AND EXIT THE KAISER

EVENTS WERE CROWDING fast on each other. The Hindenburg line had broken, and the whole Allied Front was sweeping rapidly forward into Belgium; Prince Max of Baden had formed a coalition ministry, and had been forced to include two socialist deputies, Scheidemann and Bauer. It was evident that the war was drawing to a close, and that the people of Germany were about to kick over the traces; rumours of revolt and discontent were becoming more insistent each day.

Such was the situation when suddenly we heard of the mutiny of the German sailors at Kiel, on some of the ships of the German High Seas Fleet which had been ordered to put out to sea. This was followed by reports that Liebknecht and other independent socialists were openly inciting revolution, and that local government had been overthrown in Kiel, Hamburg, and Bremen, with soldiers' councils taking its place.

Imagine my excitement when I walked into one of the cubicles at the office, and found myself facing a released pre-war British spy, and in his company an official delegate from the Hamburg soldiers' council.

'I am Johnson' – a fictitious name – said the Englishman. 'Don't you remember me? I was caught by the Germans six years ago, just as I was boarding a vessel at Hamburg, and thought I had got clear with the plans which C commissioned me to get. I have been in prison in Hamburg all these years, and was freed by the Hamburg Soldatenrat a week ago. This is Schultze, a delegate from them,' he continued as he presented his companion to me. 'He has been sent out with me on a mission to the British government.' I listened in amazement to their story, as each took it up in turn.

The prisoners of yesterday were the masters of Hamburg today. The governor of the prison was at present locked up in one of his own cells, and while Johnson and his friends were being entertained at a banquet in the Hamburg Senate House, their former keeper was being given prison fare, his own special recipe for 'socialist swine'.

How Johnson came by his new-found friend, he explained briefly. During his early days in prison, Johnson's only companions were criminals, but as the war progressed, and the Kaiser's government viewed with alarm the steady growth of socialism, members of the Minority Socialist Party began to swell the ranks of the inmates of the prison at Altona, near Hamburg. With these leaders Johnson rapidly made friends; they ate the same vile prison food; they, too, were victims of the Kaiser; they were intelligent men, a relief from the dregs he had been forced to associate with.

When they were freed by their friends, these leaders immediately rushed back to their home centres, but those from Hamburg gladly took Johnson along with them as one of their companions. He was admitted to all their councils, and found himself enrolled as a member of the Hamburg Soldatenrat.

Plans of government were suggested, and it was difficult to keep the sailors in check, but on one point everyone from Hamburg was agreed: they had had enough of Prussian domination, and wanted to be freed entirely from it. Why not revive the old Hanseatic League, a federation of the Hanseatic towns of Hamburg, Bremen, Lübeck, and Danzig? They remembered how prosperous these towns had been during the era of their independence, and how friendly they had been with England.

The leaders knew that Prussia and the rest of Germany would never willingly agree to this separation, which would cut them off from the sea, and that, as soon as the revolution had quietened down, they would be attacked, unless they obtained help from the Allies. Surely, the Allies would support them; it would be a means of removing the German fleet from the sea, never to return, and it would help in the dismemberment of Germany, which they had heard the Allies intended to accomplish.

Ways and means were discussed. Why not set up a Hanseatic League under the protection of England, and ask the British to send some part of their fleet to Hamburg and the other ports? This would prevent interference from the rest of Germany. Quick action had to be taken, while yet they were masters of the situation. A delegate had to be sent immediately to England to open up negotiations. Their eyes fell on Johnson: he was obviously the man to send along; he had been an eyewitness of everything that had happened; he could tell the British that they meant everything they said, and that they really had complete control of the local government.

I still have a mental picture of Johnson as he shouted at me in his excitement: 'There is no German fleet left – the sailors have all mutinied. On the arrival of the British fleet in Hamburg, the admiral in command will be given an official reception and he will be entertained at a banquet at the Senate House. The old Hanseatic League, under British protection, with Hamburg as its head, will then be publicly proclaimed!'

If Schultze had not been sitting next to him with his array of official documents, signed by the Hamburg Soldatenrat, giving him full power to negotiate, I would have thought that six years of detention in a German prison, in wartime, had deranged Johnson's mind; for although I knew all the events which I have already outlined, the Kaiser had not yet crossed the frontier, the Armistice had not yet been signed, and there was considerable rumour that the Germans were about to stage a revolution, hoping that the emissaries of the people would get better peace terms from the Allies than the old wartime leaders would have been able to secure.

Full details were immediately telegraphed in code to London, and I was still waiting for instructions, when I suddenly had news that the Kaiser had fled from Berlin, and had arrived at German GHQ, at Spa, only a few miles from the Dutch Limburg frontier. Leaving my assistant in charge at Rotterdam, I dashed down to Maastricht so as to be able to direct our operations at closer quarters; Colonel Oppenheim wanted short interval reports on everything we could possibly find out as to what was happening at Spa.

The German sentries and surveillance on the frontier had become demoralised, and quite a number of refugees were coming freely across the frontier; we could, therefore, arrange for a quicker transmission of information from the interior to us. Train-watchers' reports were no longer important. Every road in Belgium was now filled with the retreating German Army; the trains could no longer carry them. The roads had now to be watched; *promeneurs* had to be kept continually behind the German Army reporting their movements as they fell back. My headquarters were now in Maastricht, and I had a direct courier to Colonel Oppenheim at The Hague. Sleep was forgotten; more work was in hand than I could possibly cope with.

I never returned to Rotterdam. After witnessing the crossing of the frontier by the Kaiser, I penetrated into Belgium, throwing discretion to the winds, and from personal observation sent in reports on the retreat of the German Army as it filed past my eyes.

No wonder then that I lost track of Johnson and Schultze, whom I had left in the hands of my assistant. Many weeks later he told me that the British government had refused to negotiate with Schultze. With more political sagacity than was shown later at Versailles, it realised probably that, for a permanent peace, conditions had to be imposed on Germany which would not interfere with her economic existence. A nation of Germany's size had to have an outlet to the sea; and sooner or later, if taken away from her, she would fight to regain it. Furthermore, the British undoubtedly foresaw that the sailors of Kiel, Bremen, and Hamburg, and the Soldatenrat throughout Germany would eventually lose control of their local government, and that they were only the torch lighting the revolution which was to culminate in the formation of the German Republic.

Within a few hours of the news that the Kaiser had arrived at German GHQ in his flight from Berlin, I was on my way to take up my headquarters at Maastricht, the principal town in Dutch Limburg, and only some 30 miles from Spa, that pretty little Belgian watering-place with its fine chateaux and villas, whose comforts the Kaiser and his staff had enjoyed earlier in the war, and where those trenches and dug-outs were constructed, several hundred miles from the Front, in which the Kaiser was photographed to appear as if he were among his soldiers in the firing line. Here now the whole German GHQ had taken up its quarters.

Our agent there reported not only the presence of the Kaiser, but also of the Crown Prince, Hindenburg, Ludendorff, and a host of others. On 8 November, we heard that the socialists under Kurt Eisner had deposed the King of Bavaria, and had declared a Bavarian Republic. On 9 November, we read in the newspapers the decree of Prince Max announcing that the Kaiser had decided to abdicate, and that Ebert was appointed Chancellor.

I was not surprised, therefore, when late that evening I received a report from our agent that barricades had been thrown up around Spa to prevent revolutionary troops coming there from Aachen to fetch the Kaiser, and that the Kaiser himself intended crossing into Holland that night. I dashed to the Dutch commanding officer, whom I knew very well, and with whom I had had lunch that day at the Maastricht Club, to tell him the news.

'Yes,' said he, 'we have just been informed from The Hague that the Kaiser is coming across the frontier at Eysden, at 7 a.m. tomorrow. I have received orders about interning him. Do you want to come along with me?' I gladly accepted his offer, and at 6 a.m. I found myself keyed up with excitement on the way to Eysden, following the automobiles of the Dutch Army officers and other officials.

In my mind's eye, I can see the picture today as clearly as I saw it then. It was a fine morning, but at that early hour there was a ground mist, which made visibility somewhat difficult. I waited on the platform of the station at Eysden chatting to my officer friends. By and by, a train was signalled coming through from Visé, the Belgian border station adjacent to Eysden; it was the Kaiser's own special train, consisting of three or four coaches.

After a few minutes had elapsed, we saw several grey Mercedes cars draw up at the frontier; from them there alighted about a dozen figures in grey military uniforms, with long capes and spiked helmets. One was the Kaiser in the uniform of a field marshal, another General von Platen; the others were officers of the Kaiser's own staff and household, who were following him into exile. The group came on to the platform at Eysden, and there, about 15 yards from where I stood, they were formally interned

241

by my friend. After this the whole group entered the Imperial train, prepared and waiting for them.

It was one of the most impressive events of my life; not so much because of what I saw (the whole ceremony only took a few minutes – it might have been the internment of any group of officers crossing into Holland) as because of the realisation that I was watching the writing of 'Finis' across the life of a man who had been a demi-god in his own country, the almighty war lord, whom I had seen on many occasions riding with pomp and ceremony through the streets of Berlin, and who had so long disturbed the peace of Europe.

I wondered, as I looked at his grim white face, what was passing in his mind. He was pleasant to the Dutch officers, and outwardly appeared calm. He lit a cigarette and offered a cigar to my officer friend. Inwardly he must have been in a turmoil; it was undoubtedly a piece of clever acting. He had probably spent several sleepless nights before arriving at his momentous decision. He had been inclined to defy the politicians who demanded his abdication, but when Hindenburg and the general staff declared they could no longer protect him from an army seething with revolt, he had hastily fled. Here on the platform, however, he did not have at all the air of a fugitive. In uniform, surrounded by his officers, he was dignity personified; one would have said he had just arrived in Holland on a visit to the Dutch court.

All day, the Kaiser remained in his train at Eysden, while the Dutch Cabinet was deciding on their course of action. That night, van Karnebeek, the Dutch Foreign Minister, and Rosen, the German minister at The Hague, arrived in Maastricht. Once again I followed the Dutch officials to Eysden, but as the meeting took place in the train behind drawn blinds, my trip was fruitless. I was informed, however, by a Dutch officer, that the train would leave Eysden early the next morning to convey the Kaiser to the chateau of Count Goddard Bentinck, at Amerongen, where he would remain temporarily until a definite place of internment had been found.

Early on the morning of 11 November, I got up to watch the train go by at a crossing near Maastricht. All the blinds were drawn, as I thought they would be, but the passing of the Kaiser fascinated me; I wanted to see the very last act of this drama which I had been witnessing.

There was some mystery attached to the Kaiser's coming to Holland. I heard several rumours to the effect that the Queen had sent a secret emissary to Spa, offering him an asylum in Holland; but whether this was so I do not know. Everybody was now wandering what had happened to the Crown Prince. The Kaiser gave no definite information about him, except that he would probably cross into Holland later on. It was rumoured that there had been a family quarrel, which was borne out by subsequent events. We were not without news of him for long.

Once again I was lunching with my Dutch officer friend, after a busy morning sending reports to Colonel Oppenheim. We had just finished off an excellent partridge, and were waiting for the next course, when my friend was called out of the room. He dashed back a couple of minutes later, grabbed his sword, excused himself, and rushed away with the remark that the Crown Prince was at the frontier, at a point farther north than where the Kaiser had crossed. In the evening, he told me that the Crown Prince was staying temporarily at the chateau of Countess Wolf-Metternich. The first request of the Crown Prince, after crossing the frontier, was that he did not wish to see his father, or to be interned in the same place with him. Later, he was removed to the Island of Wieringen.

One more event was to happen which again focused my attention on the Kaiser. Months later, when I was installed in my office in the rue Stevin in Brussels, liquidating all the British secret service organisations in Belgium and occupied France, I received a visit from one Rubigny – a fictitious name – who, together with a fellow French agent, had been seized many months back by German Secret Police on Dutch soil and dragged several yards across the frontier into Belgium. The Dutch were powerless to do anything about the matter; the Germans declared that they were on Belgian soil when arrested, and as there were no other eyewitnesses, it was simply the agents' word against theirs. The two were condemned to prison in Liège, and when they were released at the time of the Armistice, three years of their life had been spent in confinement. Rubigny seemed a broken man; he raged against the Germans, especially against the Kaiser; he cursed them for the dirty trick they had played on the two of them, and swore he would get even. I tried to calm him, but without much apparent effect.

Shortly afterwards I got news from Holland that Rubigny had been arrested by the Dutch. Apparently he had tried to bribe the Kaiser's cook to poison his Royal master. I intervened with the Dutch authorities; I pleaded that his false imprisonment by the Germans had probably affected his mind. He was released by the Dutch and deported to Belgium. I never heard from him again.

CHAPTER 21

LIQUIDATION OF
THE SERVICE

T HE WAR WAS over, but not my work. At one time
and another during the course of the war, the British
secret service had employed over 2,000 agents in Belgium and occupied France, of whom more than 100 had been
shot, and several hundred had been imprisoned. The British government could not walk off and leave these people; pensions had
to be paid, some form of compensation had to be given to those
who had been imprisoned, decorations had to be awarded, and
a history had to be written of the organisations in the interior.

I was the logical person to be appointed to the task, for the
details were locked up within me, and I alone could tell in most

cases what the services were that each organisation had rendered. No written records had been kept. In the settlement of claims, my presence was necessary to decide what was authentic, and what were the merits of each case. I gladly accepted the mission. I could not wait until the Germans had got completely out of Belgium; I dashed across the border at the first opportunity to meet the brave men with whom I had been working so long. Many I had never met. I wanted to see them, face to face, to talk over the hundreds of incidents which had occurred, to compare notes, to find out reasons which had led up to arrests, to unravel mysteries which had baffled me in Holland – in short, to talk over the great adventure in which we had all played our parts.

I was deeply moved and excited at the prospect of seeing them all. For two and a half years I had sat in Holland running out invisible lines of communication, as it were, into a void, across the German barrier into Belgium, weaving to the left and to the right to make contacts one by one with those who had been so eagerly alert to serve their country. And now I was on my way to meet these hidden watchers whose lifelines I had held in my hands, whose faces I did not know, but whose innermost thoughts and anxieties had been so intimately my own. It was the most dramatic moment of my life.

The logical place for me to head for was Liège; it was the headquarters of the *Dame Blanche* or 'White Lady', the greatest of wartime Allied secret service organisations. In Liège I made my way hurriedly to an address which was engraved on my mind, one which St Lambert had communicated to me orally in Holland, and which I had never entrusted to paper. Warned of my coming, the two chiefs, and the heads of the organisation in each of the Belgian provinces, were waiting for me. As I entered the room where they were gathered, and I stood before them in the uniform of a British officer, they acclaimed me with emotion, and saluted me as their superior officer. I was overcome with their fervent expressions of welcome and loyalty. I found myself in the presence of a group of austere, almost ascetic-looking people, all much older than myself. Three were priests; the others were college professors, engineers, lawyers, and members of the professional classes.

I realised immediately why the 'White Lady' had been such a success; here were gathered together some of the most brilliant brains in Belgium, men filled with the highest ideals of patriotism. By the respect which they showed toward their two chiefs, I sensed the discipline which they had imposed upon themselves; I realised that their militarisation was not a fantasy, but that it had been carried out to the letter; these were the officers of a military organisation.

The two chiefs made an indelible impression on me. The one, tall, thin, with dark penetrating eyes and a black scrubby beard, breathed authority. I felt that here was a man who was accustomed to being obeyed; in pre-war days he had been an engineer, high up in one of the Belgian administrations, and it was probably there that he had learned to command and to organise. The other, a professor at the University of Liège, was an exact contrast – a small man with light hair, a long beard, blue limpid eyes, and a voice as soft as that of a woman.

After a luncheon in my honour, I was closeted with the two chiefs, and to them I outlined briefly my plan of action: they were to furnish me with a complete history of their organisation, showing the role played by each member; give me a list of all their members; provide me with full details concerning the two who had been shot so that I could procure for their families a pension from the British government; and, finally, so that I could arrange for repayment, they were to hand me an itemised statement showing the various sums which I had authorised them to borrow. Not a word did I say about the military status of which, on my own initiative, I had so boldly assured them; I was guiltily conscious that it was going to be extremely difficult to gain the consent of either Belgium or England to confirm such an arrangement, and I must confess to the mean hope that, now all was over, militarisation might not seem so important to the 'White Lady' as it had been in the early days of organisation.

But when I had finished outlining the requirements for liquidation, I was immediately put on the mat. I realised that the only thing to do was to tell them the truth. They were so overcome and so aghast that I promised I would move heaven and earth with the British authorities to make good their word to their followers, for they had all enrolled themselves in the organisation as British soldiers, and had even taken an oath of allegiance. Later the British Army council was eventually won over to treat these brave men as soldiers, and the Belgian authorities, after a protracted struggle, also consented to come into line.

It was late in the afternoon when our talk came to an end. From Liège, in a car which the 'White Lady' kindly put at my disposal, I set out for Brussels. It was now 25 November, and Belgium was free of the Germans. As soon as I arrived in Brussels,

I started looking for a suitable house and office. They quickly found a house for me on the rue Stevin, a stone's throw from the British embassy, and there within a few days, with a *cordon bleu* as cook, and with an excellent man as valet and butler, I was comfortably installed. My next step was to call on Sir Francis Villiers, the British ambassador, who had arrived by now, and to him I explained my mission. This fine old man, together with General Lyon, the military attaché; Gurney, the first secretary; and Charles, the third secretary, I was to see again and again during my stay in Brussels; they greatly facilitated my work, and backed me up whenever I needed any assistance or information from any of the Belgian ministries.

I was now ready to start in on the work of liquidation, but I still had to make arrangements with the chief in London about finances. Large sums were to be paid out in claims and pensions, and I had to know what documents and records were required by the British Treasury. Then, too, there was the cost of the liquidation itself: office expenses, assistants, typists, and above all, transportation, in connection with the necessary interviewing of a couple of thousand agents scattered through the whole of Belgium and north-eastern France. Finally, I had to find out what category and class of decorations would be available for rewarding those agents whom I should recommend.

I might have known that C would manage all this for me in the best possible way. I made a flying trip to London to consult him, and had the usual satisfaction of receiving instructions at once definite and flexible – above all, liberal.

'You alone know what services each individual agent has rendered,' said he,

And you alone can judge the merits of their claims. The British government wants them satisfied. Find out what pensions the Belgian government is giving the widows of its soldiers; I suggest you recommend a slightly higher figure. For those who have been in prison and need help, recommend a sum you think fair; I suggest the pay of a British soldier for each day spent in prison.

As regards your expenses, and the expenses of liquidation, I will instruct the paymaster to advance you £5000; he will then see that you keep this working balance by paying into your account at Lloyd's Bank in Brussels sums corresponding to your expenditures, as shown by the receipts you send in. As regards claims and pensions, as soon as your recommendations have been passed by the Treasury, the sums in question will be paid into your account for payment to the claimants.

The decorations to be recommended are those of the Order of the British Empire, military division, from the grade of commander down to the medal. Concerning the militarisation of the 'White Lady', I will do my best, but I am very doubtful if anything can be done about it. As for transportation, I will petition the War Office to supply you with such cars as you may need.

The chief kept his word; without a single exception, every decoration I recommended was eventually awarded, and every single claim and pension was paid without a query. It was a pleasure and an inspiration working under these conditions. It was this quality in the chief, this encouragement of initiative, and implicit trust in those subordinates who merited it, which made him so successful in running an organisation which had branches in every neutral country, and which he built up from nothing at the commencement of the war, to the vast machine it was at the end.

CHAPTER 22

EDITH CAVELL
– REFLECTIONS

I N ADDITION TO liquidating the British secret service organisations in Belgium and occupied France, I was called upon
to look after all other civilian groups which had rendered
service to the British. Of these, the two most important were
the organisation of Miss Cavell, which had cared for British
wounded and had helped them escape into Holland, and the one
headed by Piulunowski, a Belgian of Polish extraction, which
had over a period of several years supplied food packages and
other comforts to the British prisoners in their temporary prison
camps in Belgium, where they were kept until they were evacuated to Germany.

None of the members of the Piulunowski organisation risked their lives, but it was England's duty to consider them for dignified reward, since they performed a great and much needed work of charity. The work was carried out under great difficulties, and often in the face of obstruction and unpleasantness from the Germans. Food was also often contributed by Belgians who were much in need of it themselves. The pitiful condition of many of the prisoners, who had gone through the hell of battle and rough handling by the Germans, moved these hospitable Belgians to compassion and to untold sacrifices. The gratitude shown by the prisoners was now to be officially expressed by their mother-country.

The story of Edith Cavell had created such a stir throughout the world that it was with great interest I undertook the investigation of her organisation, with a view to recommending for decorations the brave companions who had assisted her. At the time of her death, apart from knowing that she was a British nurse who had been shot by the Germans for aiding British wounded to escape, the world did not know the exact details of her organisation. Since then various accounts have been written, notably by Got and by Libiez, who was a member of the Cavell organisation, but in order to make my comments intelligible it is necessary for me to review the story briefly. In my official capacity as liquidator of the Cavell organisation, assisted by Piulunowski and Cutbill, I had many interviews with Braffort, one of the legal defenders at the trial, and with Princess Marie de Croy, the Comtesse Jeanne de Belleville, Madame Bodart, and many others of Miss Cavell's brave associates. I am therefore able to write from considerable authentic information, and, from my intimate knowledge of German CE methods, can perhaps throw some light on the causes which led to her arrest.

In some sense I could not then, and cannot now, avoid the eerie conviction that I was gaining the most impressive evidence that one could have – the testimony of the resurrected. Comtesse de Belleville, who, when I met her at her chateau, gave me every impression of dedicated, nun-like restraint, had been tried with Edith Cavell, and had stood with her before the court martial to hear the ghastly sentence of execution. The commutation of her sentence had returned her to life inevitably marked by having been in the valley of the shadow of death, and her account of the Cavell organisation, emotionless as it was, affected me profoundly.

After the retreat from Mons, a great number of British wounded were picked up by ambulances, organised by local Belgian doctors and other patriots. However, according to German orders which were published throughout Belgium in proclamation form, they were forced to report these cases to the Germans. Imagine their consternation and emotion when, after they had taken loving care of these wounded, they saw them collected by the Germans for dispatch to prison camps in Germany, to endure behind barbed-wire fences the bad food, wretched and overcrowded sleeping quarters, and the spirit-breaking restrictions, which were so evident in the temporary camps already in use in Belgium.

It was quite natural that an organisation should spring up to help these wounded, quite incapable of undergoing the rigours of a prison encampment, to escape from the small civilian hospitals and homes where they had been sheltered in Frameries, La

Bouverie, Wasmes, Quiévrain, Wiheries, Paturages, and other centres in the neighbourhood of Mons. The rescuers were encouraged in this plan by the fact that some of the wounded had not been reported, and others, such as those in the clinic of Dr van Hassel at Paturages, were sometimes overlooked by the Germans. Towards the end of August 1914, Lieutenant-Colonel Gibbs organised at Wasmes a regular drainage of these officers and soldiers through hiding places in the villages and woods. The fugitives were given Belgian identity cards, food, money, and guides who evacuated them through Ostend, until the fall of Antwerp at the commencement of October 1914. This was a relatively simple task at the time, since there were considerable gaps in the German lines, and an organised control of the Belgian inhabitants had not as yet been created by the Germans; many groups of Belgian refugees were following the same route to England.

With Ostend closed, the British officers and men who still remained in the Mons area, and the Belgian friends who had nursed and hidden them and were now aiding them to rejoin their regiments, had to look to the Dutch frontier for a channel of escape. The problem was not the actual passage at the frontier, for the strict surveillance of 1916 and the electric wire had not as yet been installed, and the *passeurs* of the Campine and those to the north of Antwerp were finding it easy to pass refugees into Holland. The difficulty was to find hiding places in Brussels, mid-way to the frontier, where the men could wait until the moon was favourable and a sufficiently large group had been assembled in readiness for the *passeurs*, who often took as many as twenty men at a time. It was impossible for the *passeurs* to pick up the men in the Mons area, for the journey to the frontier had to be made at night, and the distance was too great. Besides, most of the Flemish *passeurs* could not speak French, and for the same reason most of the men and officers had to keep out of sight as much as possible.

When Dr van Hassel, whom I have already mentioned, started looking around in Brussels for assistance, it was quite natural that he should address himself to Miss Cavell, who was known to him professionally as the director of a school for nurses in the rue de la Culture; besides, she herself had been nursing the wounded since the commencement of hostilities. Miss Cavell, realising that she had a patriotic duty to perform, readily consented. Sergeant Meachin of the Cheshire Regiment was the first to reach her, and others rapidly followed. As the number increased she gradually enlisted the help of her many friends in Brussels, who each agreed to hide one or two men in their homes. This was the start of the Cavell organisation, which ended so tragically a year later.

In the Mons area the work of collecting the men and dispatching them to Brussels was undertaken by Capiau, who from the commencement had been prominent in caring for the wounded left in the area. He did his work well. He enlisted the active help of Prince Reginald de Croy and his sister, Princess Marie, who undertook to shelter some of the fugitives in their chateau at Bellignies. Mlle Louise Thuliez, a noble Frenchwoman, collected men hidden in the forest of Mormal, and even penetrated as far as Cambrai. The Comtesse Jeanne de Belleville agreed to give refuge to some of the men in her chateau at Montignies-sur-Roc. Capiau himself undertook the procuring of false Belgian identity cards, and supplied the guides to conduct the fugitives to Brussels. Another group under Libiez sometimes worked with Miss Cavell, and sometimes worked independently.

In this way, a steady flow of men went from the Borinage, or Mons area, to Holland via Brussels. At the start they were mostly recovered British wounded, but later on, they were joined by young Belgians and Frenchmen who wished to enrol themselves in their respective armies. This proved the downfall of the organisation. It became so cumbersome that it was only a matter of time until it had to blow up. In addition, many of the members were engaged in other activities of a compromising nature, such as the publication and distribution of *La Libre Belgique*, an illicit newspaper which, together with *Le Mot du Soldat,* was circulated by patriotic Belgians to offset the propaganda and false news given out in the other Belgian papers, published under German supervision.

I know definitely that Miss Cavell and the leading members of the organisation were not engaged in espionage, but some of the *passeurs* may possibly have been approached by one or another of the Allied secret services in Holland, who were exploiting every possible channel to get information out of Belgium. As I looked over the situation, I realised these mistakes which led the noble associates to disaster. Perhaps the greatest was the very thing which proved their innocence of anything like spying: the Cavell organisation as a whole really had had no specific directing head, as would have been the case with our espionage services: it was made up of a number of loosely linked groups united only by a common ideal. I was surprised that it lasted as long as it did.

Whatever was the cause or whoever was the informer the Germans eventually got on the track of the organisation, and employed their usual tactics. They did not make an immediate arrest, but contented themselves with watching the suspected members for some time. It was on Baucq, one of Miss Cavell's associates in Brussels, that the Germans focused their attention. He was intimately connected with *La Libre Belgique.* It is significant that they arrested him first and that it was not until 15 August, four days later, that the chain of evidence led them to Miss Cavell and Capiau. Were they tracking the illicit newspaper organisation or that of Miss Cavell? We can only conjecture that they first of all went off on one scent and then turned aside to investigate the more important one, which they ran across later by chance. My experience of the German Secret Police was that although they often watched an organisation for weeks to follow all the ramifications, once they made an arrest all the others followed with lightning rapidity to prevent escape. Had they known about Miss Cavell at the time, they would have arrested her simultaneously with Baucq.

Having watched Baucq closely, they knew that he was in the habit of taking out his dog before retiring for the night. To prevent his warning anyone inside the house, or signalling to the outside (as he might have done in the manner of signalling from a letter box) they cleverly waited for him in the street to make the arrest. Having secured their man, they surrounded the house and made a forced entry. There quite fortuitously they found the unfortunate Louise Thuliez, who had a few hours previously arrived from Mons. She at first gave them the false name of Lejeune, but luck was with the Germans; the indiscreet young woman had a note-book in her possession giving the names and addresses of many members of the Cavell organisation, and, in addition, from her false identity card, signed by Commissaire Toussaint of Paturages, they got an indication of what area to search for the others.

After the arrest of Capiau and Miss Cavell, that of the others followed quickly. Prince Reginald de Croy escaped. The prisoners, thirty-five in number, locked in separate cells, were each told in turn that the others had confessed, and so the Germans were quickly in possession of all the facts.

At the trial, the defenders were the three Belgian lawyers, Sadi Kirschen, Braun, and Braffort, and in addition two Germans; these attorneys divided up the defence of the thirty-five prisoners among themselves. Miss Cavell was in the Kirschen group. Stöber was the German military prosecuting attorney. Bergan and Pinkhoff, heads of the German Secret Police, were the witnesses for the prosecution. Philippe Baucq, Edith Cavell, Louise Thuliez, Louis Séverin, and the Comtesse Jeanne de Belleville were condemned to death. Eight were freed, and the rest got varying terms of from three to ten years' hard labour. Of those condemned to death, Edith Cavell and Baucq were shot at dawn on 12 October 1915; the others had their sentence commuted to life imprisonment.

Knowing that the United States had been asked to intervene by the British government, the Germans passed sentence at 5 p.m. and set the execution for dawn of the next day. Brand Whitlock, the American minister, got wind of it, however, and took immediate action. From his sick-bed, where he was confined by a serious illness, he immediately addressed pleas for mercy to the German authorities, and instructed Gibson, the Secretary of the Legation, to call on them personally. Gibson, together with the Spanish ambassador, the Marquis de Villalobar, hunted up Baron von der Lancken, the chief of the political department. He appeared sympathetic, but said the matter rested entirely in the hands of Baron von Bissing, the governor-general; von Bissing was implacable, and the execution was carried out.

According to the strict letter of the law, the Germans had a right to execute Miss Cavell and Baucq. Both of them confessed that they realised the seriousness of what they were doing, and that they had received news from fugitives after they had successfully reached Holland. The Germans had fully warned the population by proclamation that all wounded had to be reported, and that aiding their escape was a capital offence. Furthermore, one must consider the very rational motive for this rigorous order: after the Belgian and British retreat, there were left behind hundreds of fugitives who, apart from the possibility of rejoining their units, were an actual menace to the Germans. Right up to a late date in 1915, there were groups of soldiers hidden in the woods on the French–Belgian border; in civilian clothes, armed with a false identity card, they were quickly turned from soldiers into all the appearance of civilians. Many Belgian soldiers in civilian clothes had been sent into Belgium from Holland to blow up bridges and other objectives, and the Germans had reason to believe that this was the work of soldiers wounded and unwounded, left in Belgium after the retreat. This, however, is all that can be said in defence of the Germans. Miss Cavell had nursed many wounded Germans, and in helping British soldiers to escape she was only doing her duty as a British woman.

Apart from the humane work in tending the wounded, the Cavell organisation rendered the Allies the greatest service in helping to swell the ranks of their armies, not only through the 200-odd men who reached Holland through Miss Cavell's hands alone, but through the wonderful stimulus to recruiting caused by her heroic death.

The decorations awarded the Cavell organisation were those of the Order of the British Empire, civil division, as opposed to the military division of the same order awarded to agents engaged in active espionage work. As I look back now, it seems unfair that this distinction should have been made. Certainly the Cavell group had run the constant risks of those in active service, and aside from the evidence of this fact in the death sentences, all of them suffered untold miseries in prison. Although Braffort, one of the defenders at the trial, was decorated, Sadi Kirschen, the defender of Miss Cavell, was not given an award. It was difficult to recommend him at the time, for he was severely criticised by some members of the organisation. The criticism was based on the fact that he had kept de Leval, the attorney of the American Legation, away from the trial on the plea that his presence would prejudice the Germans, and that before the trial when de Leval tried to get in touch with him on the two or three days preceding the 11th, he was not to be reached. Kirschen claimed that the Germans prevented his seeing Miss Cavell or examining the documents before the court opened session, and Brand Whitlock said that he had defended Miss Cavell well.

There is no question in my mind that this savage criticism of his part in the affair was entirely unjust. Nothing he could have done could have prevented the execution of Edith Cavell. She became in the short time between her arrest and her death less a human being than a pawn of principle; the German officials were determined to make an example of her, even though in all that she had done she was so eminently worthy of mercy.

CHAPTER 23

PASSPORT CONTROL
IN GERMANY

THE LIQUIDATION OVER, I determined to relax for a time. I spent a delightful week with some friends at their chateau in Belgian Luxembourg, hunting and fishing, and then I received the eagerly awaited communication from C informing me that I had been transferred to the staff of Lord Kilmarnock, attaché and private secretary to the British ambassador in Berlin. I was to report in London immediately for instructions.

In London I was informed by the chief that in recognition of my services, he had awarded me the best of his appointments abroad in the post-war re-arrangement of the secret service. I was to open an office in Berlin, and in addition to the duties which he would give me to perform, but which would develop after I had got settled, I was to direct and organise the passport control there. For this purpose, I would be attached to Lord Kilmarnock's staff as chief passport control officer for Germany, with branch offices in Hamburg and Munich. Although Lord Kilmarnock would not be taking up his post for several weeks, I was to proceed to Berlin immediately, where I was to report to General Malcolm, the head of the British mission. Finally, the chief directed me to get full instructions from the Home Office concerning the granting of visas.

At the Home Office I was told that no visa, under any circumstances, should be granted to any German who could possibly try to get work in England, and that as regarded other applicants, I should weed them out as strictly as possible, forwarding to the Home Office for final consideration and sanction, only those applications coming from people whose good faith I had thoroughly investigated. I was shown a multitude of forms and rubber stamps, whose use was explained to me, with the assurance that a supply of them was waiting for me at the British mission. With a light heart and full of expectation, I set out for Berlin, knowing that a new field had been opened up for me. I was all excitement. I visualised the old days of Rotterdam all over again, though, of course, with new objectives and new methods. There would be the same pioneering work to be done, but it would be even more interesting. I was more experienced. I was going forward fully prepared for the battle of wits which the secret service always calls for.

Arrived in Berlin, I drove immediately to the Hotel Bristol, where I had stopped in pre-war days, but found it impossible to get a room. All the good hotels were filled, and each had a long waiting list. I secured the temporary use of a room for a few hours, and after a proper breakfast I made my way to the Moltkestrasse, the headquarters of the British mission. My interview with General Malcolm lasted but a few minutes; it was merely a courtesy call to place myself under his protection. He was a busy man, for not only had he been directing the return of several hundred thousand British prisoners of war to England, but in the absence of a diplomatic representative he was also handling all communications between the British and German governments. He was beset with a continual stream of callers, both from the other Allied missions and from the various German ministries.

He put me in touch with two of his officers – Captain Breen and Count de Salis, the son of the British envoy at the Vatican. With these two I spent the rest of the day looking around, and being shown the ropes. Breen was especially useful to me; he was thoroughly conversant with the German political situation, and, in fact, was one of General Malcolm's right-hand men.

When I broached the subject of quarters, I found that I should have to get a requisition from the Foreign Office before I could get a room in one of the hotels, for Berlin was crowded not only with Allied officers of the various military missions and control commission, but with Germans from the provinces. It was too late after my arrival to secure this necessary inch of red tape; so I spent the night on a camp bed at the British embassy in the Wilhelmstrasse, where I found the Dutch representatives, who had occupied the embassy during the war, preparing to move out before Lord Kilmarnock's arrival. The chancellery presented a

265

scene of bustle as packing-cases were filled with Dutch official records, but the rest of the embassy was wrapped in silence and darkness; shutters were drawn, furniture was covered, the servants had already been dismissed. That night Breen and I were the sole occupants. On the next day, thanks to my requisition, I found myself located at the Hotel Esplanade on the Potsdamerplatz, one of the newest and best of the Berlin hotels.

For a few days I looked around in order to orientate myself. Officers of the Allied armies were to be seen everywhere, especially in the fashionable places. I felt quite strange walking around Berlin in a uniform, when a year ago I was sending spies into Germany employing every form of secrecy. For the moment I was glad to have it on, for it seemed a protection; the people appeared sullen. I soon realised, however, that they were not aggressive; they were too cowed. Their sullenness was due to their resentment of the presence of the Allied officers, and the foreign uniforms probably had an irritating effect.

The city was filled with men still wearing their field grey soldier's uniform. Several million men had been demobilised, but vast numbers of them had not yet obtained work, nor had they the price of a new suit of clothes. My thoughts went back to Belgium, to those few days after the Armistice when I had seen these same men file past me, an efficient military machine. Then, even though dirty and tired, they looked as if they had life in them, and still could fight. Now they seemed to be derelicts, completely demoralised and in despair, more like human scarecrows than soldiers; often they wore only part uniform and part ragged civilian attire, a pair of trousers or a coat from the remnants of a pre-war wardrobe. Starvation conditions, disappointment with the situation at home, and misery in their families had done more damage to their morale in a few months than the enemy fire during the course of the whole war. The German authorities could do nothing for them, except dish out potatoes to them at the communal kitchens; the unfortunate creatures could only wait listlessly and hopelessly until such time as the German industries had picked up sufficiently for them to be absorbed.

At the big hotels, and in the better restaurants, where prices reckoned in German marks were enormously high, one could get absolutely everything, but in the ordinary establishments the food was wretched. *Ersatz*, or substitution products, were used for numerous foodstuffs: ground acorns went under the name of coffee, weak coffee under the name of Moka, and coffee such as we know it received the rating of double Moka; the difference in price between coffee and double Moka was staggering.

If the mass of the people in Berlin were poverty stricken, there were quite a number who had enriched themselves through graft or speculation. Some were war profiteers; others were fattening on the people's miseries by cornering foodstuffs and other necessities of life, or had made scandalous profits out of the sale of left-over war supplies which, through graft, had come into their hands for a mere song. These grafters, speculators, and war profiteers were collectively called 'Schiebers', a term of insult which was hurled at them on every occasion by the rest of the German people. It did not worry them in the least, however. Richly clad in furs and other finery they openly paraded themselves along the Unter den Linden and on the Kurfürstendamm; they filled the large hotels, and spent their money on a lavish scale. They were responsible also for the spectacular night life

267

of Berlin which was such a direct contrast to the misery of the poorer people. All this gave me the impression of a huge corpse preyed on by a number of vultures.

Such conditions in any other country would undoubtedly have proved a fertile breeding-ground for communism, but although I heard a great deal of talk of it, this came rather from the people who feared it than from those who should have been actively sponsoring it. There were certain sectors of Berlin, such as that of Wedding, which were entirely Red, but for the moment the communists were inactive. Noske, the Minister of War, had the situation well in hand; the flare-up of communism at the outbreak of the revolution had been firmly crushed by the Republican forces, and the mass of the German people, even those who were in abject want, were still hoping that the present government in the course of time would steer them through their difficulties. For a few months still those who filled the potato lines waited; later many were to join the ranks of the communists.

Two or three days after my arrival, having got my bearings, I started out to find an office, assisted by Breen. After looking at several houses, we finally decided on a large villa in a street facing the Thiergarten. Breen transformed the top floor into an apartment for himself; the passport control office and waiting-rooms were installed on the floor below; the British consulate eventually took over the ground floor – I believe it is still housed there.

Armed with my forms and my rubber stamps, I waited for the visa applicants to arrive. There was quite a rush at first from the many Germans who had worked in England before the war, but as soon as word got around that applicants in this category were not being considered, the numbers dwindled greatly. From time to time, after due investigation, I forwarded visa applications to London for the approval of the Home Office, but soon found that very few were being granted. I felt sorry for some of those turned down, disappointment was so plainly written on their faces; getting to England seemed to mean such a lot to them. Poor devils! Some of them had had good jobs in England before the war, and in some cases had spent almost a lifetime over there. Now they were walking the streets of Berlin. The British authorities could not be blamed, of course; they had their own demobilised men and unemployed to look after, for men were walking the streets in London too.

When the passport office seemed to be functioning smoothly, I proceeded to examine the secret service field. I discovered immediately that exactly the same conditions were prevailing here which had existed in Holland – in fact, it was infinitely worse, for here there was even more competition and overlapping. Every member of the various Allied missions was making reports, with a general sense that everybody was encroaching on important work that everybody else was doing. Yet there was no real need of competition or real cause for irritation: no finesse was needed in getting information – one simply walked in and demanded it. I experienced this myself in the course of several interviews which I had with high ranking members of the German Foreign Office. They felt helpless, defenceless, and humiliated to the point where all secrecy or even reserve was abandoned.

This condition, and the inactivity at the passport office, was so different from the picture which I had visualised on leaving London that it produced in me a severe reaction. Had I been patient the situation would probably have cleared itself, for later I was to find the chief calling me back to do urgent work for him in Germany. Disappointment, inactivity, and my old restlessness, however, got the better of me. Even though I knew that at my request the chief would have transferred me to another country, I started to search for a new field. I weighed the facts. I was now twenty-eight years old, six precious years of my life had been spent in the service of my country, and I had never intended to remain permanently in the secret service. Surely, it was time to get back to civilian life.

Had I been older, and as experienced in the art of self-advancement as I was in matters pertaining to secret service, I should have waited until I had secured a definite post, or, at any rate, had decided on what I was going to make of my future. I was brimful of confidence, however; I felt sure that with my intimate knowledge of Europe, my many foreign connections, my army and university records, and my knowledge of engineering and other sciences, there would be no difficulty in building up a civilian career in connection with one of the big engineering, business, or financial concerns in Europe. So, having made up my mind that my activities in Berlin did not offer a sufficiently active field for me, I sent in my resignation – true to form, on the moment's impulse – and asked for demobilisation.

The chief was surprised, expressed regret, paid me the compliment of asking me to find a suitable man to take my place, and requested me to remain on a week or two until Lord Kilmarnock had taken his post. I promptly departed for Cologne to interview some of my friends in the intelligence corps, any of whom

I knew would jump at the Berlin post. Eventually I proposed Captain F.; he was accepted, and probably today is still carrying out the functions of passport control officer for Germany – at least, he was there a few years ago. His duties were confined to passport control; someone else whom I highly recommended relieved me of my secret service work.

With a feeling of relief at my escape from Berlin, and anxiously looking forward to the new career which I intended developing as soon as I got back to England, I took my leave of Lord Kilmarnock, of Seeds, the first secretary, and of Thelwall, the commercial attaché. Six years of responsibility and service in the army had come to an end. I felt as if I were walking on air. I was free, and once more a civilian.

CHAPTER 24

YVONNE – AN INTERLUDE

WHAT WAS MORE natural than that I should stop off at Brussels on my way back to London?

I was crossing the Place de la Monnaie when I met her. *Yvonne.* Months before, Mlle L., a friend of mine who was a star in the *corps de ballet* at the Brussels opera, had introduced me to her. 'This is Yvonne,' she had said, 'my charming little understudy.' And then later, when we were all dining together at the Chapon Fin, she had whispered: 'Don't look at her so intently. You haven't got a dog's chance; she's Z's protégée.' I had opened my eyes wide in astonishment, for Z was one of the great men in Belgium, one of her most prominent statesmen, a man whose name was a household word throughout Europe. I was astonished that he should be the captive of this small vivacious bloom of loveliness.

Now here she was. This time there was no one to sidetrack me. I looked at her and smiled. 'You don't remember me, I am sure,' I said, as I stood facing her, hat in hand.

'Yes, I do, *mon capitaine*,' she sparkled amiably. 'I met you at the Chapon Fin. You are a friend of L.' Thus encouraged, I suggested an apéritif at a neighbouring bodega.

It was all very well for L. to have told me not to look at her. I couldn't help it. Her lustrous violet eyes, which languished and glowed beneath her long lashes, her strikingly beautiful head, crowned with smooth waves of soft gold hair, her delicate subtle grace and her happy contagious smile, overwhelmed me. I actually trembled as I sat opposite her. It was the *coup de foudre*. I knew that I was blindly in love with her, and intuitively I sensed that she reciprocated my feeling. Gone were my thoughts of London; my uncompleted ticket remained in my pocket. I met her every day for a week.

She was twenty-one, fresh and unaffected, renowned for her beauty, already an acclaimed artist. Her sparkling wit and laughter had charmed not only Z, but also some of the leading people in Europe, whom she had met through him. She had dined with a Lord Mayor of London, the Shah of Persia had awarded her a decoration, she wore the Palmes Académiques, presented by a premier of France, and she had danced at special request before royalty. And Z, her patron, was one of the most powerful men in Belgium, who could assist her in furthering a brilliant career at the opera.

Both her father and her mother objected strongly to our infatuation. He was a *maître de ballet*, and she a dancer who had had many a triumph in her day at the opera at Paris. They knew what the cost of our idyll would be, since both of them were steeped in the unromantic traditions of advancement in the European theatre. They called on me at my hotel. 'You must leave her alone. We have trained her since she was four years old. She needs Z; he wouldn't do anything for her, if you were in the picture. No artist in France or Belgium can arrive without someone backing her. You will ruin her career.' How often was I to hear that word career during the next four years?

We were both foolish; we both had our careers to consider and each of us was inimical to the welfare of the other. Yet we were in love, and for the moment that was all that mattered.

I was wrong. I should have packed my bags and gone on my way. It would have been better, both for her and for me. I was the older and more intelligent; I should have done the thinking for both of us. But loneliness had eaten into my heart. From my boyhood days up, I really had had no home. I stood alone in Europe, with no relatives and no intimate friends. I had worked intensively both at the university, and during the last six years in the army, without encouragement. And here was all the tenderness, all the love, companionship and beauty in life that I had missed. Besides, there was the setting of the ballet which had always exerted on me a romantic appeal. Pavlova, Karsavina, Lopokova, Nijinsky, Mordkin, and the many members of Diaghileff's troupe, I had seen over and over again. Apart from the technique of their art, I loved their imagery; who has seen *Le Spectre de la Rose*, or *La Boutique Fantasque* and not gone away charmed ? Most potent influence of all, I was just at that time like a diver who had come too quickly to the surface; at one stroke I had released myself from the tremendous tension of my war and post-war responsibilities, and the effect was heady.

I promised Yvonne's parents to think things over, but as I sat and watched her dance with exquisite grace and execution, in the Walpurgis scene in the last act of *Faust*, I realised that here was something stronger than I. I could not give her up. Surely I could solve the problem, as I had solved the many other problems of my life. I would remain on in Brussels and work out a scheme of things which would permit us to hold on to this great happiness which we had found. I had numbers of influential friends. I would build up a career here. Why not ?

For the next two years my life was a feverish struggle to find my footing in the hurly-burly of post-war commerce and finance. Financially I was often very successful, but my chief reward was the snatches of weeks or hours in the company of the loveliest and kindest creature I have ever known. Her engagements dictated my arrangements, her friends were my friends, her life my life.

On the evenings when she had to dance in Brussels, I took her to the opera and then slipped in to watch the ballet. *Faust, Marouf, Lakmé, Manon, Carmen, Traviata* – these were the principal operas she danced in. How often have I seen them presented! I became well known in the coulisses of the opera. I met the other members of the ballet and became acquainted with *régisseurs, maîtres de ballet,* mistresses of the wardrobe, wardrobe women and the back stage personnel. I heard all the scandal, all their joys and all their sorrows. I acquired a new vocabulary of technical terms; I learned to discourse learnedly on *fouettés,* and where to buy the best *chaussons;* everyone agreed that those Z used to get from Italy for Yvonne were the best.

In summer, when the opera season was over, she danced at one or another of the fashionable seaside resorts. When time permitted, I made a flying trip there for a few days.

During the first summer I knew her, she had an engagement at the Kursaal in Ostend. This was the first season at Ostend since the war. In spite of the enormous damage done to almost every large building in the town by Allied bombardments from the sea and air, the Digue was now repaired, and so were the Kursaal and the large hotels such as the 'Splendide' and the Hôtel de la Plage. Wonders had been worked; no one could distinguish it from the Ostend of pre-war days.

The resort was crowded not only with Belgians, but with a number of English and Dutch, with whom it had always been a favourite. Most of the summer resorts had been closed during the war, and this season those who could afford it were determined to play. Old *habitués* flocked to Ostend not only to have a thoroughly good time, but also out of curiosity to see the results of German occupation and Belgian restoration. During the day the beach was a blaze of colour with beach umbrellas, and with the latest bathing suits, often worn by mannequins sent by the best Parisian establishments, such as Lanvin, Poiret, and Patou. In the afternoon, there were races at the Wellington Hippodrome, where Horatio Bottomley, that chequered British Member of Parliament, newspaper owner, and sportsman, was an outstanding figure.

In the evening, it was the Kursaal for gambling, dancing, the concert and the ballet. Here evening dress was *de rigueur*, and beautiful women with expensive jewels and gorgeous costumes were everywhere. It was in the gambling-rooms, however, that the scene was the most brilliant. Bankers, members of Europe's aristocracy, stage favourites, and expensive mistresses all rubbed shoulders with each other, some all intent on gambling, others merely parading themselves, or making a critical appraisal of each other's clothes and companions. That season the gambling was very high; one night I saw a well-known Londoner, a great tobacco importer, lose £20,000 at the big table at baccarat.

I spent profoundly happy days with Yvonne. Often I spoke of marriage. She only laughed her quick bubble of laughter.

'You Englishmen are funny; don't you know that very few artists in Belgium or France ever marry? It would ruin my career. What's wrong? Aren't we happy as things are?' She lived, as far as her own affairs were concerned, for the day, the hour – and brilliantly sufficient she made them. I learned not to fret her by attempts to make her see my notion of established life, so different from hers, and as time went on and my business affairs became more pressing, I learned her way of enjoying pleasure without trying to make it last.

In Brussels and Paris, in her company, I met many artists in the theatrical world. There was Régina Badet, now a great dramatic actress, somewhat stout, quite a contrast to her days in 1910 at the Marigny Theatre in Paris. Who would then have thought that in later years she would be interpreting Ibsen's plays? I found her very witty and amusing. Accompanied by one of her friends, I took her to the Savoy one night, where she attracted attention not only by her famous jewels, but also by a cigarette-holder at least eight inches long, which she insisted on using while we danced.

Then there was Jenny Golder, whom any theatrical *habitué*

in those days will remember; she was the star at the Casino de Paris for several years. I knew Jenny very well. I had first met her at the 'Savoy' in Brussels, just after the Armistice, where I had been much attracted to this willowy girl with her large, somewhat sad brown eyes and auburn hair, which accentuated her ivory skin and chiselled features. She had intrigued me, too, for it was quite evident after hearing and seeing her sing and dance, that she was quite out of place in a cabaret, even though the 'Savoy' was one of the best of its kind in Europe.

'What are you doing here?' I had said to her, as she sat at our table conversing one night.

'That is a long story,' was the answer, in excellent English. She was an Australian. It appeared that shortly after her arrival from Australia, she had contracted an unhappy marriage. At this time, she was glad of any kind of engagement. 'You see,' I remember her saying rather wistfully, 'it doesn't pay for a girl to marry when she is on the stage.'

I had helped her with a small loan to enable her to get on her feet. She first of all secured an engagement in a revue which was playing at the Alhambra in Brussels. There she attracted the attention of Volterra, the owner of the Casino de Paris, who promptly gave her an engagement in his theatre. Within a few months she was playing the stellar role, a worthy successor to Gaby Delys and Mistinguett, who had preceded her.

I met her often in Paris, and then later again in Berlin. How far she had climbed since those days at the 'Savoy'! She was now a headliner at the Wintergarten in Berlin, drawing large crowds. She appeared in various numbers, but the greatest hit with her Berlin audience was 'Mr Gallagher and Mr Shean', which she sang as a male impersonator in evening dress and silk hat. As I sat one evening in her suite of rooms at the 'Adlon', we laughed over her struggles in Brussels. But whatever success had come her way she thoroughly deserved. She worked incessantly. Even a torn ligament which she endured for a whole theatrical engagement, could not daunt her.

Poor Jenny! She committed suicide in Paris a few days after a certain banker disappeared from his plane over the English Channel. I knew she had known him intimately, but I could not help wondering why the two deaths followed each other in such close succession. There seemed no reason why she should take her own life, especially as I knew she adored her mother, who was dependent upon her. She was young, she had reached the peak; but apparently success was not enough – at least, success alone.

Although, of course, many of the older families were strict as to whom they invited to their houses, or with whom they were seen in public, yet society in Europe had become much mixed. At the fashionable Parisian restaurants, such as 'Ciro's', the Café de Paris, 'Fouquets', 'Armenonville', 'Pré-Catelan', and the Château de Madrid, one often saw a mixed group of actresses, high officials, leaders of society, and members of the various embassies, all dining together – sometimes accompanied by their wives, sometimes not. In this group, too, one occasionally saw the chic courtesan, when the wives were absent, though as a rule she swept in accompanied only by the man of her choice. At the big hotels, at the races at Longchamps and Auteuil, and at Deauville and other fashionable seaside resorts, she remained the arbiter of fashions.

Such a courtesan was La belle Sabine, the name by which everyone knew her. She merited the title, for she was a beautiful blonde of striking appearance and personality. I first saw her in The Hague, where she came into prominence by marrying an English officer, who, after three years spent in a German prison camp, had been dispatched to Holland for internment in exchange for similar privileges which the British had granted to a certain number of German officers. Captain B. had not seen a woman during all these long years in Germany, and he fell an easy prey to Sabine's charms. Then he very considerately died a few months later, leaving her the whole of his fortune, the tidy sum of about £50,000. The indignant family contested the will, but the courts awarded her the money.

After the Armistice she turned up in Brussels, her blonde hair changed to auburn, and with nearly all her money changed into jewellery, chiefly bracelets which covered both arms half-way up to the elbow. She was promptly annexed by an Antwerp millionaire, who had a vast fortune in the Romanian oil wells. What pleasure he found in keeping her I do not know, for he was away half the year in Romania, and during the remaining time he was generally tied down by business in Antwerp. He probably never spent more than a month in the year with her, but I think it flattered his vanity to own this beautiful woman, as she flitted from one resort to another, apparelled in the ransom of a king, and with a dozen men dancing attendance.

I knew her quite well. With those who didn't know her, she had the reputation of being a crafty gold-digger, but as a matter of fact, she was the reverse. She was simply a big, overgrown child, joyous, and full of frolic. She had a peculiar fascination for men, which she probably could not explain herself. She merely took what they willingly gave her.

Other silhouettes flit through my memory: Isabelita Ruiz, in one of those delightful Madrid cabarets, long before Cochran made her famous at the London Pavilion; Hari Singh, later the Maharajah of Kashmir, whom all the ladies thought a darling; the Maharajah of Patiala, on the Champs-Élysées; Zographos and the Greek syndicate holding the bank at the big table at Deauville; André, the cheery Casino owner and gambling king of France, drinking his Eau Contrexéville, while he himself gaily lost a few thousands as a punter, knowing it would all come back to him; the King of Spain, watching his horses run under the colours of the 'Duke of Toledo', at that intimate little racecourse in Madrid; the brisk Dolly Sisters, gay and full of fun; Raquel Meller, the idol of the Spanish and Argentine colony in Paris, whose folk songs, sung as only she could sing them, brought back to them homeland memories; the Terrace at Monte Carlo, looking on the beautiful bay with its waters of the deepest blue, and the Hôtel de Paris and the Casino, at the height of the season; Épinard, Coq Gaulois, and Flower Shop, those three great horses, winning at Longchamps and Auteuil; San Sebastian and Madrid in summer, land of cabarets, where the meanest performer is a superb artist, and where, in the fierce heat, the people go to bed at dawn and dine at midnight; the Embassy Club, in Bond Street, under the direction of Luigi, where England's aristocracy mingles with the élite of the stage; dinner at 'Valadier's', looking down on the lights of Rome, and then the Hôtel de Russie, with its delightful gardens; the Bay of Naples, and Capri; the Lido Beach, the Excelsior, and a gondola at night on the Grand Canal; Belmonte, that ace of toreadors, and the bull fights at Pamplona.

This is the setting in which I passed those happy two years with Yvonne – now frantically engaged in putting over some financial project in order to make the much-needed money, now dashing back to Brussels in the opera season, or to France, Italy, and Spain in summer, to spend a short time in her company and to watch with pride her triumphs wherever she was dancing.

Although I suffered materially in that I was diverted from an ordered career at the most critical period of my life, yet even today I do not regret those years, for they supplied me with unforgettable memories.

CHAPTER 25

INVESTIGATING
WAR WIZARDRY

E XCEPT FOR MY army pay, I had never earned a penny
in my life. An indulgent father had almost lavishly supplied all my needs during my university days, and while
I was in secret service I had never counted costs – I had produced results and expense accounts had been met generously. I
had virtually been on an allowance all my life, with no compre-
hension of the financial pressure under which most men live.

I now became painfully aware of the fact that millions were
scrambling for a job. For each good appointment there were
dozens of candidates, and tens of thousands of perfectly capable
and willing men, with the finest educations and training, were

literally out on the streets. Besides, I was in Belgium, where salaries, even for the directors of the big companies, were absurdly low compared with the rest of Europe.

My old restlessness seized me, not merely, I think, because of financial disappointment, but because the life I was leading offered no definitely energetic action. Everywhere I faced hesitancy and vacillation, and I felt the imperative need of a clear objective and a settled chance of accomplishment. Inevitably my thoughts turned to C and the secret service. I would return to it temporarily. It would take me to a new country, and there, perhaps, at last I would succeed in finding myself.

It was with pleasure that I resumed contact with the chief and with my old colleagues, for although I had no intention of devoting myself entirely to the service, and stipulated that I should be free to continue my own commercial enterprises, my feeling upon finding myself once more a link in the adventures of secret service was very much that of the war horse who sayeth 'Ha! Ha!' among the trumpets. I had missed the excitement, the ceaseless work, and even the heavy burden of my wartime responsibilities.

For some time I had given a somewhat listless ear to proposals from my Belgian friends that I should arrange an interchange of information between the Belgian and British secret services. I now surprised them by the enthusiastic manner in which I took up the matter with the chief in England, pointing out to him that there was a great deal of information which interested both secret services, and which neither side should mind the other getting. 'Why not pool this type of information?' I urged him. The chief finally agreed, and I was asked to handle the first interchange of reports. Even though this was purely a routine job I thrilled once more at reading secret service reports. Always keenly interested in international affairs, I had been relying on the newspapers during the last two years; now once again I was getting a preview of impending events, and sensing once more the undercurrents of international relations, which as a rule come to the surface in print only after a crisis has been reached. How long this interchange continued I do not know, for I was suddenly requested by the chief to undertake some urgent work for him in Germany, which required immediate attention. Handing over my job to another intermediary, I set off post-haste to London to get my instructions.

The chief informed me that through an officer in the control commission he had just learned of a wireless-controlled robot perfected by the Germans a few days before the Armistice, which could not only guide an aeroplane in its flight, but also drop bombs on a given objective. I was to proceed to Germany immediately, secure full details at all costs, and if possible, bring the inventor over to England for an interview at the British Air Ministry.

My first step naturally was to find the officer who had supplied the information. Knowing his name, I quickly located him in Munich, and from him gained sufficient information to run the inventor to earth. To my surprise, I found my man in the Rhineland, in occupied territory. He was a sportsman, interested in speed and machines of speed; his appearance was anything but that of the typical inventor. Tall, thin, with a long, pointed, foxlike face, high narrow brow and fair hair combed straight back from it, he looked – especially in his gay tweed plus fours – the double of the German Crown Prince just off on a ski-ing expedition. Protected by the army of Occupation, I had no fear of being embarrassed by the German authorities; so I went straight to the point, explaining to the inventor what I wanted, and asking him to accompany me to England.

Without giving me a decision, he immediately launched into a graphic description of his invention, and the destruction it would cause. 'There has never been anything approaching it,' he cried, his pale blue eyes blazing, his hands spread flat on the table between us. 'The Allies were worried by the big gun, and by the zeppelin and aeroplane raids on London, but all of that was child's play to what my wireless robot could have done. Just imagine several hundreds of these aeroplanes, dropping tonnes of high explosives on London at night! Had the war lasted, my invention would have produced startling results. I was at German headquarters in Spa at the time of the Armistice,' he went on, more quietly, but with a wry grin that said much of his irritation and disappointment. 'You should have heard how the High Command cursed the revolutionaries and independent socialists for the cowardly betrayal of the country.'

I discounted a certain amount of what he had told me as inventor's enthusiasm. But I had reported the existence of torpedo-nosed motor boats at Zeebrugge, controlled by wireless operated from an aeroplane. I had also seen a model airship manoeuvred by wireless, without a soul on board, and also knew of the stabilising effect of a gyroscope. In addition to the supporting evidence of these earlier devices, which had probably led him on, this man gave me the impression of honesty and sincerity; I was convinced of the truth of most of what he had told me.

He was a typical inventor, more interested in the invention itself than in selling it. I soon discovered, however, that if he was not business-minded, his woman companion was. When we went to his house, I found myself in the presence of a young girl about twenty-one years old, a pretty blonde, fragile, but with a dynamic personality, who quickly took charge of the discussion, while he listened attentively to the very intelligent questions she asked me. What her relation was to this man, who was old enough to be her father, I do not know – I am sure she was not a blood relation; nor was she his wife. Without any comments, he accepted her final decision that he should accompany me back to London.

On our way through Belgium, and again on the Ostend–Folkestone boat, and at Scott's near Leicester Square, where I took him to dinner on the night of our arrival, he insisted on ordering champagne of the best vintage, and mixing it with Guinness's stout. 'Ah,' he kept saying, as he smacked his lips, 'this is the best drink in the world. How I missed it during the war!' He appeared surprised and a little put out when I refused to try it.

Having put him in contact with the Air Ministry, my mission was accomplished, and as I was urgently needed in Aachen, I left him to carry on the negotiations. I learned subsequently that they were entirely successful.

Some months later I met the inventor again, wrapped up in a new invention. By gluing sheets of three-ply wood together across-grain with a special glue, and by chemically treating it in a secret way, he had discovered a system through which he could mould the wood into any required shape, yet be sure of an extremely durable product when it solidified. He was using it for canoe construction, and also for the body of a new light motor car which he was experimenting with. This car, although it could seat two people, was so light that a strong man could lift it off the ground, and its construction costs were so low that it could sell at the same price as a motor-cycle. He was as enthusiastic about this car as he had been about his aeroplane, but although he drove me around the town in a model, it never appeared on the market. It was probably too uncomfortable and small, more suited to juveniles than adults. The canoe was a great success, and no doubt his wood-moulding process is now being used for a great many other articles. The world will remember him, however, by his wireless robot-controlled aeroplane, for it is an engine of destruction which must be reckoned with in the next war.

A short while afterwards I was put on the track of two other German inventions, the one a mysterious ray, the other a new light machine gun.

I had heard persistent rumours that the Germans had developed a ray which, when projected from the ground, had the power of putting out of action the magneto of an aeroplane in flight. It was whispered that several planes had actually been brought down in some very mysterious manner, with dead engines, during the last stages of the war. Finally, I got an urgent message from the chief, instructing me to clear up the mystery without fail. Whenever I tried to trace down these stories to their source, I was always met by a blank wall. No one had any definite information to give me. It appeared to be very much the same sort of legendary affair as the rumour at the commencement of the war about the Russians landing in France, which sprang from a fantastic blunder. Someone had sent a telegram from one of the Scandinavian countries to the effect that a certain specified number of Russians had been sent from Archangel to England; the sender was specifying a type of eggs, but the telegraph clerk thought that Russians were troops, and spread the tale accordingly. The whole matter had assumed the proportions of legend and the conviction of truth, which was only heightened by the mysterious quality of the affair. But on what distortion of fact could these rumours of a deadening ray depend?

I had very nearly given the matter up when one day a Russian in my employ, who had served as an aviator during the war, told me that he had met the inventor's wife, and that she had promised to talk to her husband about it. She was afraid that her solicitations would be fruitless, since her husband was a member of the Black Reichswehr, and as such would be summarily put out of the way if his negotiations with me were discovered.

Although this put me definitely on the track of the ray, the outlook seemed almost hopeless, for I had already sent in a long report of the Black Reichswehr's activities, and I knew only too well the sinister tactics of the organisation. It was a secret band founded in 1922 with the object of collecting arms and forming itself into a secret army. Its members were plotting the downfall of the government, which they accused of pandering too much to the Allies, and in order to maintain secrecy, the leaders summarily murdered any of its members whose actions seemed to them suspicious in any degree.

I persisted, however, in my efforts, and eventually, through the Russian, I finally brought the inventor to hear my offer. He was to have a big sum for the full information, and £50 down for a preliminary report, which was to be submitted to the Air Ministry as a test of his good faith. If this report proved satisfactory, I promised that the Air Ministry would make him a definite offer for the complete details. The information proved sufficiently interesting for the chief to want the man in London, so that the negotiations could take place there after a final demonstration.

When I set about to convey this message to the inventor, I was stupefied to learn that he had died suddenly. I never heard anything more of him. I did not wish to inquire into the matter generally or pointedly, and I could get nothing whatever from the Russian, who seemed afraid to discuss the subject. Whether the inventor had been killed as he feared, or whether he died a natural death; whether he suddenly grew afraid and simply disappeared; or whether it was a fake and he dared not attempt to carry out a useless trick, I never could discover. Personally, I think there was something tangible in the ray; the Russian intermediary, I am convinced, was honest. His terror at the time of the inventor's death was too real to be acted. In my own mind there persists the opinion that the inventor was done to death by Schulz, the head of the Black Reichswehr's murder squad. This fiendish butcher was eventually run to earth after the organisation had been forcibly disbanded by the government. At his trial it was proved conclusively that he had been responsible for twenty-two murders, and it was surmised that there must have been a great many more. I anxiously scanned the reports of the trial in search of the inventor's name, but nothing came to light about him.

My first knowledge of the machine gun developed by the

Germans came from old General von G. He was a fine old chap whom I had met during my first visit to Berlin in 1919. On my return to the German capital I had been glad to resume our acquaintance. I often dropped into his apartment after dinner, and over a coffee and kirsch, which he never failed to remind me was thirty years old, we discussed various phases of the war. The question of war guilt was what exasperated him the most. 'Didn't the Russians mobilise first?' he would shout in his excitement. 'It is perfectly clear; the war was manoeuvred by the Russians and the French, who were jealous and afraid of us. The assassination of the Archduke Francis Ferdinand – wasn't it instigated by the Russians?' I have never yet come across a German who believed that his country was responsible for the war, and so I never attempted to argue with the general. Germans never could understand that imperialism and militarism, to the extent that it was practised in Germany, was a menace to the peace of Europe, and, in itself, an incentive to war.

Like every other German of his class, the general's income and savings had dwindled to the vanishing point, and he was anxiously looking around for some new source of income. I should have been prepared, perhaps, to receive offers of information from him, but such violent partisanship as his quite closed my mind to the possibility. I was intensely surprised, therefore, when one day the fiery old patriot told me about a new light machine gun that had just been invented. He claimed for it the most surprising results in the trials. When I cautioned him about compromising himself, he shrugged his shoulders, and said: 'As long as the French don't get it, that's all we care about. It is no use to us; the control commission wouldn't permit its employ anyhow.' In the end, not only did he consent to procure a blueprint for me, but he also arranged a demonstration. The chief was delighted with the details. The gun proved to be much lighter than the Lewis machine gun, and just as efficient; it could be carried by one man and fired from the shoulder. The inventor received his money and the general his commission.

The general's attitude demonstrated how little interest the German government had at that time in armaments, for certainly no one could have doubted the old gentleman's loyalty. It was part of the apathy which marked much of German official life directly after the war, existing in anomalous fashion side by side with the far more positive forces of inventive activity and rebellious secret organisations sworn to avenge the German defeat.

Inventions of the sort which I have been describing, bought from foreigners, have of course a limited value to the purchasing nation. They are almost invariably sold to half a dozen other nations as well, in spite of promises to the contrary. Von G. I could trust, but I am sure that the astute little lady who figured in the robot invention did not miss any of the markets open to her. Each buyer was no doubt sworn to secrecy, as we were. The most valued invention or secret formula is that which is known, and can be known, only to the nation which produced it; necessarily it comes from one of the nation's own nationals – usually an expert employed by the government for such work, or an employee of some great engineering or chemical works which is in close contact with government activities.

However, to prevent surprise, a nation must always know of every device that can be used against it in war. This knowledge also often enables a country to make improvements on their own creations, or even give their inventors and experts the germ of an idea which might lead to some other invention; it may supply the missing link in some revolutionary device of their own, which is still in the experimental stage. The pursuit of these new devices is one of the most exciting activities of secret service, and the unusual fecundity of German genius in such matters directly after the war made the investigation unusually absorbing. But even as I moved about my work, excited and keyed up to the demands of it as I was, I could not help reflecting that it was a wasteful round of death producing means of death, the needy inventing means of destruction rather than production. I longed to harness all this brilliance and power to a concentrated force for living.

CHAPTER 26

THE GERMAN SECRET SERVICE MAKES A PROPOSAL

THE OCCUPATION OF the Ruhr was in full swing, and the separatist movement for the creation of an independent Rhineland Republic was being actively pushed by the French. The British government had protested, and the British press, with no uncertain voice, was proclaiming that the French were not out for reparations, but only for further destruction of their hereditary enemy. Its correspondents were reporting each move of the French. Feeling was running high, not only in Germany, but also in the rest of Europe. The British intelligence service in Cologne was also proving a thorn in the side of their former ally. It was no use for France to pretend that she was not sponsoring the separatist movement, for all her intrigues and plans were being uncovered by British agents. The Germans were fairly beaming with an appreciation of the British attitude, and were openly talking of a split between the Allies.

This was the atmosphere when one evening during one of my many discussions with General von G., he ingeniously switched the conversation to secret service.

'I have been told,' he said over the coffee and kirsch (its age having as usual been mentioned), 'that you were in charge of the military section of the British secret service in Holland. Are you still occupied with it?'

I looked at him astounded. My surprise did not spring from this sudden reference to my connection with the British secret service, for I was aware that the Germans knew all about me from Holland; but I could see that he was leading up to some proposal, and I was amazed that a German should fancy my former service to be of any use to their Reich.

I said nothing, however, and he went on, 'If you are, I have an interesting proposition to make to you. After the Armistice, our secret service grant was stopped entirely, and the German secret service ceased to exist. But it has been brought to life again, and the chief is one of my friends. He is seriously handicapped for funds. Why don't you get your people to allow you to co-operate with him? You need information about France, just as we do. Now wait,' he hurried on, silencing an objection he saw on the way; 'I realise perfectly that the British secret service cannot risk involving itself, but don't you see how perfectly natural it is that we should? I suggest that you get the British secret service to supply part of the funds, and we will supply the agents, sharing the information obtained with you. You would be the sole intermediary, and nothing could ever be traced to the British.'

This struck me as an extraordinarily naive proposition, for I did not agree with the general that the Germans could risk being involved in secret service activities against France; the French were in the Ruhr and so could inflict any penalties they desired. Besides, how could the Germans be sure the British would not report the matter to the French? The fact that the British opposed the Ruhr occupation was no proof that even in a matter of secret service they would support the German power. I was convinced of the general's honesty. I had been so often in his home that I knew he would not wittingly deceive me; so I attributed this very dubious plan to overzealousness on his part. I agreed, however, to meet a delegate from the German secret service so as to discuss the matter first hand.

The meeting eventually took place at the Fürstenhof Hotel, just off the Potsdamerplatz, where General von G. introduced me to one Major von Tresckow. I was faced by a man with hard steel-grey eyes, and stiff, close-cropped dark hair, whose carriage and manner immediately betrayed him to be an army officer. For a moment we stood and looked at each other, each sizing the other up. I was quite prepared for a cross-examination and a gradual leading up to the point, but instead, after informing me that he was representing his chief, he wasted no time in repeating verbatim the general's proposal. His chief evidently knew all about me. No question was asked about my identity nor about my secret service connections.

Now I was really astonished. It was obviously a serious proposition. I refrained from committing myself, but tried to draw out von Tresckow to find out how he intended operating. He refused, however, to discuss the matter further until I had found out whether on principle the British secret service would co-operate. If the answer was in the affirmative he promised to present a concrete scheme to me, but warned me that we would not be put in touch with the agents themselves; the only basis of co-operation would be the exchange of German reports for a monthly sum from the British, which could be stopped at any time if the information seemed unsatisfactory. I jibbed a bit at this, suggesting that it would please headquarters better to pay for each piece of information according to its value. But both of us agreed that no definite details could be discussed until I had the chief's permission to proceed with the negotiations.

The subject closed, the general ordered coffee. For the next half-hour we exchanged reminiscences about Holland, and discussed at some length the Cavell affair, the general loud in his denunciation of the criticism which the Germans had brought on themselves in the matter, whereas the much sharper von Tresckow saw that the execution was a colossal tactical blunder.

I eventually took my leave, promising von Tresckow to communicate with him through the general as soon as I had received a reply from the chief.

I had no idea what attitude the chief would take, for although it was a wonderful opportunity, and I knew all nations spy on each other, however friendly their relations may be, yet there were obvious complications in this case. The only possible method to employ would be one which gave both sides a loophole for complete denial in case of need, for I realised neither service would trust the other completely. Such a plan could, however, be devised, and so I waited curiously for a decision.

The chief did not keep me long in suspense: he instructed me to drop the matter completely. What his reasons were, he never told me.

In this attempt the typical optimism and miscalculation of the Germans was as obvious as it was in their attitude on the war guilt or the Cavell case; in spite of their cleverness in other fields, they have invariably failed in diplomacy, and never seem to have been able to foresee the response which foreign nations would have either to their acts or their proposals. It is not that they are deceitful. I am sure that in this matter they were acting in perfectly good faith. It was purely a case of bad judgement. They entirely misinterpreted the British motives in opposing the French concerning the Ruhr.

That the German secret service was short of funds did not surprise me in the least. It is the cry of all secret services in peacetime, and even of some during war. Before the war, the British secret service grant was negligible, and even after it, on the occasion of my transfer to Berlin, I saw C worrying over a sheet of figures to see how he could possibly cover the ground. The Belgian secret service suffered from this same handicap during the war. It would be interesting to relate what part of a country's revenue is earmarked for secret service, but that is one of the things which, as Kipling says, is another story – and it is not mine to tell.

The German proposal that we should use foreign agents to spy on another country, especially a friendly one, is common practice. When it is announced in the newspapers that an

American subject has been arrested in Europe on a charge of espionage, the one country it is certain he was not spying for is the United States. The name of Major von Tresckow was, of course, fictitious; this, coupled with the fact that I had met him in the lobby of an hotel, would have enabled the Germans to repudiate the whole affair if the British had reported the matter to the French.

General von G. was greatly disappointed with the decision; he had hoped to be appointed as the intermediary to deal with me. It would have put him once more on the active pay list, which would have increased his sadly diminished income.

I felt very sorry for the old general. In civilian life he was a fish out of water. Everything around him had changed, and he was at the age when it was difficult for him to adapt himself. With me he was a great favourite: his peppery disposition, his crashing voice, which seemed eternally ringing across a parade ground, and his grandiose mannerisms were a continual source of amusement, though I would never have dared to show it. The pathos of his situation was not limited to his own case; he was representative of a type. Formerly a masterful man of action, he was, like many an old officer of the imperial regime, reduced to the position of an opportunist, if not an intriguer. It is to his credit that his schemes were so obvious, so futile, so hopeless of results; their lack of cleverness proved them to be new and awkward channels of action.

CHAPTER 27

RUSSIAN ADVENTURE

C EASELESS ACTIVITY, AND the stirring, rapidly changing events through which I had lived during the intervening years, had already dimmed my memory of those delightful evenings which I had spent with Tania and her brother in The Hague, when I found myself suddenly plunged into the vortex of Russian life in Berlin.

One could not miss the Russians in Berlin; there were thousands of them there, more than in any of the other large capitals of Europe. Many of them, especially the wives and daughters, were very popular with the members of the control commission and with some of the attachés of the different embassies, and it was in this milieu that I first became acquainted with them.

I was delighted. All of them had travelled much, and had lived interesting lives. In addition to listening to the adventures which they had gone through during the revolution and in escaping from Russia, I heard graphic descriptions of Russia, Turkestan, and Siberia, and tales about the Cossacks and the Kirghiz. Most of them had lived at the Russian court, and had a stock of stories about the Tsar and the baneful influence of the superstitious Tsarina on her weak husband, about the Grand Dukes, the court balls, and the lavish entertainments that went on in Petrograd and Moscow before the revolution, and about Rasputin and the scandals connected with him.

Some of them had been with the White armies of Kolchak, Youdenish, Denikin, or Wrangel; they were quite willing to recognise their own mistakes, but from their recital of events, it was quite evident that they had been left in the lurch by the Allies. There was no excuse for the betrayal of Kolchak by the Czechs. It amazed me constantly to see the tolerance with which they took this major catastrophe. It was, however, the same fatalistic attitude which I had known among the Russian refugees in Paris – an air so compounded of stoicism and apparent frivolity that one scarcely knew how to judge them.

Things did not go so badly for these refugees at the start. Some had been able to get hold of a certain amount of money in foreign currencies before they escaped, others had been able to secure their jewels. Accustomed, however, to luxury and extravagance, most of them spent every penny they possessed before trying to engage themselves in some occupation which could secure for them a livelihood. Berlin had practically nothing to offer them in the way of fixed employment; thousands of its own people were out of work. They could not get out of Germany, as they had no passports; the League of Nations had not yet started issuing them, and they had no inclination to ask them of their Bolshevik enemies, who had now been recognised by the Germans as the *de facto* government.

All that remained then was to join the band of financial adventurers with which Berlin swarmed. Some were remarkably successful; the majority failed completely, and how they ever got enough to eat was a mystery to me. I felt dreadfully sorry for these refugees scattered over the face of the earth; they were not only here, but in every capital of Europe. Many years later, when I visited China, I even found them in Shanghai, half-starved, living in the filth and squalor of the Chinese quarter.

Although as a class they could be criticised for their treatment of the Russian people, and for the mess which they had made not only in governing, but in refusing to see the writing on the wall months ahead, and for their futile attempts to stop the revolution when it did come; yet, for the most part, as individuals, they were not responsible for a system which had been handed down for generations, and which they had learned to accept as part of their heritage. They endured adversity with an astounding philosophy; they were always willing to help each other by sharing whatever they had, and they were invariably cheerful, at least on the surface, even though perhaps they did not have the price of a meal in their pockets.

Some of them held up under the strain; others it broke. Prince K., a former governor of Riga, worked in a department store, and could smile at the strange tricks fate had played him, while poor Prince Pavlik O. took to drugs, and died as a result shortly afterwards. He was the son of the former Russian ambassador to Italy, and, in addition to vast estates, had owned most of the sugar-mills in Russia. For a while he lived on the money which a rich Romanian friend had loaned him. After this, he went around fruitlessly trying to sell an interest in his mills, which he was still in hopes would be returned to him someday. Von Malzahn, who was then in the Foreign Office, and who was later the German ambassador in Washington, was very kind to him. They had known each other when von Malzahn was a young attaché in Petrograd before the war. Prince O. took me around to see him one evening. As we sat and talked, I could see the look of pity in von Malzahn's eyes; he remembered Prince O. in better days.

Where you have Russians, there you will have parties, restaurants, cabarets, and clubs. They love to gather together for a celebration, and above all to talk. Every one of them is a musician; they all know their folk-songs, and love not only to listen but to participate in them. On festive occasions, in their private homes and elsewhere, the meals are always accompanied by bursts of song which produce a general spirit of camaraderie and an indescribable gaiety. Russian friends of mine will remember the palatial flat which I had just off the Kurfurstendamm; I could afford it during the inflation. Here, when I could spare the time, we assembled and sang those never-to-be-forgotten gipsy songs to the accompaniment of a guitarist who was a master. He was an old Turk, who had played before many a Grand Duke; their names and those of many others were inscribed on his instrument.

Sakuskis – hors d'œuvres which the Russians can consume by the hour – and vodka were plentiful, and we drank innumerable toasts; I learned to drink my first *charochka*, an intimate ritual among friends where each in turn has a toast sung to him while he drains his glass to the last drop.

As far as restaurants were concerned, it was at Olivier's on the Motzstrasse that we generally gathered. Olivier had been head chef to the Tsar, and his cooking gave me a taste for Russian food which ever since has led me off in search of a Russian restaurant in whatever town I have visited. Alas, I have often suffered, for every Russian is not a good cook. It was at Olivier's, too, that I heard those gipsy entertainers, the very best in Tsarist Russia, who had followed the *émigrés* into exile. Who can equal Gulescu, or even Iliescu on the violin, or Raphael on the accordion, or the deep-throated notes of Nastia Poliakova, in their rendering of this haunting music? For those who wish to hear them, they are now probably to be found in Paris at the Restaurant Muscovite in the rue Caumartin, at 'La Maisonette', or at Casanova's; some, perhaps, are still in Berlin.

It was not all amusement or self-deception with the Russians in Berlin. A good many of them seriously tried to retrieve their fortunes, and it was quite natural that they should turn their attention to their own country. Their schemes generally involved some sort of concession, which the Bolsheviks, pressed for money, were now granting to foreign capitalists. In the background, one frequently found some White Russian acting as technical adviser. At first I listened to the typical Russian enthusiasm surrounding these plans with friendly indifference, but as I thought over the possibilities, my professional interest and my personal curiosity sprang into a new hope. My affairs in Germany were hanging fire; I had options on at least a dozen interesting inventions, and had spent considerable time and money investigating them and trying to dispose of them, only to see a lack of vision and fear of losing money prevent industrial concerns from investing in them readily. Many of these companies today, I know, regret their lack of courage. It was natural, then, that I should grasp at the opportunity to find myself a new field. And here it was.

I spent hours with former Russian owners, going over plans for concessions of every description: manganese, timber, oil, river transportation on the Volga, pigs' bristles, casings, and trading in every form. Eventually, encouraged by the success of the German concessions of Dr Wirth and others, I set out for London to arrange a trip to Moscow.

In London, among the many English holders of Russian bonds, among owners of confiscated property in Russia, and in the various commercial circles, I discovered a great deal of interest in these concessions, and found myself rushed into a series of interviews at the clubs – if not at the Junior Carlton or White's, then at the Devonshire or St James's.

All this culminated in a small holding company being formed by half a dozen persons, of whom one was a peer, one the wife of a baronet, one the director of a steel works, and another a director of a large company trading with India. I was commissioned by this group to proceed to Moscow to negotiate for a general trading concession on the most favourable terms I could secure. It was planned, when this had been obtained, to float a larger company, to include manufacturers who would be interested in buying from or selling to Russia. In the new company I was to have a directorship.

On leaving London, I felt that I was undertaking quite an

adventure, for it was early in 1924, and a departure for Russia was still considered news by the papers. So far only a very few foreigners had been allowed to enter the country, and the number of Englishmen had been confined to a few isolated cases. Forced by necessity, a few European concessions were being granted, but if my journey were successful, mine would be the first trade agreement, on a concession basis, made between Russia and an English company. It was quite obvious that foreigners were not wanted at all in the country, and, of course, tourists were unheard of.

I did not think I was incurring any risks by entering Russia, but I did feel that I was taking a journey into the unknown. I had heard enough about Bolshevik atrocities and about the Cheka, or its successor, the GPU, to make me feel uncomfortable, and the long wait of three weeks before Moscow sent permission for my visa to be granted was not heart-warming. Possibly this was simply the usual Russian delay, to which I became accustomed later on; possibly my association with the secret service was known to the Russian Police, and they felt inclined to question my motives and arrange for a supervision of my movements. Watched in Russia I certainly was – but of that later; in my last days in England it was not any dread of espionage that haunted me, and kept me arguing continually to myself that, after all, mine was a simply harmless commercial enterprise. It was rather, I think, the feeling one has in walking over a trackless plain in the dark, in unfamiliar country: the new Russia was unpredictable, a completely unknown quantity, and I was uneasy before it as one is always uneasy before blankness.

On my arrival in Berlin, where I intended stopping over a

couple of days, my mission took on an entirely different aspect. No sooner did my Russian friends hear that I was on my way to Moscow, than I was besieged by requests. Each in turn wanted me to do something for him – to look up relatives or friends, or to examine some piece of property, the return of which was still hoped for. I promised to do my best, and said goodbye to them with a feeling of sadness. I realised that the very fact of my journey must fill them anew with the ache of homesickness; I was on my way to their native land, which, perhaps, they would never see again.

I was packing my bags in great haste at the Adlon Hotel when a telephone message announced that Prince M. was in the lobby and wished to see me. Asked up to my room, he announced on entering that he had an important matter which he wished to discuss with me.

'I can't give you much time,' I replied. 'I am leaving by the eight o'clock train, and it is now six; I still have to pack and get my dinner.' What he had to tell me, however, was of such interest that I delayed my departure without objection for twenty-four hours.

Prince M. was one of the few Russians in Berlin who was still comparatively well off. Before the war, he had maintained a palatial home in Paris, in which he had placed a few of the priceless old masters from his magnificent private collection in Russia. He had been fortunate enough to get a good price for them, and had been living on the proceeds. When I first met him I had mistaken him for a Scot: he spoke English with a pronounced Scottish accent, acquired from his boyhood governess. She had spent thirty years in his family, and had remained with them in Russia until about six months previously, when the family had persuaded her at last to return to Scotland. I had met her on her way through Berlin, and had been amused at the similarity of their speech.

I had seen quite a lot of Prince M. in Berlin, and from him had learned a great deal about his family history. He worried continually about his old father, who still remained in Leningrad in spite of his many endeavours to get a visa from the Bolsheviki to leave the country. 'They are after our family jewels,' he told me on several occasions. 'Our emeralds are famous throughout Russia, and the Bolsheviki refuse to believe my father's story that I escaped with them. That is why they are holding him.' Naturally then, I was all attention on the evening of my departure, when he spoke once more about the jewels.

'My father has them hidden away. The stones have been removed from their settings, and it will be simple to transport them,' he urged eagerly. 'I will give you the password which the governess brought me from my father, so that you will be secretly identified at home. Are you willing to bring them out for me? It is purely a business proposition; I can pay you £500 if you are successful.'

My first impulse was to refuse, for the money did not interest me in the least. I certainly placed a higher value on my safety. I was already nervous about my trip, and I knew that should I be caught, there would be trouble. I did not relish getting involved with the Bolsheviki; they had already demonstrated that they were not afraid to mete out the severest punishment to foreigners. My love of adventure carried me off, however, and before I was well aware what I was doing, I had told Prince M. that I would not accept the money, but that I was willing to undertake the job. Armed with the password and the address of his father in Leningrad, I continued my journey the next evening, considerably more perturbed in mind than when I had left London. I reproached myself for giving way too easily. Here I was on a trip to Russia to arrange a concession in which I hoped to build up a future, and yet I was jeopardising it right from the start by engaging myself on a foolhardy side-issue. But I knew myself well enough to be aware that, had I been able to withdraw, I would not have done so.

From everything I had heard of eastern Europe in those days, I was prepared to feel that I should be jumping from the edge of civilisation at the Russian border. The sensation arrived even earlier. At Wirballen, I crossed the border into Lithuania, the most uninteresting country I have ever been in; when I saw the mud in the streets and the huts out of which Kovno is composed, I readily understood the remark which a Pole once made to me during the Lithuanian conflict – that Poland would never bother to seize Lithuania, because it isn't worth having.

On the other hand, Riga, the capital of Latvia, was quite a city. It was built on the German plan: the dwellings were all large buildings, with a flat of nine or ten rooms to each floor. The streets were wide, and parts of the town closely resembled certain sections of Berlin. However, the best hotel, the Hotel de Rome, where I spent the night, was a great disappointment. I was nearly eaten up by the bedbugs. In the morning, when I approached the desk clerk with a grim look on my face, he smiled serenely, and before I could get a word in, he countered: 'Yes, it is terrible, I know, but we will never be able to get rid of them until we strip the papers off the walls. It is a souvenir that the

Bolsheviki left us.' One bright spot I found – a small German restaurant, recommended by Prince K. I had an excellent lunch there; it was the last good meal I was to have for three weeks.

That evening I left for Moscow, and at about 10 p.m. got to the border, where we changed into a Russian train. It was Labour Day; all the cars were decorated with red flags, and the front of the engine carried a huge sickle and hammer, the emblem of the USSR. I was to meet the same colour and the same emblem at every turn during the whole of my stay in Russia.

I was prepared for anything after my experience at the Hotel de Rome, but to my surprise, the train was clean and comfortable. The conductor provided me with tea, piping hot, at regular intervals; this was a privilege, for the few other travellers made their own from the supply of boiling water they got at the stations. Food we carried with us. I had rebelled somewhat at the annoyance of it when I departed from Riga, but I recognised it as a necessity when I saw the food that was on sale at the various stopping-places. I was thankful for the kindly advice and the ample supply of sandwiches which the Riga restaurant owner had supplied me with.

Along the railway I got my first glimpse of Russia; its rolling hills, stretches of forest – birch trees and pines – reminded me of eastern Canada. But here the likeness ceased; typical of Russia alone were the peasants, all dressed alike, dirty and ill-kept, wandering aimlessly up and down the platform, waiting for the great event of the day, the arrival of the train. From time to time one caught glimpses of relics of the old regime: a departed aristocrat's country mansion crumbling to ruin in a partitioned estate, or in the villages the church with its five minarets, a large one for Christ and four smaller ones for the gospels.

313

The hot and tiresome journey dragged on for some thirty-six hours, but at last we were in Moscow. From a distance I was dazzled by the sight – the sun beating down on hundreds of golden minarets gave me the impression of an *Arabian Nights* city. At the station, however, the first impression seemed a mirage, a mere vision which faded before the depressing reality of new Russia. The place was packed with humanity, people as usual standing about aimlessly, with apparently no reason for having come there and no reason to go away. In the enclosed space their odour was overpowering. They were like a horde of robots, with no distinctions except of age and size, to tell one from another. Their passivity, their dull lack of expression, their absence of any self-direction, made them seem cut and stamped to pattern by a machine. Not a sign of individuality, of self-respect, or taste, did I see. There was not one white collar or tie in the crowd; I did not, in fact, see one during the whole of my stay in Russia.

Outside the station I hailed a cab-driver, who took me to the Savoy Hotel, reserved for foreign visitors. I soon discovered it to be the only hotel open in Moscow. I was the only guest there. The rooms were clean and comfortable, but terribly expensive. In Russian chervonetz I paid the equivalent of £3 per day for a room, plus £1 for each bath I took; the food, which was very poor, was correspondingly dear. I made a rapid calculation of the cost *per diem*, and resolved to get out of Moscow as quickly as possible, but my resolution was in vain, for it took me three weeks to secure my concession.

I found Krassin, with whom I negotiated, a charming man; he spoke perfect English, and having been the Soviet representative in London before Rakovsky, he was thoroughly acquainted

with trade conditions in England. He had also been employed
as an engineer before the war by Siemens-Schuckert in Berlin;
it was obviously his experience there which had qualified him
so pre-eminently for the post of Trade Commissar which he
now occupied.

He quickly agreed to accord me the same terms which he said
had been granted the Germans in their concessions: namely, a
company was to be formed with sufficient capital for working
purposes – in our case, £100,000; half the shares of the company
were to be given to the Soviet government; there was to be equal
representation on the board of directors, and the chairman, with
the casting vote, was to be a Soviet member; the headquarters
of the company was to be in Moscow, and the board meetings
were to take place there; the working capital of the company
was to be deposited in the Russian state bank; the profits were
not to be exported.

These terms may have satisfied the Germans, and there was an
obvious advantage in having a government partner, who would
guarantee to buy and sell to the concessionaire, but I knew my
friends would be disappointed; they would never agree to putting their heads in the Soviet mouth in this fashion. As for me,
who had had visions of myself as an executive in a large London office handling a flood of Soviet trade, my hopes vanished
into thin air.

I smiled somewhat grimly to myself. There I was in Moscow,
paying out goodness knows how many chervonetz a day, waiting for the official seal and signature to a concession which I
was almost certain my friends would reject. However, there was
nothing to do but to remain on for a few more days; I might as

315

well take back the piece of paper which I had travelled so far to get. At least I was making history, for it was the first trade concession that had ever been granted by the Soviets to a purely British company.

During the period of waiting in Moscow I met two people whom, perhaps, I might not mention, had I not noticed their names of late in a situation which seemed a sardonic echo of my own wasted weeks in Russia. Both were figures in the recent Monkhouse trial, in which several British engineers and employees working for Metropolitan Vickers were tried for sabotage of the machinery in some of the water-power stations which were in the course of construction in Russia. One whom I had known was Anna Sergievna K. I do not deny that a slight chill ran over me when I recalled that she had acted as my secretary while I was in Russia. She was a quiet, reserved, capable woman, an accomplished linguist, and a creature of unlimited energy. I had felt rather absurdly that she was my Soviet chaperon, for she had been recommended to me by one of the staff at the Savoy Hotel, an obvious GPU agent, before whom I had made a careful parade of having nothing to hide. I asked this recommendation as an instance of good faith on my part, and I assumed that my discreet secretary was not without instructions. Yet here she was involved in a situation of more than threatening character. These reversals of fortune have been common in the new Russia from the first; I had no reason to be surprised at all – no reason, that is to say, except the human tendency to regard our own affairs and those of our acquaintances as exempt from dangers which, however regretfully, we accept as probable or inevitable for the rest of mankind.

My other acquaintance in Moscow has suffered the same reversal, but as a foreigner he has been more desperately placed, and his story is marked by a strong ironic quality which makes the remembrance of my conversations with him infinitely pathetic. This was Saunders, an English engineer, to whom I took a letter of introduction from his brother in England. He interested me immensely, for he was one of the few Englishmen who had lived in Russia continuously since before the war. He had been connected with some English Works in Moscow, and had remained through the years of war and revolution to look after their interests, though when I saw him, he was without a job. When I asked him why he did not return to England, I found him possessed with the idea that he was the only Englishman on the spot available for commercial work, and that someday this would infallibly bring him a rich return.

Saunders took me out to his home in the country, about an hour's journey by train. Here living was cheaper, he informed me, and it was much healthier for his children. Also he had a cottage, whereas in Moscow he would only have been permitted a single room. He was so concerned about his family that I am sure he would never have jeopardised their future by engaging in acts of sabotage; on the contrary, he seemed at the time I saw him painfully anxious not to displease the Bolsheviki, and was obviously afraid to discuss Soviet conditions. I confined myself, therefore, to giving him news of his brother, and to telling him what conditions were like in England, while in my mind there took root the assurance that Soviet Russia opened no future for any Englishman. Ten years and the Monkhouse affair have not altered that conviction.

After two weeks had elapsed, I was glad to get a note from Greenfield, Krassin's secretary, asking me to call at his office. Without comment, he handed me the concession containing all the terms agreed upon, with the Soviet seal affixed. I accepted it without enthusiasm. Even when one is 'making history', as I was doing in gaining this document, one is not always personally exalted. I should have been even less enthusiastic had I realised that even this official, so highly and securely placed, was to be ploughed under by caprices of Soviet fortune. He was a bit of a mystery, however, this Greenfield. Where he got his English name, I do not know; he was probably Grünefeld once, in New York or London. He spoke perfect English. I wished to draw him out on the few occasions I met him, but without success; he knew the value of silence and discretion. It was years afterwards in Paris, when I met a Russian who was well up in Soviet affairs, that I learned his fate through a passing allusion to his name. 'He was condemned to Siberia,' was the laconic comment that closed his history. Many a Soviet official has met the same end; even the highest ones were not safe from the eyes and ears of the GPU.

The concession settled, I turned my attention to my other mission, and applied for a return visa, allowing me to proceed via Leningrad. This delayed me another day, in which my nervous tension may be imagined. I was cross-examined for nearly an hour by a GPU official as to why I wanted to go by this route, instead of choosing the shorter one through Riga. It was in some ways a comic experience. Here was I, who had spent hours in my time examining spies, traitors, purveyors of information of all sorts – sitting meekly in the character of a suspect; I actually began to feel guilty of some crime or other, as people say they do at the sight of a policeman. My positive conviction that the Russian police knew all there was to know of my work in espionage made me even more self-conscious. However, I took a leaf from the book in which both spy and thief are so well versed – the art of innocence – and relied upon blank simplicity to shield my movements and my purpose. Both the address of Prince M.'s father and the necessary password existed in my memory only; nothing in my papers or bags could give me away.

I was therefore, and I repeated it *ad nauseam*, a simple English man of business, who wished to see the sights – no more. My answer did not seem to please my examiner, but eventually he told me that permission would be granted, and that my passport, duly stamped, would be sent to me at my hotel. He dismissed me with an abruptness which I fancied I understood: he had determined to have me watched on the way to Leningrad.

The journey took about twenty hours, but the instant I settled myself in my compartment I realised – with inward chuckles – that it would not be monotonous or dull. The watcher I had expected was cheerfully installed and awaiting me. Most comic of all, from Anglo-Saxon standards of privacy in compartment travel – it was a woman. She was a good-looking brunette of about thirty-five, who opened up conversation with me immediately. She began in excellent German; I found out afterwards that she spoke English and French equally well. Somewhat too carefully, she explained that she had been employed in the Soviet embassy in Berlin, and was on her way to visit friends in Leningrad.

In spite of my amusement, I was on the alert to observe that she plied me with innumerable questions about my trip to Leningrad, and seemed especially interested in the Berlin White Russian colony. Many of my acquaintances she mentioned by name. I parried with amiable but empty gossip, pretended a vastly greater ignorance than I had, and with every appearance of candour turned my share of the conversation into petitions for information on Russian life, sights, and manners. Apparently my sight-seeing role satisfied her, for after a while she confined herself to telling me the places of interest to visit in Leningrad.

I enjoyed her company; she was both attractive and intelligent, and mistress of a solid fund of interesting information. I smiled as I said goodbye to her. Our roles had been reversed, for it was to her, my quondam examiner, that I am indebted for much that I know of Soviet Russia.

As the train pulled into the city, my first impulse was to make immediately for the address Prince M. had given me, but on reflection I realised that the surveillance over me might be continued; so I decided to find rooms and pretend a preliminary round of sightseeing. The Europaiski Hotel, where I stopped, famous in pre-revolutionary days, was a distinct improvement on the Savoy. The room I occupied had been well kept up, and compared favourably with the best hotels in Europe. The same high prices as in Moscow prevailed, however. As I took my key at the desk, I spied a box of Corona cigars. I had not been able to smoke the insipid Soviet cigarettes, and I was dying for a smoke. 'How much?' I asked the desk clerk. 'A chervonetz [£1] apiece,' he replied. I succumbed; I had already grown accustomed to the prices. But I smiled ruefully as the cigar crumbled to dust in my hands. It was at least seven years old.

In the roof-garden of the hotel, palms, fountains, gipsy

entertainers, red-coated waiters darting between tables crowded with uniformed officers and lovely *élégantes*, were gone. I found nothing but half a dozen billiard tables installed; some Soviet youths, who looked like students, were crowded around the tables, all intent on those huge white Russian billiard balls, each at least four times the size of those used in other countries.

The only activity throughout Leningrad, in fact, seemed to be that of the university, where crowds of students were seen. The Soviets were doing their best to foster higher learning, and I was told that the laboratories of the university were splendidly equipped. Otherwise, Leningrad had all the appearance of a derelict city, a sorry sight with its buildings in disrepair, and with falling plaster and bricks scattered over the sidewalk.

As I drove down the Nevski Prospekt, now the Prospect of 25 October, in honour of the revolution, there was hardly a person in sight. In many places the wooden paving of the streets was caved in, leaving holes big enough to engulf cab and horse; and at night, in the darkness, the drive would have been made at the risk of one's life. The dozens of deserted factories at the edge of the town bore out what I had learned in Moscow – that hundreds of works had been allowed to go to ruin during the earlier stages of the revolution, and that later many a costly plant which was beyond repair had been pulled down to furnish scrap for the Soviet Steel Works. In the distance the Winter Palace and St Isaac's Cathedral stood out in regal majesty. Like the Kremlin, they defied the ravages of time and of the Soviets.

In the afternoon I dismissed my cab at a point discreetly distant from the hotel, and set out for my goal by a devious route on foot. In the course of it I got lost several times, not daring to ask for any information, but at length I made my way to the dwelling of Prince M.'s father, which I found to be an apartment house. In response to my knock, the door was furtively opened by a person I could not distinctly see, but who, as soon as he learned I was from abroad, let me in quickly, as if he feared someone would see me on the staircase. I found myself facing a tall well-built man with white hair and a large moustache, whose sad and kindly eyes attracted me immediately. From the way he carried himself, and from his general air of good breeding and culture, I knew that I was in the presence of the father.

He brought me into a room where he introduced me to the rest of the family: the Princess his wife, still so lovely that I could believe the legend of his having killed his brother, her first husband, in a duel for her favour; his daughter, a very plain, masculine-looking woman, a marked contrast to her handsome brother, but also with a Scottish accent; and, finally, the daughter's two sons, boys of about sixteen and fourteen years old. I was immediately plied with a battery of questions. For nearly an hour I was cross-examined by each of the family in turn. I had to repeat over and over again exactly how Dima, Prince M., looked, and I had to tell in detail everything I knew about him.

Finally, I called the father aside and asked to be allowed to speak with him privately. When the others had left the room, I told him about the mission from his son, and gave him the password. He uttered a sigh of relief. 'I was wondering,' he said, 'when I saw you, whether you were the person we had been expecting. We knew Dima would find someone.'

Without further ado, he took down from the wall an icon of the Virgin Mary, removed a small piece of wood from the frame, and from a hole bored in it, poured out twenty-three huge emeralds and diamonds. I could not keep my eyes from them. They were flawless, and worth a fortune; no wonder the Bolsheviki had tried to find out what had happened to them. I smiled at the icon; it was certainly not the best spot for a hiding place. The Bolsheviki, with their avowed anti-religious policy, might have destroyed it; but the father, a typical superstitious Russian, evidently looked for divine protection through it.

'How are you going to hide them?' he anxiously inquired. I indicated the lining of the heavy travelling ulster with which I had come prepared. Goodness knows it was very inadequate; it would be the very first place I would have examined, if I myself had to conduct such a search, but it was the best and simplest carrier I had at my disposal. Audacity and the obvious are sometimes their own protection. The Prince called his wife in, and then while we anxiously looked on giving suggestions, she quieted her shaking fingers and sewed the stones into various parts of the coat – first securely stitching each stone into a separate piece of strong black linen, and then sewing these casings in the hems, under the turned over sleeves, and under the collar. After the last careful stitches were set in, and the father had given me various verbal messages for his son, chiefly about the disposal of the stones, we rejoined the rest of the family.

They pressed me to a supper of those small Neva fish which Russians know so well. They were excellently prepared, but humble fare for this old man, who had been in the old days equerry to the Tsar, and one of the richest men in Russia. It was sad to see him in a small three-room apartment, piled high with all his worldly belongings; but he was lucky, for in Moscow the whole family would have had to put up with a single room. He told me, among other details, how once a week in this community building, which contained about twenty families, he had to take his turn at carrying garbage into the street for all the people.

They were living on the small sum which the Bolsheviki permitted Prince M. to send the family monthly. Before they had pressed their loyal governess to return to England and safety she had insisted on providing the household with sums from her savings, which, British fashion, she had put away in British banks; the cordial gifts of the family's better days made her under the new regime far better off than they. Now the welfare of the family depended on the sale of the jewels, and hence – uneasy thought – on their safety with me. What worried the old nobleman most, however, was the education of his daughter's two boys. 'We have got to teach them at home,' he said. 'They won't allow our sons to enter the university, and, of course, they cannot go abroad. A whole generation of families such as ours is lost to the civilisation we believe in.' He thanked God, however, that he was still alive after his experience in prison; like most of the aristocracy who had remained in Russia, he had spent many months in prison without any charge being brought against him.

The next evening I left for Reval, glad to be on my way out of Russia, and in the early hours of the morning I reached the frontier. A GPU agent entered my compartment. Here was the ordeal I had mentally gone through a thousand times during my three weeks' stay in Russia. After examining my papers, he carefully went through my bags. Impassively I watched him, having – oh so casually! – tossed my ulster into a corner of the seat to be out of his way. He looked at me closely, as if weighing whether or not he should search my clothes. I was afraid he could hear the thumping of my heart. But evidently my face belied the turmoil of my mind, for he turned away with a sour grin, apparently satisfied that he had done enough. The train started, and within a few minutes I was in Esthonia. I don't think I have ever in my life experienced such a relief.

In Reval, the seaboard capital of Esthonia, I found myself once again among people in individual clothes and with separate personalities; I saw smiling faces again, energetic movements of persons with some point to their *existence*, bands of active children on their way to school. The robot population of the USSR was behind me. Whether it was by contrast or not, I do not know, but the town seemed to breathe prosperity. The marketplace was crowded; people were buying and selling; money was changing hands. Most of the people were of German origin, and I found German spoken everywhere. I made for the first restaurant, and was happy to sit down to a good meal at a reasonable price. Shortly after, I ensconced myself in a comfortable *wagon lit* en route for London, via Riga and Berlin, feeling, I think, much as a man would feel who had safely returned from Mars.

Filled with this sense of lightness or ease or life resumed – whatever one wishes to call it – I set about the final discharge of my two Russian missions; the more personally pressing fortunately could come first, since I could dismiss it on the way to London.

The Baltic seaport towns were swarming with Russian spies, and as I did not wish to risk compromising Prince M.'s father in Russia, I refrained from telegraphing the Prince. Imagine his excitement, then, when he heard my voice over the telephone in Berlin, announcing the success of our affair. I hastened to his apartment, and there I handed him the stones. He wept and embraced me when he saw them. 'It is not for my sake that I am happy,' he told me. 'But it means that I shall have enough money to support my father in Russia for the rest of his days.'

The next day I set out for London somewhat despondent, for although I had the concession I had set out to obtain, it did not promise what either my friends or I had hoped for. I was considerably exercised in mind as to what I would do with the future.

My friends were remarkably kind. They had not been altogether unprepared for what I had to tell them. They assured me they had looked upon the trip as a gamble and so were not surprised at the terms granted me. What became of the concession papers I do not know. They are probably locked away in some safe. Perhaps one day they will be exhibited as historical documents – the first Soviet Trade Concession granted to the British.

As for myself, for the moment I had laid aside my cares. 'Now for Yvonne and Brussels,' thought I. 'I have certainly earned a vacation.'

During the last two years I had seen Yvonne only at odd intervals. My thoughts always turned back to her, and we had corresponded regularly; but my affairs tied me down to Central Europe, while she had been confined to Belgium and other Latin countries by her theatrical engagements. On the rare occasions we had been together, we still got the same joy out of each other, we still were divinely happy, but I was ever aware of the antagonism of her parents. She was not only supporting them, but also her grandmother, and they watched her as if their lives depended on her.

The whole situation worried me. Even if she were to change her mind, and consent to marry me, I knew she was right: she needed Z. He was not only powerful enough to make or break her at the Brussels opera, but he was instrumental in arranging numerous fêtes for visiting royalty and celebrities; he was the one who chose the artists for these occasions, and could humiliate her by not selecting her or even by ordering the opera director to make her play a secondary role to one of her juniors. Although she was a superb artist, she owed her success entirely to Z, for there is a regular order of promotion in national opera companies, and at her age, in spite of her talent, she should normally still have been in the ballet.

She loved me enough to give up the stage if I had really insisted, but I knew it would break her heart. She had been dancing ever since she was four years old, and I knew her life was wrapped up in it. On my part, too, I knew that whatever my feelings toward her were, it was when I saw her dancing that I loved her most. Her entry on the stage always gave me a thrill. The whole atmosphere of the theatre and of the circle in which she lived entranced me. As I look back now, I realise that a great deal of what I attributed to her was part of my own imagination, something beautiful that I had created and fitted around her. The theatre and the ballet were all part of the staging; and yet without her gaiety, her sparkling wit, her great beauty, her sweetness of character, and her charming companionship, all would have faded away into the realm of unreality for want of an anchorage.

At the time of these events, I was incapable of seeing matters so clearly. I knew merely that I was on my way to Yvonne, and I could have gone singing. I was like a schoolboy setting out on his vacation. As soon as we met, however, I realised that something was wrong. She was sad and wistful. Her mood was contagious, and we ate our dinner – as usual at the Savoy – in semi-silence. That evening it was *Faust* again that she danced, the ballet in which I had first seen her. Normally, it would have enchanted me, but now it only filled me with sadness, for she had promised that after the performance she would tell me the reason for her depression.

As we sat together in her house over the dying embers in the fireplace, she explained, with tears in her eyes, that she had promised not to see me any more. 'Z is dreadfully jealous of you,' she faltered, 'and you know how dependent I am on him. Besides, I have seen you so rarely during the past few years. You have your career and I have mine. There are my parents and my grandmother, too; they have worried me incessantly about you until I cannot stand the strain any longer.'

I told her that I understood. I was to come and say goodbye to her on the morrow, to see her just once again. I would leave Brussels on the evening train. I kissed her good night, trying not to think of the last farewell so close upon us.

When her maid ushered me into her sitting-room the next afternoon, I was astounded to find Z there. Her eyes implored me; I knew he must have dropped in inadvertently. It was an extraordinary situation. I had never seen Z at her house before, though we had often met officially during the time I had been stationed in Brussels, and we both knew of each other's affection for Yvonne. How should we not, when the whole of Brussels knew about it? We looked at each other without a word being spoken. Neither of us had the right to reproach the other. I knew what he had done for her; he knew that I loved her, and that I had made her happy.

At last I broke the silence. 'I am leaving Brussels tonight,' said I. 'Perhaps I shall never return. I have come to say good-bye to Yvonne.' He shook my hand. 'I understand,' he replied; 'I am dreadfully sorry.'

I kissed her farewell and left the room. Then my reason seemed to break. I could not leave her. I came back into the room, and took her once again in my arms. Again and again I kissed her, with the futile clinging of one who embraces the dying. At last she put me gently away from her, and I heard a door close. I stumbled blindly down the steps into the street.

What was I going to do? I had no plans. Events had been moving rapidly in my life. I had left Berlin. My mission in Russia had proved a successful failure. I had been cut adrift from Yvonne.

As I sat in my room in the Hôtel Daunou in Paris, I looked back over the last ten years of my life. I could only see suffering; the wounded dying of tetanus in the hospital at St Nazaire; dying comrades as they were shot down next to me; the dead, as I crawled among them on the slopes of Notre Dame de Lorette; the suffering of the French and Belgian people in the occupied territories during the war; agents shot or imprisoned for espionage; the look of despair on the faces of the German deserters; Russian refugees, deprived of their families, their homes, and all their worldly possessions; millions of half-starved people in Germany and Russia. It was a ghastly picture of man's inhumanity to man.

As I looked forward, I could see the dance going on: the Central Powers striving to hold their heads up under the burden of the Versailles and other treaties, and hoping to get back something of what they had lost; France and the countries of the Little Entente, in a circle around them, grimly determined to hold on to what they had got, and still carrying on a war in peacetime, grinding down their hereditary enemies by relentless political and economic pressure, and by unceasing propaganda; Italy, not satisfied with her share, and trying to grasp an additional portion; Russia, writhing under new masters, even more stern than those she had thrown off; and England alone trying to get on with business as usual, and striving to wipe out the scars of war, yet anxiously attempting to maintain her traditional policy of holding the balance of power.

There was also my career, that objective which had dragged me on relentlessly ever since I was a boy, but which had grown somewhat dimmed during the last years. It was still there beckoning me on, as I caught glimpses of it in the mist of the life which had enveloped me.

Now it seemed to shine out brightly. 'Why not give it all up?' it whispered to me. 'Go home to South Africa to your own people.' I weighed what I had achieved in Europe during the four years since my demobilisation, but in the maze of my activities I could see no promise of a definite career there.

And so I listened. The rolling veldt called to me once more, and so did my grand old pioneer father. I knew a great deal about government; I had gained unique experience of it in many lands; there were my university qualifications; I was sure I could get into one of the ministries. I would dedicate the rest of my life to my native land.

Having made my decision, hope seized me anew; I packed my bag, and within twenty-four hours I was on board the *Armadale Castle*, steaming past the Isle of Wight, en route for South Africa.

CHAPTER 28

SABOTAGE IN
THE USA – BLACK TOM
BLOWS UP

AFTER LEAVING EUROPE I spent several years in South
Africa, my native land, before journeying to the United
States in 1927.

Because of my war experience in the British secret service, and
the unique opportunities I had had of learning the methods
and psychology of the German secret service, I was invited to
assist the American claimants in their investigations in connection with the Black Tom and Kingsland cases. These were the
two most spectacular and devastating acts of sabotage known

to history, and the only ones, with the exception of an explosion in Tacoma harbour, in which any attempt has been made to prove German complicity, and to collect damages.

In the course of my investigations I got to know intimately many of the principal characters involved, and have obtained from them their personal stories. In addition, the voluminous records of these cases, consisting of exhibits, briefs, oral arguments before the Mixed Claims Commission, and reports of the various American investigators have been at my disposal.

Elsewhere I have written in detail about the evidence. Here I merely present to the reader the salient features of the two cases. It is not for me to indict Germany. Many arguments can be advanced in support of her contention that, while the United States was technically neutral during the neutrality period, actually she was affording material and financial aid to Germany's enemies and that Germany was justified, therefore, in the use of sabotage to impede the flow of munitions and supplies to the Allies. In wartime every nation adopts the most expedient methods to guard its vital interests, and American unpreparedness in the field of counter-espionage was an open invitation to Germany to conduct a campaign of sabotage in the United States.

At 2 a.m. on the night of 30 July 1916, New York City was rocked by the greatest explosion in her history. Over 2,000,000 lbs of munitions stored on Black Tom Island in New York harbour blew up in a series of explosions. Two of the blasts were distinctly heard in Camden and Philadelphia, nearly 100 miles away. The tremendous concussion shattered practically every window in Jersey City, and in Manhattan and Brooklyn thousands of heavy plate-glass windows fell from office buildings and skyscrapers into the streets. Buildings trembled; some of the inhabitants were thrown from their beds; and the population, panic-stricken, emptied itself out into the streets.

For hours the sky was lit up by the fierce fire which raged on Black Tom Island; and for three hours a steady stream of high explosives and shrapnel shells were hurled from the conflagration as they exploded, some of them landing as far off as Governors Island. Buildings on Ellis Island were wrecked, and all immigrants there had to be evacuated. During these terrifying hours Black Tom and its vicinity might well have been part of the Western Front during a gigantic battle. The residents of Greater New York and northern New Jersey were shaken badly by the blast, but fortunately the terminal was just far enough away to prevent the metropolitan area's being razed.

To follow intelligently the tragic events which happened on that night, it is necessary to understand the layout of the terminal and also the conditions which prevailed there at the time of the explosion.

Black Tom is a promontory, nearly 1 mile long, which juts out into the Upper Bay from the New Jersey shore, about opposite the Statue of Liberty. It was originally an island, but at the time of the explosion was joined to the shore by a fill about 150 ft wide.

On Black Tom the Lehigh Valley Railroad company had built large warehouses, numerous piers, and a network of tracks. Within a short time after the commencement of the war, Black Tom became the most important point in America for the transfer of munitions and supplies to Allied vessels. Loaded freight cars were run into the northern part of the terminal, and from

there the munitions were loaded into barges hired by the con-
signees and tied up at the adjoining piers.

As it was not always possible for the representatives of the
Allied governments to determine beforehand the exact time
steamers would be ready to receive the loads of ammunition, it
was quite usual for the munitions cars to be kept there for several
days, sometimes a week, waiting to be unloaded. Thus, on the
night of the explosion there were thirty-four carloads of munitions on Black Tom, consisting of eleven cars of high explosives,
seventeen of shells, three of nitro-cellulose, one of TNT, and two
of combination fuses; in all a total of approximately 2,123,000
lbs of explosives.

At the north pier, bordering on the tracks, ten barges were
tied up, most of them loaded with explosives which they had
taken on at other terminals and piers in New York harbour. They
had tied up at Black Tom, some to take on additional explosives,
others to stay there during the night and over the following Sunday until their loads could be shifted to steamers. One of these
barges, the *Johnson* 17, was loaded with 100,000 lbs of TNT
and 417 cases of detonating fuses – a veritable floating bomb.

During July 1916 Black Tom terminal was guarded at night by
six watchmen provided by the Lehigh Valley Railroad company,
and by private detectives furnished by the Dougherty Detective
Agency and paid for by the Allied governments, owners of the
munitions. These men went on duty at 5 p.m. and remained
until 6 a.m.

There was no gate on the tongue of land connecting Black
Tom to the mainland; consequently it was an easy matter for
a person to reach the terminal; and, unless of a suspicious

appearance, he would not have been stopped by the guards as this passageway was also commonly used by the barge men whose boats were tied up at the pier. Furthermore, the terminal was in an isolated spot and unlighted, thus making it difficult to see a person prowling about. In addition anyone could reach it at night in a boat with little danger of being observed.

On Saturday evening, 29 July, at 5 p.m., all work stopped on Black Tom; the workmen departed for their usual Sunday holiday; and all locomotive engines were sent to the mainland. The terminal was a dead yard.

A gentle wind was blowing from the south-west. The night was quiet, and the guards placidly made their periodical rounds.

At 12.45 a.m. a fire was suddenly noticed in one of the munitions cars. At the first sight of it the guards raised the fire alarm and fled in a panic.

Five independent witnesses on Black Tom Island at the time made affidavits that the fire started inside the car and that the fire burned for about twenty minutes before the first explosion. A witness on Bedloe's Island, who had a view of the pier as well, later stated that another fire appeared almost simultaneously in a barge about 300 yards away, presumably the *Johnson* 17.

At 2 a.m. the first explosion occurred, and this was followed by a second terrific blast at 2.40. In the confusion no one was able to tell whether the barge or the munitions near the car blew up first. However this fact is established: the *Johnson* 17 was 325 feet away from the pier when it exploded. This was determined by the crater which soundings of the river-bed disclosed. The depth of the river at that point was found to be 21 ft; whereas a geodetic survey made a few days before the explosion had established a depth of 7 ft at the same spot. How the barge drifted so far away from the pier is not known. Only Johnson, the captain of the barge and the only man on board at the time, could tell whether its mooring had been burned away, or whether he had cast it loose. Both he and his barge had disappeared, however. Three months later his body drifted up on Bedloe's Island.

Another huge crater was found at a spot near where the burning car had stood. Thus it appeared that the two major explosions had been caused by the detonation of the munitions near the car and on the barge, the two places where the fires had been observed.

The two explosions and the conflagration which broke out destroyed the entire Black Tom terminal together with all the munitions and rolling stock which happened to be there that night. The damage was estimated at $14,000,000, and three men and a child were killed. These included Leyden, one of the night watchmen, and a policeman named James Doherty.

The immediate outcome of the Black Tom disaster was that several suits were filed against the Lehigh Valley Railroad company by the Russian government, which owned most of the munitions that had exploded, and by the property owners in the neighbourhood. The plaintiffs maintained that the railroad had been negligent in not providing better protection for the property in view of the fact that it was known that German sabotage agents were at work in this country.

The Lehigh Valley based its defence on the theory that the explosions had been caused by spontaneous combustion, a defence which seemed the most expedient at the time, but one which rose to plague it later; for this was the very defence which the Germans raised when, after the war, the railroad and other American claimants in the Black Tom case filed their claims against Germany for damages with the Mixed Claims Commission. At these early trials, however, experts proved to the satisfaction of the jury that spontaneous combustion was impossible. It was established that the smokeless powder contained in the shells was manufactured in accordance with the specifications of the United States Army and Navy; that it was all new powder, treated with a stabiliser known as diphenylamine which prevented spontaneous combustion. Dr Free, United States government expert, testified that he had examined nearly 2,000,000,000 lbs of powder manufactured in this way and that it was inconceivable that spontaneous combustion could have occurred. It was further shown that even untreated smokeless powder would require a temperature of 356° Fahrenheit before it would ignite.

As regards TNT, experts testified that it was impossible for it to ignite spontaneously. Finally, it was pointed out that if the shells had gone off by spontaneous combustion, the guards would not have seen flames destroying the freight car for eighteen minutes before the first explosion at 2 a.m. Besides all this there was evidence to show that before either of the explosions occurred another fire had broken out almost simultaneously with the first at a point nearly 300 yards away from the car – the distance between it and the barge *Johnson* 17. This fact alone indicated that the origin of the explosions was incendiary. In most of these cases the jury found that the Lehigh Valley Railroad company had been negligent in not having sufficient guards to protect the property.

But there were other developments. The local police were busily searching for leads. A Mrs Chapman, a resident of Bayonne, New Jersey, who since her childhood had known Captain John J. Rigney, of the Bayonne police department reported to him her suspicions that a cousin, Michael Kristoff, was responsible for the destruction of Black Tom. She related that Kristoff, who had formerly lodged with her and at the time lodged with her mother, Mrs Anna Rushnak, at 76 East 25th Street, Bayonne, did not return home until four o'clock in the morning of the night of the explosion. Hearing him pace the floor, her mother went to his room. She found him in a state of great excitement and near nervous prostration. To her anxious query as to what had happened, the only reply she could get out of him was 'What I do! What I do!' This he kept repeating over and over again as he ran his hands through his hair.

According to Captain Rigney, Mrs Chapman also told him that 'Kristoff had been in the habit of going away from time to time and that everywhere he went there was an explosion.' She referred to some place in Columbus, Ohio, where he had gone and said that whenever he came back from any of these trips he always had plenty of money. She also said that she had seen maps and charts in Kristoff's possession while he had been staying with her at her house at 114 Neptune Avenue, Jersey City, New Jersey.

The result was that after shadowing Kristoff for some time, Captain Rigney arrested him near Mrs Rushnak's home on 31 August 1916 and turned him over to Lieutenant Peter Green of the Jersey City police department.

All that was known about Kristoff was that he was born in

1893, in Presov, then in the Slovak region of Hungary, now a part of Czechoslovakia, and had been given the surname of Michael. When he was six years old his parents immigrated to the United States, where his mother had several members of her family living. By 1916 he had grown into a tall, slimly built young man, with light reddish hair, pale blue eyes, fair complexion, and a weak receding chin. For some months prior to July he had been working for the Tidewater Oil Company at Bayonne, New Jersey, close to Black Tom.

When examined by the Bayonne Police authorities, his story ran substantially as follows: on 3 January 1916 he was sitting in the waiting-room of the Pennsylvania railroad station, 33rd Street, New York City, when he was accosted by a man who asked him the time and then inquired where he was going. Kristoff informed him that he was waiting for a train to go to Cambridge, Ohio, where he intended to visit his sister. This man, who then gave his name as Graentnor, offered him a job at $20 per week, which he accepted. He went with Graentnor to the Hotel York, and on the next day they started off on a series of travels which took them in turn to Philadelphia, Bridgeport, Cleveland, Akron, Columbus, Chicago, Kansas City, St Louis, and finally back to New York. After arranging to meet him in the lobby of the Hotel McAlpin Graentnor disappeared, and he never saw him again. Kristoff stated that during these journeys his job was to carry Graentnor's two suitcases, which contained blueprints of bridges and factories, also money and books. He had no idea whom Graentnor saw in these towns, but ventured an opinion that the plans were 'to show people how to build bridges and houses and factories'.

His whole story sounded so unintelligible to the police authorities that they got the impression Kristoff was half demented; and, therefore, they called in a specialist to examine him. It was finally decided that he was not altogether sane, but not dangerously insane. Whereupon, in spite of the fact he had furnished several false alibis as to where he had been on the night of the explosion and had admitted working for the Eagle Oil Works, adjacent to Black Tom, and not returning for his pay after the explosion, he was released on 25 September 1916 after promising to look for Graentnor.

But the Lehigh Valley Railroad officials were not convinced. To them the strange story of Kristoff was not that of a crazy man but that of a man attempting to cover up his tracks. They felt that in his clumsy evasions he had admitted some truths. Factories were being blown up all over the country, and Graentnor and his two suitcases filled with blueprints sounded real.

From the payroll records of the Tidewater Oil Company in Bayonne, where Kristoff had been employed prior to his work at the Eagle Oil Works, they discovered that he had been absent for five work-days in January 1916. Subsequently he had left the employ of the company on 29 February 1916, and had not returned to work until 19 June. After working there for a month he had transferred his services to the Eagle Oil Works. In addition, Mrs Chapman later made an affidavit to the effect that while cleaning Kristoff's room one day shortly before the Black Tom explosion she had found an un-mailed letter to a man named 'Grandson' or 'Graentnor' in which he had demanded a large sum of money. The Lehigh Valley Railroad therefore hired Alexander Kassman, an employee of the W. J. Burns Detective Agency, to shadow him.

For almost a year Kassman lived in close contact with Kristoff; they worked at the same chocolate factory and met nightly. Kassman posed as an Austrian anarchist, took Kristoff to anarchists' meetings, and thus won his confidence. At regular intervals Kassman reported to the Burns Agency. A perusal of these reports shows that Kristoff on numerous occasions admitted to Kassman that he had assisted in blowing up Black Tom.

In May 1917 Kassman lost track of Kristoff. Records discovered long afterwards revealed, however, that he employed a well-known ruse to divert attention from himself: on 22 May 1917 he enlisted in the United States Army. A later entry in his army record shows that he was discharged on 12 September 1917 because of tuberculosis and for having enlisted under false enlistment papers.

Kristoff now vanished completely until the spring of 1921, when he was located in prison at Albany, New York, where he had been committed for larceny under the name of 'John Christie',

Once again the Lehigh Valley attempted to get from him further information about Black Tom. Through the co-operation of the county officials of Albany County, a detective of the Washington detective bureau was placed in a cell next to Kristoff, and together with him was assigned to work in the prison bakery. The detective remained there nineteen days, but Kristoff was on the defensive when approached about Black Tom. He was well aware that a murder charge was involved. He repeated the same story about Graentnor and the blueprints which he had told to the Bayonne police five years previously; and, although he refused to make any admission that he had blown up Black Tom, he did admit that he had been working with a German group for several weeks and that they had promised him a large sum of money.

Shortly after this he was released from prison and for the time being disappeared.

Of the various investigations which were conducted at the time by the Department of Justice, the Interstate Commerce Commission, the local authorities, and the owners, none was successful. It was not until after 1922, when the Mixed Claims Commission was established, that the American lawyers employed by the owners gradually began by exhaustive investigations to lift the curtain of mystery which surrounded the destruction of Black Tom, and by piecing the intricate clues together began to build up their case against Germany. The story of their dogged fight against the German secret service and their immense difficulties in collecting the evidence is told elsewhere. The evidence they collected led the American investigators to the conviction that Graentnor was Hinsch or at least that Hinsch knew a Graentnor whose name he borrowed as an alias; that Jahnke and Witzke rowed across to Black Tom from the New York side to assist Kristoff in blowing up the terminal; and that two of the Dougherty guards were paid agents of Koenig's.

CHAPTER 29

THE KINGSLAND FIRE

O N THE AFTERNOON of 11 January 1917 New York City once again heard the thunderous roar of exploding munitions. For four hours northern New Jersey, New York City, Westchester, and the western end of Long Island listened to a bombardment in which probably half a million 3-inch, high explosive shells were discharged. This explosion took place in the shell-assembling plant of the agency of the Canadian Car & Foundry company, near Kingsland, New Jersey, about 10 miles from the docks in New York harbour. A fire originated suddenly and inexplicably in one of the assembling sheds, Building 30, to be exact; and within a few minutes the whole plant was ablaze. As the flames reached each case of shells and exploded the projection charges, the missiles shot high up in the air and then rained down in the vicinity of the factory.

343

Luckily the shells were not equipped with detonating fuses; therefore they fell as so much metal without exploding. Kingsland and Rutherford were soon filled with hundreds of refugees who had fled from their homes. Fortunately there were no casualties. The 14,000 workers in the plant and all others nearby, mindful of the danger, fled in a mad rush at the first peal of the fire alarm, escaping only just in the nick of time. The entire plant was destroyed. Here the material damage amounted to $17,000,000.

To understand events it is necessary to know something about the plant at Kingsland and the history of the company.

The war had been in progress but a few months when enormous munitions orders started pouring in to the Canadian Car & Foundry company in Montreal. Large contracts were signed both with England and Russia for the delivery of shells. The Canadian factory was working to capacity when, in the spring of 1915, the company secured an $83,000,000 contract from the Russian government for 5 million shells. In order to fulfil this contract the parent company in Canada formed a separate agency and incorporated it under the laws of New York. In March 1916 the huge plant of the agency was erected close to Kingsland, in Bergen County, New Jersey. Shells, shell-cases, shrapnel, and powder were shipped to Kingsland from over 100 different factories and there assembled for shipment to Russia. At the time of the fire the plant was turning out three million shells per month – it was a worthy objective for the German saboteur. The company was well aware of this, and as a safeguard had erected around the plant a 6 ft fence which was patrolled night and day by guards. None of the 1,400 workers were allowed to enter without a preparatory search, and it was strictly forbidden for any of them to carry matches on his person.

Building 30, where the fire originated, was entirely devoted to cleaning out shells. The building was furnished with forty-eight workbenches, along which stood the workers. On the bench in front of each worker was a pan of petrol and a small rotating machine operated by a belt. The cleaning process consisted, first, in dusting out the shell with a brush; then, in order to clean out the thin coating of grease with which the shell had been covered on shipment from the factory, a cloth, moistened in the pan of petrol, was wrapped around a piece of wood about a foot long and, after the shell had been fitted on to the rotating machine, inserted into the shell as it slowly turned; finally, a dry cloth was wrapped around the stick, and the shell was dried in a similar manner. It was in the vicinity of one of these machines that the fire was first noticed.

So rapidly did it spread from building to building that within a few minutes the whole mammoth plant was ablaze. Four hours later all that was left of it was a smouldering mass of ruins. 275,000 loaded shells, 300,000 cartridge cases, 100,086 detonators, 439,920 time fuses, large stores of TNT, and more than one million unloaded shells that were either in the shops, or waiting shipment to Russia, were completely destroyed.

Immediately after the fire, the officers of the company commenced an investigation to determine the cause of the blaze. Various workmen were called in and examined by Mr Cahan, one of the directors of the company. It was quickly established that the fire had broken out at the bench of Fiodore Wozniak, one of the workers. A gang foreman, Morris Chester Musson,

who was at the end of the building when the fire originated,
described what he saw as follows in an affidavit:

> *One of the men at the place where the fire originated was Fiodore
> Wozniak, whose photograph I recognise and which appears below
> as follows:*
>
> *[A photograph of Wozniak appeared here in the original affidavit.]*
>
> *I noticed that this man Wozniak had quite a large collection of rags and
> that the blaze started in these rags. I also noticed that he had spilled
> his pan of alcohol all over the table just preceding that time. The fire
> immediately spread very rapidly in the alcohol saturated table. I also
> noticed that someone threw a pail of liquid on the rags or the table
> almost immediately in the confusion. I am not able to state whether
> this was water or one of the pails of refuse alcohol under the tables.
> My recollection, however, is that there were no pails of water in the
> building, the fire buckets being filled with sand. Whatever the liquid
> was it caused the fire to spread very rapidly and the flames dropped
> down on the floor and in a few minutes the entire place was in a blaze.*
>
> *It was my firm conviction from what I saw, and I so stated at the
> time, that the place was set on fire purposely, and that has always
> been and is my firm belief.*

Thomas Steele, another workman, described his observations
as follows:

> *I was working in No. 30, No. 2265. The fire broke out in the liq-
> uid pan in front of an Austrian workman just after three o'clock.*

This Austrian had been there working for at least three weeks.

I saw the fire burning up in his pan about four or five inches high. The Austrian said nothing, but ran for his coat and taking it, ran through the freight car opening out into the backyard. I was the third man from the Austrian.

Mr Cahan also gave his impressions of an interview he had with Wozniak:

I told him [Wozniak] that most of his fellow workmen agreed that the flames had first been seen at or near his table. He admitted to me that the flames had originated there and he said that they had started in some cloths which he was using to clean one of the shells.

Wozniak told me that several days before the fire occurred he had found matches deposited in one of the shells, among the cloths, 'rags', he called them, which he used for cleaning shells. He seemed to lay singular stress on this fact which at the time, created suspicion in my mind that he was developing a story to throw suspicion on one of his fellow workers ... He said that he was taking the third step in the process of cleaning a shell, that is, drying the inside with a clean cloth, when a flame burst from the opening of the shell...

I questioned Wozniak about the man who had worked at the bench next to him and he said that the man working next to him, on the day of the fire, was a new man who came on that bench that day for the first time ... He said that he did not know his name...

I found the man who usually worked at the second table next to that of Wozniak. He was No. 1208, named Rodriguez, who claimed

*to have been originally from Porto Rico. He gave his residence No.
105 West 64th Street, New York City; and when I had him brought
to the office of the company he declared that he had been absent from
the Works on the day of the fire and that he had been home all day
with his family...*

*Other workmen in Building 30 alleged that the fire started in
the pan of gasoline mixture, which was fixed in front of Wozniak's
wooden roller ... others who were farther away only saw the flames
shooting from the pan of gasoline mixture high towards the ceiling.*

*...I had the impression from his [Wozniak's] nervous behaviour,
from his demeanour when led into apparent contradictions, and from
other incidents in our interviews which were significant to me but difficult to describe, that he knew that the fire was no accident and that
he personally was implicated in its origin.*

G. W. A. Woodhouse, who acted as interpreter for Mr Cahan at
some of his interviews with Wozniak and who also interviewed
Wozniak, separately stated:

*I obtained the same impression from the interviews which are recorded
by Mr Cahan ... I also know that the company made great efforts later
to try to shadow Wozniak and to locate the other workman who was
said to have been employed that day for the first time at the adjoining
bench, but Wozniak disappeared entirely shortly after the detectives
were put on his trail, and we never were able to locate either him or
the workman who had been at the adjoining table.*

Wozniak said that, though he had entered the company's employ
as a Russian, he was actually an 'Austrian Galician'; he admitted

that he had served his time in the Austrian Army and that he had at one time been an Austrian gendarme.

Wozniak was told by Mr Cahan that he would be needed in New York in connection with further investigations regarding the fire and that he would be kept on the company's payroll during that period. Detectives were then employed to watch Wozniak. He went to live at the Russian Immigrant Home on Third Street, New York; but shortly thereafter he eluded the detectives and disappeared.

Other investigations by the owners and the police proved abortive; the disaster was left unexplained as yet another mystery of the war. The insurance companies paid out several million dollars in claims, and the owners had to bear the rest of the loss.

The years rolled by, and it was not until after 1922, when the Mixed Claims Commission was formed and the owners of Kingsland filed a claim against Germany for recovery, that the mystery of the fire was largely dispelled. The American investigators finally produced the evidence which they believe proves conclusively that Hinsch procured the services of Wozniak, and that Wozniak, acting under instructions of Herrmann, fired Kingsland, either by the use of incendiary pencils or rags saturated with phosphorus dissolved in some solvent. On the other hand, the Germans claim it was an industrial accident.

The Mixed Claims Commission met on 18 September 1930 at The Hague to render a judgment on the evidence presented by Germany and the United States in the Black Tom and Kingsland cases.

The umpire was the Honourable Roland W. Boyden; the Honourable Chandler P. Anderson was the American commissioner;

and the German commissioner was Dr Wilhelm Kiesselbach. On
behalf of the government of the United States there appeared:
the Honourable Robert W. Bonynge, American Agent, and Mr
H. H. Martin, Counsel to the American Agent. On behalf of
Germany: Dr Karl von Lewinski, German agent; Dr Wilhelm
Tannenberg, counsel to the German agent; and Mr T. J. Healy,
assistant counsel.

After making appropriate reference to the Peace Palace in
which they were assembled, an edifice dedicated by the donor,
Andrew Carnegie, to the cause of peace and the settlement of
international controversies by judicial tribunals, Mr Bonynge
outlined the charge:

> *That during the period of American neutrality, the Imperial Ger-*
> *man government, in accordance with the policy now admitted to*
> *have been inaugurated by the Foreign Office of the Imperial German*
> *government, authorising and directing sabotage against munitions*
> *and munition plants in the United States, did employ, through its*
> *agents thereunto duly authorised, men who actually set fire to the*
> *Black Tom terminal and to the Kingsland plant of the agency of*
> *Canadian Car & Foundry company.*

He then went on to point out the difficulties which Germany
had set up in the way of the American investigators to prevent
their obtaining information, and quoted the numerous instances
of obstruction and lack of co-operation, and stressed specific
instances.

What the outcome of the Black Tom and Kingsland cases
will be, no one yet knows. It is one thing to feel convinced that

Germany is guilty in both cases; it is another thing to prove it in an international court of law, which almost inevitably is inclined to believe the word of a government as against that of individual witnesses. Furthermore, German agents did not stand on street corners and advertise what they were doing. By 1916 Germany's sabotage directors in the United States had become veterans in the field and were sufficiently well versed in secret service methods to cover up their tracks. A Hinsch would not reveal his identity to a Kristoff. He would employ just the methods that Graentnor used.

Starting out on a cold trail nearly six years after the destruction of Black Tom and Kingsland, and after most of the German agents and officials involved had scattered to the four corners of the globe, the American investigators have had an almost superhuman task. Precious years had been lost during which many of the contemporary clues had disappeared. The Germans had also been given a breathing spell; and by 1924, the period when the investigation really got under way, the German secret service had once again come to life, the backbone of the German government had been stiffened, and both were ready to fight tooth and nail.

Had the American investigators been on the scene in Berlin just after the Armistice their task would have been simple. They could have demanded and would have received the sabotage documents which the German government has since either destroyed or secreted. Proof that the German secret service files were intact at the period was furnished by a British officer attached to the Inter-Allied Control Commission, who examined the archives and took the Edith Cavell file, which he still has in his possession.

HENRY LANDAU

It has also been especially difficult for the American lawyers
to convince the three judges of the Mixed Claims Commission that a sovereign country such as Germany would resort
to fraud and trickery; yet such artifices are the stock-in-trade
of all secret services; and in the Black Tom and Kingsland
cases the American claimants have had to cross swords with
the German secret service. The German government is the
façade; it is her secret service which has supplied the organisation which has kept a close eye, not only on all the German
wartime sabotage agents involved, but also on the movements
of the American investigators. In the opinion of this author,
who spent several years of his life combating the German secret
service, the methods it has employed fighting the American
claimants run true to form.

In no large country other than the United States could Germany have carried out the wholesale sabotage campaign which
she conducted there during the neutrality period. Even a country
like Holland, caught between the Germans and Allies as though
in a nut-cracker, would not have tolerated for a moment any spy
or sabotage activity conducted against her. The secret services
of all the belligerents used Holland as a spy base during the war,
but all of them were extremely careful to avoid any act which
might have been interpreted as directed against the Dutch. Her
police knew the identity and whereabouts of the directors of the
various secret services, and, precarious though Holland's position was, they would quickly have been held responsible for any
hostile acts of their agents.

The weakness of the United States both then and now is that
there was, and still is, no American counter-espionage service.

The Department of Justice does investigate whatever reports of suspected spy activities are sent in from time to time by private citizens, but there is no check-up on spies in any way comparable with that which exists in other countries. Foreign spies can operate there in comparative safety.

At least $150,000,000 damage was done in the United States by sabotage agents during the war – not to mention the huge loss in potential profits caused by the destruction of factories holding millions of dollars' worth of contracts. The same objectives exist today and are just as vulnerable. Twenty men willing to give their lives could probably put the Panama Canal out of action. Furthermore, germ warfare was in its infancy twenty years ago. But tremendous strides have been made since, both in developing more deadly and concentrated strains of disease bacteria and in perfecting superior and easier methods of disseminating them. It would be too late to start organising a counter-espionage defence after the outbreak of hostilities, for in a few days a handful of agents could initiate a nation-wide epidemic of plague, cholera, or other deadly diseases. A grim portent of this coming form of attack is the recent news from Spain that several secret agents have been sentenced to death for spreading sleeping sickness and typhus behind the Insurgent lines.

A counter-espionage service cannot be created overnight. Its efficiency depends on an experienced personnel, on the possession of accurate records of suspects, on watching these suspects, and on piecing together information obtained from all parts of the country. Twenty-four hours after the declaration of war in 1914 every suspected German spy in France either was under lock and key or had been escorted across the frontier.

Foreign key agents for sabotage and espionage are already in the United States waiting; and when needed others will be quickly recruited from among those Fascist, communist, or other alien organisations which, through the chance of war, happen to be lined up on the side of the enemy. All this was demonstrated during the war. Foreign spy activities in Mexico are also of special interest. We have seen how Mexico was used as a spy base during the war, and it is probable that today, even in time of peace, it is still being used as such.

Apart from protecting naval and military secrets from the foreign spy, and being ready to combat the saboteur in the event of war, an American counter-espionage service would amply justify its existence by keeping a watchful eye on internal subversive movements. In addition it would serve to co-ordinate all pertinent information collected by the various law enforcement agencies of the government, by the local police forces, reserve army intelligence officers and the American Legion. Under present conditions such information tends to be hidden in water-tight compartments. The immigration and naturalisation service, the FBI, and finally the secret service division of the Treasury could all be used as channels of information and action without in any way interfering with their present functions.

When we turn to the field of secret service, we find the United States in an even weaker position. She is the only large nation that does not employ such a service to obtain the war plans of prospective enemies and learn about their new weapons. The small intelligence units maintained by the army and navy are the only organisations of the kind, and their principal object is to serve as a nucleus for expansion in time of war. The military intelligence, a small section of the general staff, consists of a few officers and stenographers. When we consider that its yearly grant is only $30,000, we are not surprised to learn that its sole function is to act in an advisory capacity to the staff and to digest the information from foreign press clippings and such data as the military attachés are able to gather by keeping their eyes and ears open. The cryptographic bureau, which functioned so efficiently during the latter part of the war and immediately afterward, has been discontinued.

Today, nearly every European country not only has large and active military and naval intelligence services, as well as effective counter-espionage organisations, but also a central secret service operating an army of spies whose reports are distributed to the navy, army and Foreign Office.

The combined efforts of American armament manufacturers, research laboratories, and the specialists of the army and navy have probably succeeded in keeping equipment up to date and may possibly have developed some surprise weapons of their own; but in these times of rapid changes it is truly dangerous for any country not to be fully posted on the military developments of the rest of the world. It is futile to think that weapons which are considered inhuman will not be employed. Military experts and foreign statesmen agree that all international laws will be broken and the most destructive weapons that can be devised will be used. Effective defence against new weapons can be prepared only if they are known in advance.

Before the war, there was an interchange of information between the different international armament manufacturers.

The result was that the heavy siege guns used by the Germans in their attacks on Liège and Antwerp were the only weapons of any importance which were not common to all armies at the outbreak of hostilities in 1914. Today almost every country has an Official Secrets Act which prevents the interchange of information.

Spying is undoubtedly on the increase. Hardly a week passes without the European press reporting some important spy arrest; and yet those who have secret service experience realise that these newspaper reports only reflect the bubbles at the surface – that underneath, secretly and cautiously, extensive spy organisations are being established in every country.

In France alone more spies have been caught since the Armistice than were arrested throughout the whole of Europe during the twenty-five years preceding the war.

For an annual expenditure of less than 1 per cent of what America lost from German sabotage during the neutrality period a secret service and counter-espionage organisation could be maintained – the peer of any in the world. This indeed seems a low rate of insurance to pay for rendering the United States safe from military surprise and from the ravages of subversive agents both foreign and domestic.